*THE CYCLICAL NIGHT*

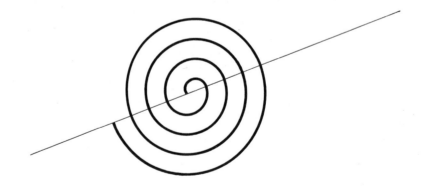

# THE CYCLICAL NIGHT

*Irony in James Joyce and Jorge Luis Borges*
## L. A. MURILLO

*Harvard University Press  Cambridge, Massachusetts  1968*

*A Portrait of the Artist as a Young Man*, by James Joyce. Copyright 1916 by B.W. Huebsch, 1944 by Nora Joyce. Copyright © 1964 by the Estate of James Joyce. All rights reserved. Reprinted by permission of The Viking Press, Inc, and Jonathan Cape, Ltd. *Finnegans Wake*, by James Joyce. Copyright 1939, © 1967 by George Joyce and Lucia Joyce. Reprinted by permission of The Viking Press, Inc, and The Society of Authors. *Ulysses*, by James Joyce. Copyright 1914, 1918 by Margaret Caroline Anderson. Copyright 1934, by The Modern Library, Inc. Copyright 1942, 1946, by Nora Joseph Joyce. Reprinted by permission of Random House, Inc, and John Lane The Bodley Head. *James Joyce: A Critical Introduction*, by Harry Levin. Copyright 1941, © 1960 by New Directions Publishing Corporation. Reprinted by permission of New Directions Publishing Corporation, and Faber and Faber, Ltd. *Obras completas de Jorge Luis Borges*, © 1953–1964 by Emecé Editores, S. A. Extracts in Spanish reprinted by permission of Emecé Editores, S. A., Buenos Aires. Excerpts in English from "El jardín de senderos que se bifurcan," "La muerte y la brújula," "Emma Zunz," and "El inmortal" are published by permission of The New Directions Publishing Corporation, New York, publisher of Jorge Luis Borges, *Labyrinths*, Donald A. Yates and James E. Irby, eds., and Laurence Pollinger, Ltd., London. "Jorge Luis Borges: 'The God's Script' (*La escritura del dios*)" translated by L. A. Murillo, © 1964 by L. A. Murillo. Reprinted by permission of New Directions Publishing Corporation, New York, publisher of Jorge Luis Borges, *Labyrinths*, Donald A. Yates and James E. Irby, eds., and Laurence Pollinger, Ltd., London.

ACKNOWLEDGMENTS

I gratefully acknowledge permission from the Society of
Authors, as the literary representative of the Estate of the late
James Augustine Aloysius Joyce, to use quotations from his
works, in particular *Stephen Hero* and *Finnegans Wake*; from the
Executors of the Estate of James Joyce, and Jonathan Cape Ltd,
to use quotations from *Stephen Hero* and, in addition, The Viking Press Inc, to use quotations from *Dubliners* and *A Portrait
of the Artist as a Young Man*; from Faber and Faber Ltd, and The
Viking Press Inc, to use quotations from *The Letters of James
Joyce* and *The Critical Writings of James Joyce*; from John Lane
The Bodley Head, and Random House Inc, to use quotations
from *Ulysses*; and from The Viking Press Inc for permission
to use quotations from *Finnegans Wake*.

I am also grateful to The Viking Press Inc for permission to
reproduce quotations from *Transition, Essays on Contemporary
Literature* by Edwin Muir; to New Directions Publishing

Corporation, Faber and Faber Ltd, and Harry Levin, for permission to reproduce quotations from *James Joyce: A Critical Introduction*; to Chatto and Windus Ltd, Barnes and Noble Inc, and S. L. Goldberg, for permission to reproduce quotations from *The Classical Temper, A Study of James Joyce's "Ulysses"*; to Chatto and Windus Ltd, Indiana University Press, and Hugh Kenner, for permission to reproduce quotations from *Dublin's Joyce*; and to Faber and Faber Ltd, Northwestern University Press, and Clive Hart, for permission to reproduce quotations from *Structure and Motif in "Finnegans Wake."*

I am grateful also to Emecé Editores for their permission to use quotations in Spanish from the volumes of *Obras completas de Jorge Luis Borges*, and to New Directions Publishing Corporation for permission to reprint, from *Labyrinths, Selected Stories and Other Writings by Jorge Luis Borges*, edited by Donald A. Yates and James E. Irby, my translation of "The God's Script."

I wish to express my gratitude to the Department of Romance Languages and Literatures, Harvard University, for the grant from its Solomon Lincoln Fund which has aided in the publication of this book, and to Professor Juan Marichal for his liberal auspices and encouragement. Lastly, I wish to acknowledge my indebtedness to friends new and old whose aid and advice furthered, and immeasureably improved, my efforts: my deepest thanks to each and all.

L. A. M.

Cambridge, Massachusetts
April 1968

# CONTENTS

*INTRODUCTION*

Somewhere, at a point coincident to their two orbits, Joyce and Borges meet, but this book is not that occasion. At best this study of their irony hypothesizes that event. Perhaps it even brings it nearer to us in time. Consider, for a moment, how their lives and books move on similar, tangential planes. Both have worked on their respective cities, Dublin and Buenos Aires, like mythographers resurrecting from sounds, local sights, houses, and streets, a timeless vision of their inhabitants. And, although at home in several languages and literatures, a shocking parochialism locates the center of their cosmopolis. Both are Daedalian architects of word structures, of labyrinths. Both are exorcists of the shadowy feelings and meanings, the mystery and power of words: literary exorcists of consciousness. Both betray that predilection for compounding the erudite and trivial, the esoteric and the oecumenical, implicating, at its most sensitive, our twentieth-century sensibility. And of course both have pressed an obsession with form, with style and technique, to bounds that dazzle even where they seem familiar. Some of their most brilliant moments are strictly parasitic and parodistic, and even self-parodistic. There is, moreover, an influence of one on the other, for Borges, in the twenties, was one writer of that vanguardist generation feeling the full impact, the contemporary impact, of *Ulysses*. His essay on Joyce and a translation of a fragment of the closing monologue comprise a singular event in literary history.[1] Borges' experiments with style, in his poetry of the twenties, reflects a Joycean awareness of a new sensibility in search of expression. Several of the structural ideas of *Finnegans Wake* acquire a dialectical form in some of Borges' stories, essays, and poems. His poem *"La noche cíclica"* owes at least the adjective of its title to Joyce. Perhaps the decisive point of comparison is that their interpretative vision of the intellectual, social, and moral world of man is esthetic, and that their attitudes, tastes, literary ends and means are apolitical, frequently hermetical, and heretical. It is this affinity of nonconformists that attracts attention to their use of irony for fusing style to subject. Also, we owe to a similar use of the cyclical view of time, history and personalities, some of their most inimitable and intimate revelations about themselves as writers. And a final point: Borges, like Joyce in his later years, suffers from blindness.

Yet, conceding that their literary worlds have much in common as work of "artists," of practitioners of a fine art, some basic differences between them severely restrict the possibilities of a comparative study of their attitudes, their themes, and their craft. Both are "critical" as well as "imaginative" writers. But Borges takes a genuine pleasure in working upon ideas, and in working out a style for compressing his meta-

[1]"El *Ulises* de Joyce," and "Traducción de James Joyce, La última hoja del *Ulises*," published in *Proa* (Buenos Aires), no. 6, January 1925, pp. 3–9. An introductory note on Borges appears in the Notes, p. 245.

physical speculations into an exact organization of concepts. He is everywhere clear, concise. The ideas are never obscure; what they point to, what they constitute, often is. Joyce is almost the reverse. His obscurity resides in his means, in his "using" certain ideas "for all they are worth." Once those obscurities are overcome, his meanings leap up at us, self-evident. Borges' early work was poetry, but his critical and speculative interests found more decided expression in the literary essay. Thus, from the literary essay (in the thirties) to the short narrative (in the early forties) provided a decisive line of evolution more like that of a traditional man of letters than Joyce's. And Borges has been creative in more ways and forms. For Joyce, after 1922, literary creation became such an onerous, restricted labor that he was almost incapable of creative expression in any of the conventional forms: narrative, essay, or poetry, even his personal letters. Each of his major books represents a massive advance in complexity and innova-tion, but also the exhaustion of the possibilities inherent, for him, in each form: the short story, the autobiographical novel, the naturalistic novel. At best only a semblance of this can be traced in Borges, who refused to write novels, from 1922 to 1962.

Thus, although they are brought together here, for critical and theoretical reasons, their works are studied separately. A study striving to focus on their use of irony in narrative prose is, on all accounts, a restrictive enterprise. The similarity of themes, resources, and attitudes becomes tenuous under the weight of the practical demands of a comparative method. Both authors compress enormous amounts of literary material by means of reiterative techniques, but they do so for ends quite as separate and unique as their means. One may say, in theory, and as the basis for bringing them together, that both authors have worked on irony as a mode of apprehension, but to ex-pand on this, to explicate it from various directions, to deal practically with it, one must confront the precise relation of theme to style, of meaning to form, in two sets of works. And each of these works poses its own internal problems and also represents a stage of evolution.

Precisely because Joyce and Borges match one another in the exactness of a relation of subject to style, are the works of each too exclusive for practical comparisons of the significant, but minute details. Borges' iterative form of compression, for instance, aims at preserving the clear outlines of the conceptual basis of his speculative arguments. As a conveyance for symbolical meanings, his words—their order and syntactical structure—preserve inviolately, almost in spite of oddities, the correctness demanded by Spanish syntax, lexicon, and grammar. The release of their associative meanings is thoroughly dependent on this, and likewise their potential for releasing an ironical meaning. This is a structural necessity, for Borges, with his equipage of antitheses and warring coincidences, is always underway on the cycling motions of imaginative metaphysical conjecture. Compactness, concentration of idea and image, are aimed, as their effect, at immediate conversion into symbol. Borges can condense, and therefore intensify and dramatize, the exposition of massive intellectual and imaginative questions on a few hallucinatory pages. In contrast, Joyce's obsessive need for enlarging the dimensions of one day and night of Irish life and myth has given us the encyclopedic proportions of *Ulysses* and *Finnegans Wake*. Joyce expands, elaborates, in his mature styles, by accretions within a simple, unitive pattern, and with a wealth of incidental and referential detail. He took unprecedented liberties with English, and, in *Finnegans Wake*, with a score of other languages, but his compression of the sensible, imaginative materials he chose to work with is permissibly complicated and involuted because, according to his own words, "the thought is always simple." In Borges the prose surface is always explicit, crystalline, but the thought is often hermetically compressed, even distorted, and charged by the tensions of an imaginative power thrusting for sustained symbolical expression. To put it into the terms of the essays that follow: Joyce, in the evolution of his styles, points the uses of irony toward an encompassing equipoise of myth; Borges, through the techniques of reiterative compression, pivots them on the instability of symbols.

Equally imperative, as a reason for two separate essays, are the demands posed by the critical concept under consideration: irony. If irony, as a full-bodied concept, is to enjoy the prerogatives of critical legitimacy, it must prove that it is capable of closing in, unaided, on the core of literary works; that is, capable as an independent topic of analysis to go unaided by comparative supports to the core of books. And it must show, moreover, that it is useful to elucidate that core in just this way. Few will argue, in the present state of literary criticism, that irony is a concept in need of justification or proof of its legitimacy. So long as it is treated as an ancillary feature of an author's work the question is hardly important. But irony, it needs saying, is not a concept like tragedy or comedy. These are more self-subsistent and self-evident. Irony must be seen as a contingent or intervening thing, as a mode establishing or intervening to convey the unexpressed "ironical" meaning. Tragedy expresses, we may say, the substantive "tragedy," or "the tragic." Irony does not in the same sense express a substantive meaning. Irony is modal, and an ironical meaning is one modally or circumstantially. It is a perceptive mode, a neutral or functional mode, that permits a writer "to say as little and mean as much as possible."[2] But then irony as a

[2]The quip is from an introductory page in Northrop Frye's *Anatomy of Criticism* (Princeton University Press, 1957, p. 41). My conception of irony as a perceptive mode does not of course fit neatly into (even less does it derive from) Frye's theories. I am not conscious of any decisive contradiction between his theory of modes of fiction and categories of plots (where irony occupies the fourth, wintry, position) and my efforts to deal, at close quarters, with the "circumstances" of irony in narrative prose.

mode can intervene to establish almost any variety or degree of meaning, and moreover intervene in any of various ways, devices, or uses.

The first essay attempts to focus on *what*, and *how*, Joyce accomplished by his use of irony. It is to some extent a study of the entire evolution of his narrative styles and a particular study of the involutions of style of his final work. There is general agreement among Joyce's critics about what irony is, and where it occurs in his writings. There would be no need for an essay on irony in Joyce's books if it were only a question of particularizing its being there. My concern and interest is *how* does it do what it is doing there? Or rather, *what* is it doing there in such a way that we take it for the thing it is in general and for the thing Joyce makes of it? Questions of this sort are not likely to occur to the critics of Joyce's works so long as they do not assume that the study of an author's irony involves the sustained and systemized pursuit of a critical question to its inherent and necessary solution, and not an analysis, however valid otherwise, pursued under the auspices of collateral concepts. As Joyce moved from the writing of *A Portrait* to *Ulysses* and then to *Finnegans Wake* he was moving, and carrying with him, the art of the novel into the realm of myth. An analytical approach to Joyce's irony and the ironical in his works will need to encompass that complete journey in order to ascertain the layout of the critical problems involved. The whole journey, and only the whole, can furnish the literary critic with the completeness that is requisite to a claim of critical legitimacy. The study of Joyce's irony then becomes by necessity an approach to the total significance of his works. Joyce, in his techniques of imitative form, used irony to establish, not dissolve or destroy, myth. Thus my main interest is to specify the quality or qualitativeness of his irony; that is, to specify in the core-area between the *what* (his intended meaning) of an ironical disclosure and *how* (his techniques of indirection) so as to produce in our perceptions the effect of an opposition of meanings resolvable in and along with the expression of that opposition. This is unique with Joyce, to his strange way of elaborating works of fiction outward from his personal and inner needs to an objectivized and impersonal form or focus. My approach to Joyce's irony, then, has had to differ from those of my predecessors not only in method and scope but essentially in this: that having followed its development and progression through the whole journey from the earliest *Portrait* to *Finnegans Wake*, my estimates of what to study as ironical expression and how to proceed would be qualified by the Joycean *whatness* and *howness*, the intended meaning and the techniques of verbal simulation establishing that meaning in the final book.

The case for my essay as a valid piece of Joycean criticism rests on my arguments deriving the qualitative effect produced by his irony from a resolution of the multiple meanings stated or expressed simultaneously. If irony may be said to occur when a writer expresses two meanings simultaneously, one of them explicitly stated, the other implied or concealed, then a similar operation involving more than one pair of opposed, incongruent, or antithetical meanings may similarly be called and be considered irony, or at the very least a kind of irony. The point is delicate, but not really difficult.[3] In my at-

[3]Our textbook conceptions of irony have scarcely recognized, much less provided for, the literary practice of a simultaneous expression of multiple and opposed "ironical" meanings conveyed by techniques of prose to a reader's perceptive resources as a simulation of that meaning they are designed to establish by the totally indirect means of the techniques which convey it: the *what* identified and identifiable by the *how* of the verbal, metaphorical or conceptual simulation of it.

The unity of my two studies rests on the application of a concept that considers irony a comprehensive mode for conveying and fixing a resolution as well as an opposition of meaning. My appraisals of the irony of Joyce and Borges are concerned with our perception of the multiple or total means for establishing that resolution and the full bounds of its "meaning." They are not concerned with classifying or analyzing the different species of irony

tempt to specify the irony of *Finnegans Wake* I had perforce to come to grips with the Joycean processes of the multiplicity of meanings and with the simultaneity of their expression. But of course these are inherent in Joyce's techniques of verbal simulation carried out on a large scale—so large a scale that in order to deal with them with any practical aim in mind one must deal with the whole laborious, controvertible question of the structure of the dream book. Irony in *Finnegans Wake* is operative on so many levels that the only really practical approach to it is to study how on different levels it intervenes to do its part in accomplishing for the reader a total apprehension of the book's themes and structure. It occurs in the simpler forms of verbal irony, as a more complicated irony in the techniques of verbal simulation of Joyce's imitative form, but also as a comprehensive irony of outlook or attitude governing the dramatic situations of his characters. And then beyond these, as an all-inclusive irony of the cyclical structure with inward and subjective aspects, and outward, impersonal dimensions.

The essay on Borges is equally concerned with a simultaneity of expressing multiple, conflicting meanings. In Joyce it is related closely to his techniques of verbal simulation; in Borges, to his techniques for producing a simulation, a cognitive and intuitive grasp, of reality. If the processes of mythical enlargement in Joyce call for a study of an entire evolution of themes and style, in Borges the reverse is the case. Here the sustained techniques of compression and reiteration call for exhaustive analysis of relatively few pages. And since, to English readers, his writings are not as well known as Joyce's, a close and detailed analysis must be made of his texts. Accordingly, I have analyzed one story, "The Garden of Forking

---

these authors employ, but with specifying the frame of meaning which any of these ironies may convey and establish. Irony, according to my conception of it, and the sense in which the term appears in the title of this volume, is a comprehensive mode, assimilating the various forms or types of irony, and providing for their relations to the form and content of an entire work of literature.

Paths," in detail, and furnished less detailed discussions of four other representative stories.

While we proceed in the two essays by different means of analysis, the unity of the essays rests on the analogy between the reflective act that both authors accomplish through irony. The reflective act, that is, rendered an esthetic act. Here are two writers who intensify our awareness of the intellectual and esthetic phases by which irony communicates an unstated "impersonal" and "objective" meaning. Here irony, as a mode, is inseparable from the significance of works in prose and from the means of our access to that significance. We find here the *how* of ironical expression increasingly provoking and drawing attention to itself. Increasingly the effect becomes that of provoking the reaction that this *how* is attempting to simulate both the thing represented and our intellective and esthetic notions arrested by (Joyce) or converging upon (Borges) our apprehension of the thing represented. The more immediately it provokes our awareness of the mechanics of its operation, the more intensified and effective this *how*. Its aim is both to produce a counter-reflection through the impulses of the reader and to redirect them in a conspiratorial action between him and author back upon the facets of reality or life represented. In Borges' stories we shall find that our perceptions of the multiple relations between things and persons, and the causal connections between events, constitute the "meaning" of events, of lives and things, their *whatness* established by the *howness* of Borgian irony and its quality. The residue of mockery and ridicule in this mode is directed as humor or play at our impulse to attempt and to possess an omniscient view of human events and an infallible understanding of the universal laws of causality. The result of the conspiratorial action, as part of an impersonal and objective resolution of meanings, is to betray "reality," "fact," "life," into exposing themselves in our perceptions as image, or symbol, or, to use Borges' term, a *simulacrum*.

At the center of the analogy between Joyce and Borges are the effects each produces by redirecting the representation of certain states of consciousness onto the perceptions of their readers. Yet here precisely lies the cause for proceeding on two separate essays. The analogy results from their techniques for attaining a simultaneity of expression and multiple equivalences of form to subject. The underlying contrasts are harder to trace to their source. A basic one is the central position held by metaphysical speculation in Borges' dialectical designs. Or we could compare the dreaming consciousness of *Finnegans Wake* with the hallucinatory ordeals of some of Borges' heroes. Both, as dream structures, are labyrinthine and cyclical. But the verbal obscurities of Joyce's dreamer-narrator are controlled to work their way from the irrational inconclusiveness of a sleeping mind toward coherent resolutions of rational statement; whereas in Borges style and idea impel his rational disquisitions out to fantasy, non-reason, and hallucination. In more conventional terms, we may say that in Joyce's verbal patterns we have a "stream," in Borges' compact, conceptual ones, a "structure" of consciousness.

The states of consciousness in *Finnegans Wake*, however verbally obscure, appear transparently evident in their linear and sequential movement because they are conceived in the dream as states of nonviolence. They are inner reflections of the human *mea culpa* taking place or projected upon a glass of innocency. The Borgian states of consciousness, nearly always scared by acts of violence, are radical conflicts between the subjectivity of will and illusion and their objectivization in time, conflicts between dimensions of being and the process of their impersonalization that gives rise to archetypes and symbols. Thus Borges furnishes what I call "total" conflicts because the progression and movement of their warring tensions build up and impart to us through reiteration and recapitulation (a horizontal and vertical compression of themes) a total opposition between all of their components as that dichotomy of symbolical realities that is human consciousness, both personal and collective. The effect is to heighten the reader's perceptive awareness of his own consciousness, so to speak, as a counterpart to that antagony of irresolvable forces and symbolical dissonances. The Joycean effect is then quite unlike the Borgian because, although both authors impel the inductions of ironical readings to a highly logical and, stylistically, logistical point of resolution, the tensions of the Joycean ironies which I call dis-tensions neutralize their opposition at this point to provide entry into the myth that *Finnegans Wake* enacts; whereas in Borges' stories the conflict of tensions remains irresolvable in order to produce, in their mutual annihilation or effacement, the effect of a predicament of consciousness compounded, localized, and centered in the reader's intellective and emotive response.

The over-all unity of my presentation, then, and the interconnections between chapters and analyses, is to guide my reader to a "total" apprehension of the contents of *Finnegans Wake* and then to bring him to an analogous understanding of salient features of Borges' narratives.

## SCHEME OF REFERENCES TO JOYCE'S WORKS

When American and English editions are not identical, reference is made first to the page number of the American edition and then to the English edition (thus, *SH* 41/45-6).

| | | |
|---|---|---|
| *D* | *Dubliners* | Quoted from *The Portable James Joyce*, New York: The Viking Press, rev. ed. 1966, and *The Essential James Joyce*, London: Jonathan Cape, 1948, edited by Harry Levin. |
| *P* | *A Portrait of the Artist as a Young Man* | |
| *CW* | *The Critical Writings of James Joyce*, edited by Ellsworth Mason and Richard Ellmann | New York: The Viking Press; London: Faber and Faber, 1959. |
| *FW* | *Finnegans Wake** | New York: The Viking Press, 1958; London: Faber and Faber, 1949. |
| *L* | *Letters of James Joyce*, edited by Stuart Gilbert | New York: The Viking Press; London: Faber and Faber, 1957. |
| *L^{II}* | *Letters of James Joyce*, Vol. II, edited by Richard Ellmann | New York: The Viking Press; London: Faber and Faber, 1966. |
| *SH* | *Stephen Hero*, edited by Theodore Spencer; rev. ed., with additional material, edited by John J. Slocum and Herbert Cahoon | New York: New Directions, 1955; London: Jonathan Cape, 1956. |
| *U* | *Ulysses* | New York: New Random House Edition, 1961; London: John Lane, The Bodley Head, 1949. |

*Page/line references to *Finnegans Wake* indicate the line on which quotations begin. Book/chapter references, in accordance with the practice now established among Joyceans, refer to the four main sections of the *Wake* and their divisions, e.g., III.4 (Book III, chapter 4).

# JAMES JOYCE

*The Way of Irony to the Threshold of Myth*

*FROM A PORTRAIT TO FINNEGANS WAKE*

# JOYCE 1

*Mastery of art had been achieved in irony*

In January of 1904, at the close of his twenty-first year, James Joyce wrote a short prose piece entitled "A Portrait of the Artist." In this first version of *A Portrait* the following appears: "Beneficent one! (the shrewdness of love was in the title) thou camest timely, as a witch to the agony of the selfdevourer, an envoy from the fair courts of life. How could he thank thee for that enrichment of soul by thee consummated? Mastery of art had been achieved in irony; asceticism of intellect had been a mood of indignant pride: but who had revealed him to himself but thou alone?"[1] A reader acquainted with the final version of *A Portrait of the Artist as a Young Man* will recognize that "envoy from the fair courts of life" as the girl wading in the rivulet and gazing out to sea in the climactic scene. We shall have occasion, in the course of this essay, to refer to the significance of this scene which is based on an incident in Joyce's adolescent life in 1898.[2] The first attempt to give literary form to the experience produced the apostrophic revelations in which the statement about irony is conspicuous.

The statement, first of all, looks back. "Mastery of art had been achieved in irony." In this earliest sitting for a self-portrait the young artist conceives both his life and his art as having arrived at a point of consummation. This point, it is clear to us now, was reached when Joyce discovered he could create literary works by writing of the process by which he became conscious of himself as the literary artist. However, as a factual statement about the young writer it is so highly optimistic as to be nearly false. At twenty-one Joyce had written some critical pieces, a few poems, and almost nothing of consequence in artistic prose. The tri-part sentence does not reappear in *Stephen Hero* or in the final version of *A Portrait*. It represents the initial stage of that process by which Joyce is to repossess his inner life by recreating it in the detachment of fiction. The prose piece is the moment of conception for Joyce's as yet unnamed artist-hero, and if the phrase about achieving the mastery of art in irony is applicable to the young Joyce, it is so only in part to the poems of *Chamber Music* and to the highly tentative prose *epiphanies*, and, of course, to the very process by which the prose piece, neither essay nor narrative, has emerged. Our sentence, then, belongs to the earliest stage of Stephen Dedalus, the self-image and *persona* whose significance Joyce will deepen and refine through the years of composition of *A Portrait* and *Ulysses* until, in 1921, he disappears as the cold and enigmatic youth of June 16, 1904, under the icy stars of "Ithaca."

If the phrase about achieving the mastery of art in irony is hardly applicable to Joyce in 1904, it is entirely so to the works of certain literary greats of the waning nineteenth century, the distant models the artist-hero set out to emulate. The high estimate of the esthetic possibilities of irony could have been corroborated by the young Joyce in the works and testimonies of a select group of writers in France, Germany, and England, but most likely it is the impersonal manner of the mature Ibsen that he had in mind. In French literature, from Stendhal and Flaubert to Renan and Anatole France, the ironic attitude had erected, on the support of uncompromised intimate beliefs, bridges between the sensibility of art and disillusionment with the moral and political realities of "life." As a precept, and by the example of *Madame Bovary*, Flaubert could say, in his correspondence in the 1850's, that "irony dominates life;"[3] and that beyond disillusion with a bourgeois moral order there existed "the ironical acceptance of life and its plastic and complete recasting by art. (*L' acceptation ironique de l'existence et sa refonte plastique et complète par l'Art*)."[4] Renan had advised, in the face of scientific relativity, the indulgent smile of skepticism before the absolutisms of the past. "We owe virtue to the Eternal, but we have a right to join to it irony, by way of personal reprisal."[5] And it was Anatole France, one of the dominant figures of the literary scene in Paris visited by Joyce in 1902-1903, who had written in *Le Jardin d'Epicure* (1895): "The more I consider human life, the more I believe we must give it for

witnesses and judges Irony and Pity.'[6] There are distinctions of
purpose and ends between the ironic temper of the French and
Ibsen's, and even greater ones between them and the German
tradition of Romantic irony the young Thomas Mann was to
expand, but all shared the conviction that their works were concerned with the decisive relations between private and social
beliefs and actions, with the central moral questions of their
century. The young Irish admirer of Ibsen who, in *Stephen
Hero*, declares the artist to be a self-chosen "intense centre of
the life of his age," conceives the "impersonal manner of the
artist" rather as a state of moral balance the artist achieves
between the social alienation to which he is driven by the
"formulas and machinery" of society and the inexorable affirmation of life to which he is impelled by the human spirit,
*SH* 80/85.

"The minds of the old Norse poet and of the perturbed
young Celt," we read of Stephen's discovery of Ibsen, "met in a
moment of radiant simultaneity," *SH* 40/45. The young discov-
erer of 1898 is fictionalized, in a chapter of *Stephen Hero*
completed in 1905,[7] as an isolated youth who finds in the spirit
of Ibsen the equanimity of a great human personality perfectly
united with a impersonal artistic manner. It was not only the
excellence of Ibsen's art which captivated Stephen:

> It was not that which he greeted gladly with an entire
> joyful spiritual salutation. It was the very spirit of Ibsen
> himself that was discerned moving behind the imper-
> sonal manner of the artist: [Ibsen with his profound
> self-approval, Ibsen with his haughty, disillusioned
> courage, Ibsen with his minute and wilful energy.] a
> mind of sincere and boylike bravery, of disillusioned
> pride, of minute and wilful energy.* Let the world solve
> itself in whatsoever fashion it pleased, let its putative
> Maker justify Himself by whatsoever processes seemed
> good to Him, one could scarcely advance the dignity of
> the human attitude a step beyond this answer. Here and

not in Shakespeare or Goethe was the successor to the
first poet of the Europeans, here, as only to such purpose
in Dante, a human personality had been found united
with an artistic manner which was itself almost a natural
phenomenon: and the spirit of the time united one more
readily with the Norwegian than with the Florentine.
*SH* 41/45-46*[8]

It seems safe to say, in the absence of any explicit reference
of the kind,[9] that for Joyce the ironic attitude was a factor in the
Ibsenian dramatization of moral values and spiritual liberation, a factor identifying what Stephen calls "the temper of
Ibsen"; and that the esthetic possibilities for irony would be
greatest in the "dramatic art" of Stephen's, and Joyce's, theories—that art "whereby the artist sets forth his image in immediate relations to others."       *SH* 77/82, *CW* 145

2

In *Stephen Hero* the discussion between the President of the
University and Stephen about Ibsen and the ideas on esthetics
in the essay the student has written is an example of the "impersonal" exposure that Joyce, already in 1905 the "voluntary
exile" (*L*[II]84)[10] could perform on his own experiences at the
same time that he propounded the equanimity, the "security,
satisfaction and patience" of the "classical temper," *SH* 78/83.
It is a dramatic scene, technically speaking, where the full
significance of the dialogue and of its forced subtleties are
conveyed through the momentary elimination of nearly all
assertive elements. The character of Stephen, the moral and
intellectual weight of his motivation, turns on the enigmatic
manner of his defense. A clue to this manner is that at various
moments Stephen ascribes an ironic manner to Ibsen, Newman, Aquinas, and, as we shall see presently, to his own love-
poems. The esthetic theory of Stephen's essay "Drama and

Life" insists on the freedom of the poet's purpose and on the freedom of the poet's conception of beauty from moralistic considerations. "I mean," says Stephen, in calculated defense of his admiration for Ibsen before the Jesuit priest, "that Ibsen's account of modern society is as genuinely ironical as Newman's account of English Protestant morality and belief."

—That may be, said the President appeased by the conjunction.

— And as free from any missionary intention.

The President was silent.

—It is a question of temper. Newman could refrain from writing his *Apologia* for twenty years.

—But when he came out on him! said the President with a chuckle and an expressive incompletion of the phrase. Poor Kingsley!

—It is all a question of temper—one's attitude towards society whether one is poet or critic.

—O, yes.

—Ibsen has the temper of an archangel.
. . . . .
—I have only pushed to its logical conclusion the definition Aquinas has given of the beautiful.

—Aquinas?

—*Pulcra sunt quae visa placent.* He seems to regard the beautiful as that which satisfies the esthetic appetite and nothing more—that the mere apprehension of which pleases . . .

—But he means the sublime—that which leads man upwards.

—His remark would apply to a Dutch painter's representation of a plate of onions.

—No, no; that which pleases the soul in a state of sanctification, the soul seeking its spiritual good.

—Aquinas' definition of the good is an unsafe basis of operations: it is very wide. He seems to me almost ironical in his treatment of the "appetites."

The President scratched his head a little dubiously—

—Of course Aquinas is an extraordinary mind, he murmured, the greatest doctor of the Church: but he requires immense interpretation. There are parts of Aquinas which no priest would think of announcing in the pulpit.

—But what if I, as an artist, refuse to accept the cautions which are considered necessary for those who are still in a state of original stupidity?

—I believe you are sincere but I will tell you this as an older human being than you are and as a man of some experience: the cult of beauty is difficult. Estheticism often begins well only to end in the vilest abominations of which . . .

—*Ad pulcritudinem tria requiruntur.*

—It is insidious, it creeps into the mind, little by little . . .

—*Integritas, consonantia, claritas.* There seems to me to be effulgence in that theory instead of danger. The intelligent nature apprehends it at once.

—S. Thomas of course . . .

—Aquinas is certainly on the side of the capable artist. I hear no mention of instruction or elevation.

—To support Ibsenism on Aquinas seems to me somewhat paradoxical. Young men often substitute brilliant paradox for conviction.

—My conviction has led me nowhere: my theory states itself.     *SH* 92-6/97-101

The little drama comes perilously close to farce. The implied reservations sustaining it are insufficient for exposing the barrenness of Stephen's environment by a focus through the emerging consciousness of the artist. That focus, in the light of the final version of *A Portrait*, is a question of style, or, more precisely, a question of narrative stylization, and in 1905 the self-exile is struggling to dispossess himself of Stephen's moral and intellectual limitations in order to find the center, and hence the initial point, of his own artistic purpose.

3

The poems of *Chamber Music* give us the most integral commitment to artistic form of the young Joyce before *Dubliners*; the proper context for their understanding, as Richard Ellmann invites us to consider,[11] is the personal situation Joyce faced or failed to face in the events leading up to the alliance with Nora Barnacle and departure from Dublin in October, 1904. "I wrote *Chamber Music* as a protest against myself."[12] "It is a young man's book. I felt like that. It is not a book of love verses at all, I perceive."[13] The comments are from the mature Joyce, or at least the Joyce who has fathered a son. That the romantic and lyrical elements in some of the poems are highly vulnerable to a comic-ironic interpretation is more a symptom of the sensibility of the young poet than a defect of the poems themselves as love poetry. "One reason *Chamber Music* doesn't really come off," Hugh Kenner says, "is that the author for all his irony toward the glamorous feels an irony still greater toward the quotidian."[14] To proceed to elaborate a Freudian-like interpretation of the imagery as a symbolism derivable from *Finnegans Wake*, as W. Y. Tindall does,[15] however, is to make the poems overly intelligible in the context of the later Joyce, who is completely serious and even theoretical about his comedy.

The Joyce of 1903-4 who delights in the Irish conceit of "Chamber Music" for the tinkling sounds of a lady's pot is not serious about the esthetic possibilities of his self-exacerbating comedy; he is committed artistically to the integrity of rhythm and form, and it was perhaps this unreserved commitment to "sincere" lyrical expression that elicited the onanistic allusions in the scene of morning inspiration, "O what sweet music! His soul was all dewy wet," in *A Portrait*, 485/338, the self-deprecating reference to "Chamber Music" in *Ulysses*, 282/268, and "shamebred music" in the *Wake*, 164.15. Stephen acknowledges, on the plane of self-exploration in *Stephen Hero*, an ironical attitude toward the "feudal terminology" of the love verses, but the ironical vein in the poems themselves does not conflict with the commitment to lyrical form. The context of his admission to an ironical attitude is the artistic dedication to his poetry as a serious effort at self-integration and self-possession: "it was always a mature and reasoned emotion which urged him," *SH* 174/179. That such a "reasoned" emotion was not purely lyrical in most instances invites Stephen to toy with the ulterior significance of his efforts. "He toyed also with a theory of dualism which would symbolise the twin eternities of spirit and nature in the twin eternities of male and female and even thought of explaining the audacities of his verse as symbolical allusions. It was hard for him to compel his head to preserve the strict temperature of classicism," *SH* 210/215.

It is significant that Stephen's esthetic theory is mainly concerned with "esthetic ends" and the analysis of the act of esthetic apprehension in which the qualities of beauty become manifest and the epiphany occurs. The "impersonal manner" of the Ibsenian artist is apparently the result of the emergence and the completion of the act of esthetic creation as an act of esthetic apprehension. What Stephen is unable to grasp is that the fulfillment of "esthetic ends" as he conceives them implies likewise that it is an act of self-apprehension. Detachment, impersonality, objectivity, these qualities fulfill the act of esthetic apprehension; they cannot be, for the "classical temper," simply a prerequisite to it. The artist, that "centre of life" Stephen aspires to be, as the moral condition of his art ought then to be detached, impersonal, and objective toward himself, toward his creative and apprehensive faculties, as well as toward that society of which he writes. Stephen, however, is but groping toward the conclusion that the apprehension of the artist is simultaneously a self-apprehension in the esthetic act of extricating the "literary image" from the "mesh of defining circumstances" around it. The artist is a "mediator" more than he is a creator, and making the literary image is preeminently an act of apprehending those converging circumstances which, as in the scene on Eccles Street before "one of those brown brick houses which seem the very incarnation of Irish paralysis," have brought the artist and the world of his experience to the moment of "focus," *SH* 211/216. Stephen, we know, sought

> to establish the relations which must subsist between the literary image, the work of art itself, and that energy which had imagined and fashioned it, that centre of conscious, re-acting, particular life, the artist.
>
> The artist, he imagined, standing in the position of mediator between the world of his experience and the world of his dreams — <a mediator, consequently gifted with twin faculties, a selective faculty and a reproductive faculty.> To equate these faculties was the secret of artistic success: the artist who could disentangle the subtle soul of the image from its mesh of defining circumstances most exactly and <re-embody> it in artistic circumstances chosen as the most exact for it in its new office, he was the supreme artist. This perfect coincidence of the two artistic faculties Stephen called poetry . . . The term 'literature' now seemed to him a term of contempt. . .    *SH* 77-8/82.

We may consider that Stephen is theorizing on what Joyce in 1904-5 is developing into the technique of exposure of the earlier stories in *Dubliners*. The term Stephen uses, "perfect coincidence," may be applied to the result striven for by the "classical temper," which has chosen "to bend upon these present things and so to work upon them and fashion them that the quick intelligence may go beyond them to their meaning which is still unuttered," *SH* 78/83; *cf. CW* 74. Once accomplished the "perfect coincidence" of the two artistic faculties would presumably place, in "dramatic art," the "epiphany" and the "literary image" in "immediate relation to others," that is to say, in immediate relation to the reader's intellectual and esthetic "appetites," CW 147. In the epiphany on Eccles Street we can perceive the two extremes from which the onlooker or reader must first proceed to frame the scene, the triviality of the moment and the metaphysical implications of the Irish paralysis it reveals; while the operative context which then brings them to a "focus" is the sensitivity, the developing consciousness, of the "artist."

> By an epiphany he meant a sudden spiritual manifesta-tion, whether in the vulgarity of speech or of gesture or in a memorable phase of the mind itself. He believed that it was for the man of letters to record these epiphanies with extreme care, seeing that they themselves are the most delicate and evanescent of moments.

And to Cranly, in front of the Ballast Office, Stephen says:

> Imagine my glimpses at that clock as the gropings of a spiritual eye which seeks to adjust its vision to an exact focus. The moment the focus is reached the object is epiphanised. It is just in this epiphany that I find the third, the supreme quality of beauty.     SH 211/216-7

These few pointers from *Stephen Hero* and Joyce's note-books provide an early clue to what is going to distinguish the dimension of irony and the ironical in Joyce's works: his ef-forts to bring off, as the "perfect coincidence," an equivalence between subject matter and form which accomplishes the self-illumination from within of the narrative. This equiv-alence has numerous aspects, and one we can explain by ref-erence to the notebooks is that it equates the creation of "the truthful and the beautiful" to an esthetic mode defining their apprehension. The esthetic act becomes the apprehension of those relations within its parts which constitutes the unity —integrity, symmetry, radiance—of the complete and com-pleted work of art. Hence this act also prescribes that the making of the work of art is embodied as an element of structure into its wholeness and, moreover, that the corresponding mode of apprehension will infer the "howness" of the work of art as adequate, even equivalent, to its *whatness*. Thus, from the direction of the onlooker or the reader the Joycean "literary image" will approximate to the stages of creative apprehension of the beautiful which brought it into being as "*that* thing which it is" to the objective contemplator, *SH* 213/218. Stating matters this way provides us with a better notion to start with of how "detachment," "impersonality," and even "indifference" are to be operative and objectivizing attributes of the ironical in the arrestment of the intellectual and esthetic appetites of the Joycean reader.

# JOYCE 2

*On the continent as in Eironesia*     *FW* 411.11

When Joyce and Nora Barnacle left Dublin on the night of the 8th of October in 1904 for Paris and Switzerland there began to develop those circumstances — self-imposed exile replacing rebellion — which were to modify the temper of alienation in which he had begun *Stephen Hero* and *Dubliners*. As the arbiter of his personal designs Joyce would not live in Dublin, but as an Irishman he would write only of the life there which had shaped his soul and mind to the point where fidelity to its essence as a human complex was the other side of the conviction that to attempt the life of a writer in Dublin was to cultivate hostility and betrayal.[16] The stories in *Dubliners* give us a reproduction of Irish life as Joyce knew it in the impersonal manner of naturalism, and the ironic quality in the stories written in 1904-5 is confined to the restrictive maneuvers of "a style of scrupulous meanness"[17] in which the humorous note is the exception. Their structure, moreover, discloses an incipient Joycean symbolism which some critics tend to consider more revealing as such and in itself than the unrelenting exposure of the naturalism. The characteristic tendency of Joyce's symbolism as it matures, anchored consistently in a naturalistic situation, is toward a comic context for the symbol, a comic widening or diffusion of its contexts. In *Dubliners*, with but few exceptions, Joyce cannot afford or allow this diffusion, though he is capable of many shades of humor toward the Irish and himself at any stage of his writing, because he has not yet come to terms with the forces which shaped him as a man and artist and forced his liberation from them; that is, he is not sufficiently disengaged from his subject — the moral condition of Ireland — to isolate it as the object of his techniques of exposure according to the mode of its apprehension. To a large extent that disengagement, as we shall see in the period leading up to the writing of *Ulysses*, is proportionate and corresponds to the accumulation and refinement of devices for achieving the equivalence between form and content.

Accordingly, the ironies of *Dubliners* are operative in an

exposure of "the soul of that hemiplegia or paralysis which
many consider a city," L 55, an exposure which appears "critical" so long as we adjust our vision to the author's moral
premises. The naturalism of the tone and metaphorical detail
is adjusted to precisely this purpose of moral stripping, since
the compromising undertones of pity and sentimentality are
not likely to be redirected by the reader to the author as a
qualification of his vivisective maneuvers. Of still greater
interest in the stories, however, is the movement of the naturalistic narrative toward a focus that is in every basic respect
an intended symbolism, and where this symbolism is discern-
ible as better accomplished we find that this is due to a more
complete and complex set of motives behind the critical tones
and the affective undertones. In striving toward a focus in the
arrangement of his materials, Joyce is striving toward an impersonal precision of statement and metaphorical reference
that will fix or "arrest" the naturalism into a symbolic illumination. This focus, moreover, implies a critical attitude on the
part of Joyce so long as we understand that "critical" applies to
the adjustment of our apprehension to what the story discloses
as well as to the way in which the exposure is achieved. This
adjustment is of course a matter of both moral and esthetic
considerations. In "The Dead," conceived and written in
1906-7, much of the story's merit is a result of a delicate balance
between the moral attitudes which work out its inner meaning
and the mode by which that meaning is directed to us. "The
Dead" is not only the most personal and most skillful of the
stories, not only the story in which Joyce's sentimentality and
pity emerge as a quality of evanescent pathos unusual in an
author of twenty-five or six, but likewise the story in which his
irony coheres most evidently with the intended symbolism.

2

The ironical dimension in *Dubliners* is then rather explicitly grounded in the "impersonal manner" of an attitude that

sees in Irish social convention and religion the cause of private frustrations and failure. From the opening page of "The Sisters" Joyce is determined to enlarge his naturalistic techniques and details to fit the frame, the paralytic *corpus*, of Irish public life. The words "paralysis," "gnomon," "simony," possess the deliberateness of an intended analogy and correspondence between the candor of the boy narrator, the ruin and failure of the dead priest, and the enervate life of the living. A number of critics have gone through the stories with one intent or another; nearly all have put their finger on the techniques that multiply and radiate the ironical significance of an inconclusive end or plot.[18] In "The Sisters" the moment of focus for the reader occurs when the incidents, comments, and perceptions which the sensitive boy assembles as the fragments of the inscrutable and even hostile adult world, accomplish the oblique exposure of the paralysis of Irish spiritual energies. The effect at the close is one of inconclusiveness, but this effect is simply the esthetic suspension or condition in which the naturalistic details are meant to become an operative symbolism. While the narrative is moving toward this focus we experience a certain tension between the impersonal manner and the ethical poles delimiting the subdued drama of "paralysis." But since the effect of inconclusiveness at the moment of focus is meant to arrest the naturalistic movement—Joyce's "criticism" of life—into a symbolic exposure, these tensions are necessarily slackened or suspended. This is a result of the intended correspondence, the suggested equivalence, between "paralysis," "gnomon," "simony," as uttered by the boy who does not comprehend the depth of their human significance, and that depth itself which the words illuminate from within the story.

In the three stories devoted to childhood, "The Sisters," "An Encounter," "Araby," the weight of the opposition between a joyless reality and the boy's fears and uneasy desires, of the moral implications of deformities and frustrations, falls on the sensitivity of the boy, and the oblique effect of the inconclusive end permits us to see in the exposure the suggestion that the boy has been brought to an intimation of what his experiences mean in a broader framework of human existence.[19] In other words, the boy, as perhaps only one or two characters in the stories which follow, grasps an intimation of the kind of self-knowledge that descends on Gabriel Conroy at the close of "The Dead." In the boy's "chalice," the "Pigeon House," a bazaar called "Araby," the "dis-tensive-ness" between realistic detail and symbolic contexts is the result of a technique which has confined the range of perceptions to the probing sensitivity of an adolescent who seems more mature than Stephen in the first chapter of *A Portrait* because he narrates his own experiences.

In the stories that follow, all of them "third person" narratives, the degree to which the techniques of exposure ensure a release of multiple ironical contexts varies significantly from one story to another by reason of the basic arrangement of their components. "Eveline," the first of the next group, offering the least complicated arrangement, illustrates in assertive fashion a paralyzing terror and distress of heart in an ordinary girl.[20] "Two Gallants" gives us a complete and yet economical arrangement of subject matter focused at the close by ironical exposure and the story's central symbol. In "Two Gallants" Joyce is scrupulously engaged in the "moral history"[21] aspect of a phase of Irish romance, which accounts for the callous superiority toward his characters. Lenehan gazing at the gold coin in Corley's palm is the final moment of a carefully developed equilibrium between the rhythm of the diction and the subtle variants of the dialogue. The ironical effect of the exposure radiates from the symbolic coin. The contexts of the symbol are diffused, as the after-effect of focus, with a humor that is only sufficiently grim to relieve by way of caricature the corrupt and servile manhood of the two youths. Yet the symbol is not accomplished in a way that distinguishes the story from many good ones of its kind. The gold coin can refer with equal effect to the girl who is betrayed as well as to the two gallants exposed, but as a Joycean symbol it clearly lacks the more subtle quality of the fire in "Ivy Day" and the snow in "The Dead." The explanation lies partly in the too deliberate approach to the subject which has produced an ending that is too conclusive even for Joyce. The "critical" superiority of the moralist is wholly unrelieved in that Lenehan, for all the servile disquiet of his emotions, is not permitted even the slightest glimpse of the awareness and self-knowledge that it must have cost Joyce to write the story.[22]

In the stories largely dependent on explicit statement for producing the moment of focus, we have Joyce's vivisective attitude toward Dublin life least complicated by the equivocal attachment of his loving contempt. In their case the ironical lies on the surface. A partial explanation may be that the techniques are adequate only to the sentimental side of Joyce's attitude and to the ironical-sentimental depiction of his subjects and his moral theme. In "The Boarding House" the surface movement of explicit statement—such as: Mrs. Mooney "dealt with moral problems as a cleaver deals with meat: and in this case she had made up her mind," *D* 74/59—is arrested at the moment of exposure by the probing understatement: "Then she [Polly] remembered what she had been waiting for," *D* 80/63. Joyce's concern with the isolation of individual sentiments, dreams, and desires places them against a social stagnation centered in the spiritual barrenness of family life. The joylessness of Bob Doran's future life with Polly is that marriage and family will fail to displace the bleakness of soul of the celibate. In "A Little Cloud" a prudent marriage has failed to empower Little Chandler with an identity of husband and father, so that his adult life becomes for him the remorseful frustration of adolescent dreams and desires for romance and adventure. "Counterparts" gives us the isolation of a less temperate Dubliner in which drink fails to relieve the dreariness of a mechanical existence at work and at home. In "Clay" these themes are gathered in the symbolism surrounding the figure of Maria, where the emphasis shifts to the implicit and the symbolical; and, accordingly, the exposure is less harsh, more nearly a balance between sympathy and dispassionate apprehension. The technique here is not so much to insure exposure at a central or closing moment as it is to prolong or sustain and thereby complete obliquely the "image" of Maria.

The theme of "A Painful Case" is a more sensitive one for Joyce, and therefore has required a greater concentration on disengagement. The result is that the emotional weight of the implied meanings falls more nearly on the situation than on the characters. Hence the exposure of Mr. Duffy's "incurable loneliness" of soul is accomplished less obliquely than is the case in the other stories. We apprehend that Mr. Duffy has grasped the void of sterile isolation in his celibate's life, that the unhappy outcast "from life's feast" intuits the moral framework of inadequacy and fulfillment in which we see him. One measure of Joyce's compassion is that his cathartic detachment from the subject has not depended on the elaboration within the story of a symbolic parallel or correspondence like the myth of Ulysses, which he thought of for the story he did not write, but that proved to be the embryo idea for *Ulysses*, L 146.[23] The technique in "A Painful Case" is that of refining the narrative diction to the extremes of what it can convey to the reader's most sensitive perceptions without the aid of the symbolism of "Clay" or the oblique art of reproducing dialogue.

Dialogue is the prominent technique in the first three stories devoted to Dublin public life, but the superior merits of "Ivy Day in the Committee Room" and "Grace" are due to an economy of symbolism that provides both precision and control and thematic flexibility to humorous nuances of psychological and social allusion.

"Father Purdon? Father Purdon?" said the invalid.

"O, you must know him, Tom," said Mr. Cunningham, stoutly. "Fine, jolly fellow! He's a man of the world like ourselves."    D 179/131

Mr. O'Connor tore a strip off the card and, lighting it, lit his cigarette. As he did so the flame lit up a leaf of dark glossy ivy in the lapel of his coat. The old man watched him attentively and then, taking up the piece of cardboard again, began to fan the fire slowly while his companion smoked.

"Ah, yes," he said, continuing, "it's hard to know what way to bring up children. Now who'd think he'd turn out like that! . . .    D 131/97-8

In "Ivy Day" the juxtapositions of past and present, of Parnell's heroism and his present death-in-life, are arranged so as to diffuse their meaning in the climatic "Pok!" of Mr. Hynes's bottle of stout, which has been heated against the regenerative fire even as his sentimental poem has heated the emotions in the Committee Room. The ironies of "Ivy Day" and "Grace" become operative in the tensions conveyed to us between the parochialism of Dublin's public life and the moral understanding which exposes it as a spiritual decay and paralysis. These tensions, we may go on to say now, proceed from the conception Joyce has of his stories as dramas of apprehension which achieve their moment of exposure with the arrestment of the naturalistic details in the reader's perceptions as a symbolic manifestation. The ironies, then, are qualified by this end which they serve within the story. Their tensions are subsumed in or cohere with the accomplished symbolism, and from it they acquire the qualitativeness of Joyce's equivocal attitude. In the imagery of the fire in "Ivy Day," the arrestment of naturalistic detail produces what we may call the symbolizing qualitativeness of the fire. Thus to see the fire and the contents of the bottles as the governing symbols of the story is to adjust our apprehension to the focus that is intended in the final comic "Pok!" The irony then acquires its quality from this magnetizing of our apprehension as a moral and esthetic requirement to the governing symbols. For this reason we can say that the tensions which actualize our responses have not arisen from an opposition between abstract concepts or categories of thought but from the presentation of concrete realities as intuited by an artistic sensibility which seeks their common point of rest in the complete — moral-esthetic — apprehension of the subject.

The symbolism of the snow in "The Dead" brings us to the stage of Joyce's artistic sensibility where we can clearly perceive that the governing symbol is to become operative in the correspondence between the mode of its presentation and the mode of its apprehension. This correspondence, or equivalence, is the determining factor of the quality of his irony in the story. In a fine chapter on "The Dead," Richard Ellmann suggests,[24] on the evidence of a letter from Joyce to his brother Stanislaus from Rome in 1907 ($L^{II}$ 212), that the ironic structure whereby the meaning of the story is illuminated by a character who does not appear is similar to the ironic method of Anatole France in "The Procurator of Judaea." The similarities between the two stories are curious but not decisive. The method of Anatole France depends for its effect on a sudden illumination, in which the absolutism of Christian conviction is countered by skepticism and historical relativity. Joyce's irony is operative through the symbols accomplished by the arrestment of his naturalist's precision and is accessible in its qualitativeness only through the symbols and not through an awareness of conflicting or opposed presumptions of an abstract kind.

In the closing scene of "The Dead," Gabriel's consciousness of his own person is disintegrating as he becomes aware of the overpowering presence of the dead among the living. The image of falling snow is so accomplished as to equate the exterior, descriptive and naturalistic "world" and the drama of a reconciliation to his insufficiency as lover and husband. Thus, as his perceptions, and ours, succeed and complete one another to the final period, the image enacts a verbal, rhythmical representation of Gabriel's awareness of this more complete person that he becomes, upon swooning, among the shades of the dead.

> His soul had approached that region where dwell the vast hosts of the dead. He was conscious of, but could not apprehend, their wayward and flickering existence. His own identity was fading out into a grey impalpable world: the solid world itself, which these dead had one time reared and lived in, was dissolving and dwindling.
> A few light taps upon the pane made him turn to the window. It had begun to snow again. He watched sleepily the flakes, silver and dark, falling obliquely against the lamplight. The time had come for him to set out on his journey westward. Yes, the newspapers were right: snow was general all over Ireland. . . It lay thickly drifted on the crooked crosses and headstones, on the spears of the little gate, on the barren thorns. His soul swooned slowly as he heard the snow falling faintly through the universe and faintly falling, like the descent of their last end, upon all the living and the dead.        D 241-42/174 .

Joyce has brought the "antithetical" elements by which he has presented the drama to a focus that "reconciles" them while establishing a state of *dis*-tension between them. Once we perceive that the antitheses between the living and the dead, between Gabriel and Michael Furey, or between any of the metaphorical elements, desire, fire, light, snow, and the gravestones, are to be attributed to Gabriel's acceptance of the revelation that comes upon him, we are obliged to accept the accomplished symbol as that focus bringing about and maintaining an equilibrium between a complex of significances and

our responses to them. An irony operative under these circumstances and by these methods becomes indicative of the temper of reconciliation to Ireland, to his exile, and, as Richard
Ellmann has made admirably clear,[25] to his private life as father
and husband in which Joyce conceived and completed the
story in 1906-7.

3

The question of Joyce's irony toward his artist-hero in the
final version of *A Portrait* is destined apparently to be a con-
troversial one among his critics for as long as it continues to be
of interest. As Hugh Kenner discovered,[26] a discussion of it
must take into account that Joyce was reluctant or unable to
bring the book to completion before he devised Stephen's
situation in *Ulysses* as a sequel. It is not incumbent on us to
review the differing opinions on the subject.[27] For the purposes of this essay we need to understand that the ironical
dimension of Joyce's attitude toward Stephen is essential to
the kind of work *A Portrait* was intended to be and also turned
out to be. The definitive version was begun in Trieste late in
1907 and completed late in 1914, or even as late as 1915.[28] The
first three of the five chapters were completed within a period
of a few months in 1907–8; the last two were five years in
gestation and composition. The fourth chapter, begun probably in 1909 and completed in 1914, is the shortest of the five
and contains the climactic scenes of the narrative; the fifth,
perhaps not completed until 1915, is the longest, and in it
Stephen, having developed into the "young man" of the title,
becomes vulnerable to what most of Joyce's critics agree is
ironical and even comical exposure, not as *a young man* alone,
but as the immature or even sham *artist*[29] who, with only two
little poems to his credit, sets out to the Continent to create in
"silence, exile, and cunning" the "uncreated conscience" of a
benighted Irish race.

The stylization of the narrative in *A Portrait*, the imitative accuracy, temper, and metaphorical adequacy of its representational mode to the stages of Stephen's moral and intellectual development, is hardly in need of emphasis from any quarter. The ironical dimension of the novel is part and parcel of this stylization, is operative within it and qualified by it, so that we need, nonetheless, to approach Joyce's irony toward Stephen and toward Stephen's Dublin environment by considering the stylization as the adequate focus. It is apparent that the narrative proceeds in each of the five chapters toward a climax which, when accomplished, acquires a dialectical significance in relation to the others, so that the fifth chapter becomes the final point of convergence for the contents of the other four, the dialectical point where the young man's "past" can be apprehended both as the fluid succession of events it has been as well as the personal and social factor with which he must struggle in order to win intellectual and moral liberation from "home, fatherland, and church." The narrative, then, is so arranged that its prose surface relates the story of Stephen's developing consciousness directly, but the arrangement itself is a complex of indirect significances, analogues, images, motifs, and symbols, which the reader is obliged to organize into the whole they constitute at any given point, in order to attain to the mode of apprehension indicating or pointing to the meaning or intention behind the entire artifice. One approach to this focus, I suggest, is to consider what Joyce called an "individuating rhythm" in the first paragraph of the narrative essay of January 1904,—the rhythm, as I see it, individualizing the complex of specific emotional and intellective matter being represented, and, in Joyce's words, reproducing the "features of infancy" in the "adolescent portrait."[30] In the arrangement of the five chapters we can distinguish two "individuating rhythms" which work toward juxtaposition, or counterpoint, in chapter IV, and then proceed to coalesce in the completely "dramatic" representation of chapter V, ending with the highly charged diary entries. One rhythm equates the representation with Stephen's consciousness, with the way he senses things or the way they affect him. The other is the rhythm of a representation, more or less naturalistic, of the external world. In the following, from the scene of the second sermon in chapter III, the two rhythms are juxtaposed.

> Every word for him! It was true. . . A wave of fire swept through his body: the first. Again a wave. His brain began to glow. Another. His brain was simmering and bubbling within the cracking tenement of the skull. Flames burst forth from his skull like a corolla, shrieking like voices:
> —Hell! Hell! Hell! Hell! Hell!
> Voices spoke near him:
> —On hell.
> —I suppose he rubbed it into you well.
> —You bet he did. He put us all into a blue funk.
> —That's what you fellows want: and plenty of it to make you work.    P 380/267–68

To say that an ironical exposure of Stephen emerges from the juxtaposition is surely to overread the passage, at least with regard to the boy's feelings as the sincere and unequivocal feelings of a sensitive adolescent. Nor is Joyce's purpose here simply to expose the materialism and the crude terror of the grotesque religiosity surrounding Stephen. If we apprehend it rightly, the juxtaposition is more of a balance than it is a contrast; or, rather, it achieves a balance of the two rhythms to the extent that we apprehend how such an experience as the boy is undergoing leads ultimately to the *non serviam* of chapter V and to his rejection of the hangman God of Irish Catholicism.

The two rhythms are juxtaposed most pointedly in the climactic scene on the beach in chapter IV—the scene usually cited as an instance of ironical "deflation" of Stephen's soaring "lyrical," "heroic," or "romantic" aspirations.

—Stephanos Dedalos! Bous Stephanoumenos! Bous Stephaneforos!

Their banter was not new to him and now it flattered his mild proud sovereignty. Now, as never before, his strange name seemed to him a prophecy. So timeless seemed the grey warm air, so fluid and impersonal his own mood, that all ages were as one to him. A moment before the ghost of the ancient kingdom of the Danes had looked forth through the vesture of the hazewrapped city. Now, at the name of the fabulous artificer, he seemed to hear the noise of dim waves and to see a winged form flying above the waves and slowly climbing the air. What did it mean? Was it a quaint device opening a page of some medieval book of prophecies and symbols, a hawk-like man flying sunward above the sea, a prophecy of the end he had been born to serve and had been following through the mists of childhood and boyhood, a symbol of the artist forging anew in his workshop out of the slug-gish matter of the earth a new soaring impalpable im-perishable being?

His heart trembled; his breath came faster and a wild spirit passed over his limbs as though he were soaring sunward. His heart trembled in an ecstasy of fear and his soul was in flight. His soul was soaring in an air beyond the world and the body he knew was purified in a breath and delivered of incertitude and made radiant and com-mingled with the element of the spirit. An ecstasy of flight made radiant his eyes and wild his breath and tremulous and wild and radiant his windswept limbs.

—One! Two! . . . Look out!

—O, cripes, I'm drownded!

—One! Two! Three and away!

—Me next! Me next!

—One! . . . Uk!

—Stephaneforos! . . .    *P* 430–31/301–2

The degree to which this juxtaposition produces an ironi-cal exposure of Stephen depends on precisely how we adjust the two rhythms to one another, on the degree to which we resolve the discordant contrast by an apprehension adequate to what they portray as a whole in the juxtaposition and as a part of the entire narrative of five chapters. The unitive element here is the mythical analogy, to which both the bantering and the ecstatic thoughts and feelings of the boy are to be referred. The scene and the complex of juxtaposed rhythms are an extremely important instance of a use by Joyce of such an analogy for establishing an equivalence between the representational mode of his narrative and the mode of its apprehension by the reader. There is nothing like it in *Stephen Hero* and nothing really quite like it in *Ulysses*. Stephen, in his adolescent excitement, consciously identifies himself and his name in a "timeless . . . impersonal moment" with the name of "the fabulous artificer," and by the identification and its verbal simulation he experiences the freedom and radiant ecstasy of beauty "romantically" and, of course, "uncritically," but discovers thereby, and as an adolescent, the vocation of the artist. The analogy is accomplished by a juxtaposition of the two rhythms, but it is not intended to convey a contrast, satirical or otherwise, between them, or to convey an opposite meaning, from either direction, to the mythic figure of "a hawklike man." The balanced adjustment of the two rhythms to one another is accomplished by the reader when he understands that the analogy is there as an objectivizer of Joyce's meaning, which is not expressed but represented. As the objectivizer of his meaning, the analogy is also operative as a neutralizer, and a qualifier of whatever tensions the juxtaposed rhythms will incite in our responses to the contents of the entire passage. The analogy, a complex of poetry and erudition, is meant to arrest our responses from diverting to the extremes of complete sympathy and identification with Stephen's "esthetic experience," or the satirical rejection of him as an Icarus who never gets off the ground. It is, as a *mythical* analogy, meant to arrest and thereby complete our responses, by equating to the mode of its representation our understanding of the narrative; and, as such, is a measure of the impersonality and objectivity Joyce was capable of by the year 1914 in the writing of fiction dramatizing his youthful artistic gestation to the year 1904. In *Ulysses* the entire process is dramatized in the distance separating the insufficiency and instability of Stephen's rebellion from the adjustments of Leopold Bloom as husband, father, and member of society. At this point in our essay we may say that the emergence of such an "objectifying" analogue—the operative sense of which is mythical—is a significant moment in the process of Joyce's artistic disengagement from the subject matter of his fiction through the intense contemplation of himself as the externalizing agent rendering a particular and personal experience a universal, dramatic, and impersonal one.

In chapter V of *A Portrait* Stephen has matured to the stage where the dramatic representation of his development is narrated directly in the way he expresses his ideas and attitudes, and the two rhythms which cannot now be kept apart have converged and coalesced. At this stage Stephen's own self-awareness becomes bitterly self-critical and even self-deprecatory: "His mind bred vermin. His thoughts were lice born of the sweat of sloth,"*P*504/352. It is also the stage where Joyce's withdrawal permits a genuinely humorous treatment of Stephen, indeed to the point where the young man may direct a comical irony to his own "heroic" pose and self-glorifying attitudes: "Asked me, was I writing poems? About whom? I asked her. This confused her more and I felt sorry and mean. Turned off that valve at once and opened the spiritual-heroic refrigerating apparatus, invented and patented in all countries by Dante Alighieri," *P* 525/366.

The narrative in chapter V becomes fully dramatic and impersonal to precisely the degree to which we apprehend that what is here objectivified are the qualities in the young artist that isolate Stephen from his family, friends, fatherland,

and the religion which has informed his mind but is no longer adequate to his conception of what "life" is or what it is for: his intellect and sensitivity, his courage and pride, and the impulsion that his soul derives from the stresses within him between an unyielding self-confidence and a critical self-awareness. That isolation is expressed most dramatically in the entries, where each of the book's major themes is brought to a final focus with an economy of means. The entries are the "exposure" of an artistic consciousness groping toward the "new personal experience" Stephen mentions to Lynch in the exposition of his esthetic ideas ("When we come to the phenomena of artistic conception, artistic gestation and artistic reproduction I require a new terminology and a new personal experience," *P*476–77/332). This will be the very partially fulfilled experience that Joyce permits him to have in the course of the action of *Ulysses*, for the complete "new" experience is none other than the constantly enlarging apprehension of the relations between "art" and "life" of the artist as he commits his personal experience to the ends of an impersonal art. Stephen, perforce, does not understand that his liberation, the moral liberation of the artist, is but the condition from which there will evolve the moral and artistic apprehension of life which is the work of art in Joyce's terms of 1914-21[31] — that is, *Ulysses* — although he states the rough grasp he has of it, and one that the young Joyce of 1904, or even 1907, would have been incapable of, in the bitter and cold pride of his declaration:

> "You talk to me of nationality, language, religion. I shall try to fly by those nets."     *P* 469/327
> "I will not serve that in which I no longer believe, whether it call itself my home, my fatherland, or my church: and I will try to express myself in some mode of life or art as freely as I can and as wholly as I can, using for my defence the only arms I allow myself to use — silence, exile, and cunning."     *P* 519/362

Joyce permits Stephen a number of uneasy intimations of what, in "Proteus," for instance, the new experience will exact from him in terms of his own dedication to "art" and to "life," as when the youth reflects on the lyrical entry of a previous night (10 April), expressing his feelings and apprehensions in the rhythms and image of "liberated emotion," and finds the entry insufficient as objective insight into his total circumstances, his moods, and his analytical awareness of them: "Vague words for a vague emotion," P 524/366.

A final focus to the book, the diary entries are directed simultaneously to the reader as an affirmation of the young artist's quest and sense of liberation as he experiences them and an exposure of his limitations due to his immaturity. Of major interest, with regard to an ironical reading, is the quality emerging from a "howness" focusing and completing the *whatness* of the fiction. The simultaneity of the direct and indirect functions of the illuminated whole produces a diffusion and a balance of reference points proportionately greater or less as that simultaneity becomes operative as the objectivity itself of our private apprehension equated to Joyce's mode of representation. With this as our basis, we may go on to say that the ironical dimension in *A Portrait* becomes operative according to that mode of apprehension by which we can separate the drama of liberation going on within Stephen's consciousness from the drama of repression without: from the first page, where the forces of repression, which are equally the forces to be mastered in artistic creation, are indicated in the father's story as the minotaurish[32] "moocow coming down along the road," to the last page, where the youth, invoking the image of the "old father, old artificer," goes forth to encounter "life" as the "reality of experience" for the "millionth time."

Once we understand that the "exposure" of the ironical dimension pertains to the structural unity of the book, because of the way its parts relate to one another, we perceive also the

the ulterior design and the intention that have qualified the
operations of irony, by elevating them to the luminosity of
esthetic apprehension. We shall have, then, an irony qualified
by the relations of balance and wholeness between the multiple elements we are obliged to suspend and equate. This will
be an irony directed more to the balance our apprehension is
to achieve between the elements offered for our contemplation
than a contrast between what is expressed and what is implied. Hence, putting it into a nutshell, we can say that, to the
objective contemplator, the overall effect of Joyce's irony in *A
Portrait* cannot be the one-sided exposure or deflation of
Stephen's rebellion as the futile isolation, negative impulsion,
and attempt at self-sufficiency of a barren, "indigestibly
Byronic"[33] esthete any more than it can be a Swiftian pro-
phetic exposure of Ireland in Stephen's vision of her, in "cold
violence," as "the old sow that eats her farrow," *P* 470/328.

S. L. Goldberg strikes one as the most judicious among
Joyce's critics, the most responsive to the book's complexity.
Joyce, he says, "in the very terms of his novel . . . could not
dramatise more of the deeper vision to which Stephen is grop-
ing than is embodied in the portrayal of his groping itself.
Hence the need for a sequel, *Ulysses*."[34]

# JOYCE 3

*The irony of the stars*     FW 160.22

The irony of a great author can be distinguished for the quality of the perceptions it instigates. Critical usage dating from the eighteenth century has commonly ascribed to irony, or its presence has been perceived in, a certain kind of detachment, an impersonality, or even indifference. But the truth of the matter is that the irony of a great author—Plato, Shakespeare, Goethe, or Thomas Mann—is one of the most personal and unmistakable attributes of his art. It is as if the impersonal means which traditionally have been identified with irony in the abstract sense were the surest, even the sole, means for preserving and conveying a sense of personal intimacy. In the case of *Ulysses* this paradoxical question becomes central to our enquiry. The sensibility behind the total meaning of the novel is apt to be baffling to the reader who does not grasp the fundamental, encased "impersonal" structure of its comic-ironic potential. It is not exaggerating things to say that we do not penetrate fully to the ironical nerve of *Ulysses* unless or until we can assimilate the "impersonality" of its large-scale verbal techniques and parodies, its multidimensional stylization, and arrive thereby at the apprehension of *how* (technique and artifice) Joyce provokes *what* his irony conveys. The ironical dimension in *Ulysses* pivots on the tensions provoked in a reader's awareness of the dissonant, because simultaneous, validity of double, parallel, or opposed meanings; of analogies, correspondences, and dichotomies suspended in a situation directing, almost completely, the dramatic resolution of the narrative events as a total meaning to the reader's resources for bringing to a focus the inconclusive events in the lives of Stephen Dedalus, Leopold and Molly Bloom on June 16–17, 1904. On its most inconclusive level *Ulysses* appears to be a naturalistic novel, a parallel—but in some ways one in opposition—to the Homeric epic. Likewise, its structure is both a dichotomy of the symbolic and naturalistic methods and an analogy, or correspondence, between them.

The surface detection of irony in *Ulysses*, however, is

hardly a serious problem for the reader; indeed, irony is one of its most conspicuous attributes. Joyce's critics have paid more than adequate attention to it, but they have not bent their efforts consistently to specify for themselves and for readers of *Ulysses* what it is about that irony that makes it distinctly and decisively an ingredient of the novel, or how it is related to the book's significance as a work of art.

In 1926 Edwin Muir, whose essay on Joyce in *Transition* is faithful to the critical reaction to *Ulysses* of the post-war generation, singled out a *quality* in Joyce which he explained as the result of an "objectified" expression of the artist's "uncompromising opposition" to the Zeitgeist of the emerging twentieth century.[35] There were many superficial resemblances between the works of Joyce and those of his contemporary Aldous Huxley, the "best example of the fashionable writer" passively reflecting that same Zeitgeist. Both writers were irreligious, disillusioned, and ironical, and the temper of the age was all three. Broadly speaking, Huxley's disillusionment was an "attitude" of fashion, an habitual, self-evident assumption which the reader, if he chose, might assume and take for granted. Huxley's work depended for its effect on the fact that his audience tended to make the same assumptions he made, but once his attitude or mood was not accepted as self-evident, his irony became empty, and the reader was left with a mere attitude, shared by a great number of persons who questioned it as little as did the author. In *Ulysses* Joyce had objectified his disillusionment so completely that the reader could not take it for granted or assume it as self-evident; he was compelled to reckon with it, "for this disillusionment is no longer an attitude, but rather all that an attitude by its nature hides and keeps us from seeing." Thus *Ulysses* depended very little for its comprehension on the mood with which its readers approached it, "for their floating disillusionment, half-conscious and vague, is there so profoundly grasped and completely objectified, that the general mood fades, evaporates, becomes unreal, beside it. We feel that this attitude has been radically modified, that henceforth it must become more real, or, if it persists, more unreal."

Edwin Muir was perhaps the first observer to relate the surface detection of the ironical in *Ulysses* to what was there objectified and to consider that this relation constituted a *quality*. This *quality of objectification*, I suggest, ought to be interpreted as a positive effort, if not a kind of obsession, on Joyce's part to relocate the spiritual inheritance of a disintegrating Christian belief and the Humanism evolved from it upon a broader base of value, upon "Life" understood as a value in itself. To speak of an objectified "disillusionment" is to see only one side of the many-sided impersonality of *Ulysses*. It has always surprised me that even some of Joyce's most sympathetic critics have been content to see this impersonality and this quality of objectification as satire, social criticism, parody or mock-something, mock-epic or a mock-something else.

One of Harry Levin's specialities in *James Joyce, A Critical Introduction* is a recurring, persuasive comment on the subject of Joyce's irony. It will be remembered that in the chapter on "The Personal Epic" Levin ascribes the effect of Joyce's irony in *Ulysses* to the "contradictions" of an ambiguous view of man as "a ribless wretch exalted to Homeric stature, and a legendary hero fallen upon evil days." "Out of these contradictions," he says, "Joyce's characters derive their special irony and pathos."[36] While he warns that Joyce's irony is "two-edged," he seems to have considered the mock-heroic side of the sword—or scalpel—as sharper and more durable. "Joyce's irony—he never lets us forget—is two-edged, and is constantly cutting back to the sources of his pathos. The immediate effect of this method, we have seen, is to reduce his characters to mock-heroic absurdity. A further and quite contradictory effect is to magnify them, to treat their little habits as profound rituals, to attach a universal significance to the

most minute particulars."[37] What Levin does not seem to
consider is that we do not have two effects, one following and
contingent upon the other, but that Joyce may have attempted
to produce a highly radical *single* effect intending an immediate and simultaneous perception of the unity of the realistic
detail and its symbolic overtones. Thus Levin's treatment
stresses Joyce's center of reference, "his dual formula of irony
and pathos,"[38] producing in the reader, for example, an awareness of ironic pathos in Rudy's apparition at the close of the
brothel hallucination, *U* 609/574, and one of pathetic irony at
the point (literally the large dot) at which "womb weary"
Bloom falls asleep at the close of "Ithaca," *U* 737/698. But the
other center of reference (though aware of it, Levin does not
stress it) must be the reader's perception of what Joyce has
objectified. The reader's emotions must not only be provoked,
they too must be distanced, objectified, impersonalized; that is
to say, adjusted through the "howness" of the verbal techniques to the *whatness* of the dramatic narrative. In short, what
Levin's treatment seems to lack is the emphasis on what he
preferred to leave as a brilliant suggestion: that the "material"
Joyce spoke of and the resources of his techniques were complicated in order to produce a precise effect simultaneously
with the release of the "simple" thought, and that the immediate resolution of one and the other produced that effect (in
Levin's phrase) of the thought "constantly aspiring toward the
permanence of myth."[39]

No critic has made more intense efforts to explain and to
defend the artistic sensibility behind *Ulysses* than Hugh Kenner, and none has conceded a higher quantitative estimate of
its ironical potential while fixing its qualitative resources at a
comparatively minor level. In *Dublin's Joyce* Kenner's point of
departure is Joyce's method of "double-writing." By this he
means the techniques of parody and their effects.

Joyce's Dublin was in fact an eighteenth-century parody. The technique he developed, the technique which underlies everything from the first pages of *Dubliners* to the end of *Finnegans Wake*, came out of the subject: parody: double writing. The music-halls parodied the heroic dramas; Joyce parodied the music-halls. Journalism parodied heroic elegance: Joyce parodied journalism. He focussed, that is to say, on what was actually there, and strove so to set it down that it would reveal itself as what it was, in its double nature: a distortion, but a distortion of something real.[40]

Joyce's irony in *Ulysses* is an inevitable result of the tensions instigated between Dublin's distorted human matter, embalmed in its language, and the mind and sensitivity engineering that parodic vision. It is a comprehensive irony whose potential is in exact relation to the depth and scope of Joyce's analogical perspectives. Its complete assimilation and the resolution of the naturalistic action of *Ulysses* by the reader will reproduce for the reader Joyce's comical, superior, and negative evaluation of his characters and their city—that is to say, his repudiation of them. The total sense of his irony, it follows, is derived from his complete apprehension of what Dublin and its inhabitants signify in the modern world; the complete apprehension of his subject is the equivalent of his complete repudiation of it.

Thus in the chapter on "How to Read *Ulysses*" we are told that, by a saturation in the ironies of Joyce's analogical vision, Bloom's character will focus for us at a "matrix of irony,"[41] which occurs in the suspensions of the interior monologue. The perception of this matrix involves the exploring of the "magnetic field" established by Joyce's controlling ideas. One of these ideas, and according to Kenner one of the most inclusive, is that "no Dubliner acts from his nature, no Dubliner knows what his nature is; he acts on the promptings of *idées reçues* and talks in words that have for too long been respoken."[42]

Stephen and Bloom are visited all day long by teasing fragments of ideas, and it is easy to read *Ulysses* in a mood of
languid assent to these incompatible and unrealized
modes of thought. Wyndham Lewis' assertion, correct in
one sense, that the book contains no "ideas" whatever,
the contrasting excesses of Stuart Gilbert's Bloomesque
introductory chapters on its esoteric philosophy, should
warn us that it is precisely the pathetic absurdity of
Bloom's and Stephen's bits and pieces of speculation that
is being exposed. Such conceptions as Karma and Metem-
psychosis apply with ironic punctilio both to Bloom's
and Stephen's quasi-hypnotized actions and to the
emotional quality of their thought. And these conceptions
are implicitly evaluated by the quality of those actions and
that thought. This evaluation in turn brings us into the
realm of the controlling ideas of the book, the rational
ethics and metaphysics of the free intelligence, gestured
towards by Stephen in his sententious appeals to Aquinas
and Aristotle, and by Bloom in the fidelity of his thought,
despite its negligible penetration, to empirical reality;
belied by Stephen and Bloom alike in their, respectively,
hubristic and masochistic narcissism. The controlling
ideas are never stated. They exist, like magnetic fields,
behind and around the words, apprehensible through
perspectives of triple analogy. Joyce's irony goes deep
indeed. Not only does Bloom not know that he is Ulysses
(the meaning of his own actions); he does not know that
he is an analogue of Christ inhabiting a sacramental
universe (the meaning of his own thoughts). Stephen
on the other hand is aware that he is Hamlet, but his
awareness is put to the wrong uses. It provides him with
no insight. It merely feeds his morbidity. It is a role in
which he is imprisoned. He is constantly aware of an
infinitely extending perspective of future selves to be
traversed and assimilated.[43]

According to Kenner's exegesis, the spiritual values of
Joyce the Catholic artist are not in the book or in the life fic-

tionally represented in the book; they are outside the book, to
be inferred, as Kenner does in the passage above, from the
equation of critico-moral judgment to artistic detachment.
Joyce's repudiation of Dublin, and of the modern world insofar as Dublin is representative of it, is spiritual by reason of
the values that inform his ironical vision of it. The measure of
Joyce's spiritual supremacy over Dublin is the extent and
depth to which he has transformed his materials into the
comical representation of it. This is best seen in the inane
"pseudo-impersonality"[44] of the catechism of "Ithaca," Joyce's
funniest episode because in it, presumably, he can be most
comic about his aloofness toward Bloom and Stephen. The
reader who assimilates the ironical perspectives of his analogues and resolves the naturalistic action according to Joyce's
terms, will perceive his supreme spiritual aloofness from the
whirling mechanism of the comic inferno of Dublin, and will
thereby arrive at the ultimate, cathartic effect of his comedy.
The quality of his irony pertains to the assimilation of the
scope and depth of the analogues (Ulysses, Christ, Shakespeare, Hamlet, and so on) down to the most vulgar and
trivial, ant-like Swiftian detail, in order that we may resolve
their meaning as the antithesis to the total contents of the
book, and whose total sense is Joyce's repudiation. The
cathartic value of the irony lies in the genius of Joyce's techniques of "epiphany," in the artifice of mock styles; the sensibility of this demiurgic Joyce is released in the cogency his
symbols have for illuminating the sacramental distortion in
the vulgarity of modern life. Thus the artifice of parodic styles
is an equilibrium by which Joyce can affirm his critical and
total renunciation of modern "industrial" civilization and
confirm the sacramental nature of the Word. It follows that we
cannot read *Ulysses* as a novel, but as a mock-novel, if not a
mock-myth (Bloom "is the most inadequate Messiah imagina-
ble"),[45] and that its irony is not operational in the disclosing of
a dimension in the lives of the characters which is not ulti-

mately to be resolved in Joyce's spiritual, but comical repudiation of them.

2

Kenner's views have been answered at length in *The Classical Temper, A Study of James Joyce's "Ulysses,"* by S. L. Goldberg,[46] who takes an opposite view of Joyce's book and its irony. It was, in fact, his criticism of Kenner's arguments, and the remarkable circumstance that those arguments leave Wyndham Lewis's criticisms of the novel intact, which prompted Goldberg to undertake the most extensive and by all counts the most significant treatment of irony in *Ulysses* that we have from Joyce's critics.

Goldberg's problem, as I see it, has been to resolve the dilemma posed by an irony understood as the intervention of a negative attitude and quality in the critical apprehension of *Ulysses* and what he understands as the positive achievement of Joyce. His task might have been easier had he not started from the premise on which Kenner's conception of irony in *Ulysses* stands: that Joyce's irony is a "critical" instrument, a diagnostic exposer, charged by the author's denunciation and activated and sustained by "critical" and corrosive tensions imparted to the reader—tensions whose purpose it is to "dissolve" their object, the values represented by Bloom, Stephen, and Molly. Briefly put, Goldberg's perplexity has been this: how can those "negative" and corrosive tensions account for the positive and imaginative re-creation of myth which is the total meaning of the novel arrived at through the resolution of the dramatic action? (See pp. 197ff) How is it that Joyce's ironic vision of life comes to resolve itself, through the dynamic and dramatic development of the action, into the impersonal *"stasis* of mythic contemplation?" Irony dissolves, corrodes, destroys. Myth, we are disposed to believe, is generic and cohesive, indestructible. I do not intend to produce here more than the barest schema of Goldberg's demonstration and arguments, whose intrinsic merits of clarity and thorough critical assimilation of *Ulysses* are as rewarding as they are evident.

Goldberg's first step is to declare and to demonstrate that Joyce's irony is a "qualifying criticism, which does not imply a total rejection of its object in the least" (p. 110), and that it is a compassionate irony derivable from an outlook neither exclusively tragic nor exclusively comic, but including both; derivable, that is, from Joyce's *classical temper* (p. 118). The second step is to consider that the "modes of irony in *Ulysses*," at their richest a poise or balance of moral attitudes, relate the values which are Joyce's own to those his protagonists represent. The next step is to demonstrate how the central moral activity of the author Joyce expresses itself in the "dramatic organizations of his materials, enacting its values" in his art (pp. 118–144), so that "the action of the book comprises not only the physical and mental acts of its protagonists but also the acts whereby the artist, looking back over his world within, evaluates theirs by shaping them; that is to say, it includes Joyce's manipulation of narrative techniques, his parodies, his intrusive parallels" (p. 143).

Goldberg's interpretation of *Ulysses* rests on the tenet that the book is foremost and unequivocally a representational novel (a very unusual one, of course), and that much, if not most, of its meaning is expressed in and through its representational mode (p. 107). It is to be read and understood as a representational novel, not as a complex, symbolic poem. As a novel, its protagonists must possess and execute the autonomy, the moral freedom, of human beings, and it is the dramatic presentation of this freedom with which Joyce's *classical temper* is concerned. One aspect of Joyce's artistic achievement is an innovational kind of character development in depth within an action limited to the events of a single day. The Homeric parallels, and the other purely associative analogues,

such as the parts of the body, which are outside the consciousness of the protagonists altogether, can be related to the
inner development of character only as perspectives derivable
from the protagonists' moral actions, and on this essential and
delicate maneuver depends the resolution of the dramatic
action as a re-creation or transposition of the "myth of Ulysses"
*sub specie temporis nostri* (the phrase is Joyce's, *L* 146–47)
(p. 203). The reader's comprehension of the events of the day
does not approach the full potential of Joyce's ironical vision
until "Ithaca," at which point the "mythic vision" of the work
becomes evident as the result of the superior position in time
of the author and reader, who can see, impersonally, the comprehensive, universal whole of past, present, and future which
the action and events of the day, this "now and here," comprise in the lives of Bloom, Stephen, and Molly (see pp. 188ff).
Detachment and impersonality acquire their significance from
the creative activity of the artist who contemplates his
world—his characters and his own experience—in spiritual
*stasis*, accepting it in his mature self-knowledge as the element
in which he lives, yet free from complete bondage to its values
(pp. 143–44). Thus the imaginative truth that most deeply
moves the book is pointing to the synthesis of Bloom and
Stephen in the comprehension of the artist; and it is in and by
that comprehension that Joyce's readers "behold the process of
human life, now and here, in its perennial condition." This
truth is what most deeply moves the reader and at the same
time underlies Joyce's "impersonal, comprehensive irony."
"Not only does the work achieve the completion and freedom
of a universal imaginative symbol, but the dramatic action of
Stephen-Bloom-Joyce achieves completion in the *stasis* of the
'mythic' contemplation of life" (p. 209).

A major point of Goldberg's contribution is that it has
moved the discussion of Joyce's irony over much firm ground
to an estimate of its imaginative potential and quality, from
what Joyce "dissolves" or criticizes to what he objectifies in

imaginative terms. Goldberg investigates and discriminates between "modes" of irony in the novel, but his conclusions as to its effect and quality do not rest on the specification, the separate validity of these "modes," but on the quality established by their balance, and this balance cannot be explained as "criticism" emerging from "critical tensions" because, as he acknowledges, Joyce does not have critical ideas with which to criticize and expose modern society, nor is this his intention. Joyce, he tells us, has moral attitudes, and the heart of his irony is a "poise," a balance of these attitudes. The tensions of Joyce's irony are "critical" for a purpose, but criticism is clearly not that purpose, for where we find them "balanced" we encounter something altogether beyond a context of moral or social criticism. Hence one ought to discuss equally the effect that the "balance" or "poise" produces on our discriminations, as well as the attitudes from which it derives and into which it will refract. It seems to me, then, that the way to Joyce's irony in *Ulysses* is to attempt to explain how we receive its effect as a "balance," or *stasis*, of tensions—that is to say, as a resolution of those tensions.

Goldberg has diagnosed and understood the effect conveyed by those tensions, and has illuminated the moral action of the book accordingly; yet he has not modified his conception of irony as primarily providing isolated satirical and conflicting effects rather than a resolution of these in the condition of *stasis*, or balance. The modes of irony in *Ulysses*, he argues, operate between the two extremes of the Homeric parallels (as proposed by Harry Levin), the most obvious mode being the exposure of the protagonists' inadequacies and contradictions, "the sharp, diagnostic irony that underlies Joyce's comparison of the noble and spacious world of Homer with the flaccid corruption of the present" (p. 118). The other extreme is the other side of the Homeric analogy, proceeding from genuine parallels between the "resourceful, insinuating, multi-faceted heroes of the *Odyssey* and *Ulysses*, between the common life of men and women in one age and the other, even between the gusto and vivacity of the two books . . . Joyce's irony also cuts back on the supposed grandiosities of the past in order to reveal the living clay of humanity in every age" (p. 119). Between these two extremes Joyce maintains a "poise," or complex balance of attitudes, toward his two protagonists and their ambiguous relations to society and to each other that is "far too little understood," for it is by this "poised comprehension," in which his protagonists are both the object and the means or vehicle of his criticism of life (pp. 120–121), that Joyce sees life steadily and sees it whole and achieves a dramatic presentation of it in the portrayal of Bloom and Stephen, and precisely in the technique of the interior monologue (p. 123; see also pp. 37, 248ff). Joyce's irony is richest when it "includes and balances," when it responds to the complexity of its object, rather than in its sharp hostilities and in its rejections of the preponderantly parodic irony of "Wandering Rocks," "Lestrygonians," "Nausicaa," and "Eumaeus."

The complexity of Joyce's ironic modes responds to the completeness of his vision. Bloom's limitations seem ignoble only because they are treated so completely; but because they are partly the limitations of his time and place, they are also the limitations of ordinary humanity itself. We distort Joyce's meaning if we fail to see his completeness, "if we fail to discriminate between the kind of irony he directs at the accidents of his protagonists, their 'now and here' as it were, and the kind he directs at their substance."

> To take one crucial case: when Bloom, at the end of "Circe," stands protectively over the homeless and unconscious Stephen, the physical situation of the two men forms an obvious symbol of the spiritual. Bloom imagines the figure of his dead, "unseeing" son, Rudy, resurrected, and dressed with a generously appalling sentimentality—"a fairy boy of eleven . . . dressed in an

Eton suit with glass shoes and a little bronze helmet . . ." The style of this clearly marks Bloom's sensibility, but that is not the only, or even the major, point of the passage. The substance of his "wonderstruck" perception is genuine. The only irony that affects *it* is that which encompasses the paternity theme as a whole—the fact that neither Bloom nor Stephen can understand their relationship properly. In other words, despite Bloom's petty beliefs, his occasional sentimentality, his frustrations, his exile from other men and from clear ideals of spiritual relationship, it is probably more accurate to stress his moral stature (despite his limitations) than his limitations (despite his moral stature). The difference is only one of emphasis, and we must beware of pressing either side too far, for Joyce's ironies maintain a subtle and delicate balance (pp. 136–37).

We have only to compare this passage with the efforts of previous critics to deal with one of the finest moments in the book to recognize the advantage Goldberg holds over his predecessors. Goldberg locates two "kinds" of "critical" irony that maintain a balance contingent upon a necessary suspension of emphasis. This balance is nowhere in the action itself, of course, nor in its representation, but in the apprehension of the action, in the objectified resolution of all its parts within the framework of style; that is, in its significance as art. Once we focus the physical action through style into a symbolical meaning we no longer have a quality of conflicting tensions between a kind of "critical" irony directed at the accidents of Bloom's limitations and another kind directed at his substance. For the reader to achieve the wholeness of the objectifying *stasis* of comprehension leading to "mythic contemplation," and to grasp (in Goldberg's phrase) the themes Joyce has realized dramatically, those tensions must be resolved; their resolution in fact is necessary for and no small part of that act of apprehension itself. In other words, I am pointing out the requisite development from *kinesis* to *stasis* which stipulates Joyce's irony in *Ulysses* and fixes its quality. It is this quality which Joyce's critics attempt to define when they qualify his irony with the attributes of pathos, like Levin, or, like Goldberg, as an "encompassing irony" of "compassion."

I venture to propose that beyond the critical analysis of the kind establishing "the modes of irony" in *Ulysses* there lies the consideration of "poise," or balance, as the determining factor of the quality of Joyce's irony. This, I think, is the decisive feature about it for both Joycean reader and critic. My contention is that Joyce's "structural" symbolism—the shifts of "style," points of view, and parodic techniques—are intended to converge, as it were, in our act of apprehending *how* he provokes through these very means our apprehension of the world of his characters. The ironical dimension of the novel lies exactly where Goldberg says it does, in the "gap" between the moral freedom of the three principal characters and the esthetic freedom, the encompassing vision, of the author.

> *Ulysses* portrays, as well as objective reality as we all may see it more or less, the symbolizing power that, under its given circumstances and conditions, projects its own reality: what we may call the Bloomworld, the Stephenworld, the Mollyworld and finally the Joyceworld. Thus the deeper encompassing vision of the author is in one sense external to his dramatic action, and in another its natural product—and measure. The pervasive irony generated in the gap between is not the savage irony that an ideal Reality casts on Appearance, but the kinder, more humorous and tolerant irony that Achievement casts on Potentiality. What meanings are enacted by *Ulysses* are rooted in the life enacted in it, the activity by which humanity apprehends its world and so informs it with significance. Its symbolic structures are founded in its presented reality as the epiphanies apprehended by the characters ripple out, deepen, and are enriched and interrelated in the apprehensions of the author (p. 264).

Such an irony deserves to be understood—indeed, requires to be understood—by its quality, which is to say its esthetic distinctiveness and particularity. Otherwise, as well-intentioned readers or ill-advised critics, we shall attempt to specify about Joyce where one cannot specify, in a tiresome circumlocution about an ingenuous Joycean ambiguity and ambivalence.

3

Few matters that concern the literary critic are as intangible as the quality of an author's irony. As we have noted, a reader's alertness to the intimate insights of an author's irony is a subtle process of assimilating its quality, its decisive particularity. Joyce offers the critic the advantage of a quality which can be specified as it developed to something like its potential in the writing of *Ulysses* and *Finnegans Wake*. Heretofore it has been impossible to specify the quality of Joyce's irony, or of any writer's, for that matter, without attempting to exhaust the entire content of what he ironizes, as will be apparent to any reader of Joycean criticism who cares to explain for himself what a critic (like Richard M. Kain,[47] for instance) is actually doing when he elaborates on what Joyce's characters do and say because Joyce has written their narrative. We may say at this point, even at the risk of seeming to precipitate if not beg the question, that this quality can be specified critically as the effort on Joyce's part to equate the means by which irony can provoke its apprehension to what, as "the human disposition of sensible or intelligible matter" (*CW* 145), is to be apprehended in his books. Considered in this light, his "styles" and "techniques" assume a kind of importance different from that usually attributed to them, and one that could conceivably permit some new insight as to why they were the indispensables Joyce demanded for himself.

A convenient way to state the matter is to say that by representing the actions of his characters by means of multiple techniques and encyclopedic correspondences, and by obliging the reader to suspend, as an act of apprehension, the tensions provoked by opposite or conflicting meanings and intentions, Joyce expects to accomplish the complete objectification of his materials, that is, of both the narrative of human beings and the artistic form of that narrative. The degree of objectivity, however, does not simply depend on a greater number of correspondences and analogies, on a quantitative elaboration, but on the quality proceeding from their resolution. It is that resolution, balance, or "poise," that will reveal the everyday actions of his protagonists in the form of their narrative as possessing the objectivity and impersonality of myth.

"I am writing *Ithaca* in the form of a mathematical catechism," Joyce wrote to Frank Budgen in February of 1921.[48] "All events are resolved into their cosmic, physical, psychical etc. equivalents, e.g. Bloom jumping down the area, drawing water from the tap, the micturating in the garden, the cone of incense, lighted candle and statue so that the reader will know everything and know it in the baldest and coldest way, but Bloom and Stephen thereby become heavenly bodies, wanderers like the stars at which they gaze," L 159–60. Joyce's statement gives some indication of how the encyclopedic and quantitative range is to produce a qualitative effect. In "Ithaca" the form of a mathematical catechism is not only representing the actions of Bloom and Stephen but enacting on the level of "style" an encyclopedic and universalizing enquiry on the significance of the events of the day and resolving two major themes of the book, the Hamlet-paternity theme and the theme of the "slaughter of the suitors." It closes with the "universalizing" of the Blooms' bed, "the bed of conception and of birth, of consummation of marriage and of breach of marriage, of sleep and of death," U 731/691. The contents of "Ithaca" complete the particularization of the myth of Ulysses and of the opposite, the mythification of the particular lives represented in the book, by establishing what we shall call here a "coincidence" between the two processes. This "coincidence," the Joycean equivalence between form and content, is, furthermore, the basis of Joyce's "comedy" in the episode and of his parodies. It follows, then, that the effect of this "coincidence" will fulfill its potential as a resolver of the ironical juxtaposition of the naturalistic and the mythical to the degree that our perceptions are engaged, as the minimal requirement, in direct quantitative relation to the Joyce's multiple perspectives and attitudes. If Joyce's enquiry into the meeting of his two protagonists in Bloom's home is both intensive and encyclopedic — that is to say, quantitative — even to the point of absurdity that Hugh Kenner chooses to stress, our perceptions must respond initially in a quantitative respect also. But beyond the initial response we recognize as purely quantitative lies the assimilation of the multiples they constitute as the Joycean quality of impersonality and objectification. The proper response to the whole effect, it appears to me, is to accept the "coincidence" of the two processes as the focus of moral attitudes, which  is another way of describing the detachment and objectivity shared by Joyce and his readers. What we mean by detachment, objectivity, or impersonality is, after all, simply the concrete engagement between a plurality of meanings and intentions in the narrative and our capacity to imagine what they constitute as an understanding of life.

The techniques of "Ithaca" seem inhuman and cold in their comedy because we are requested to endow the moral perspective implied by each set of question and reply with equal importance. We expect an author to discriminate, to endow significance upon his work through selection. Joyce of course does select and discriminate, but not on the level of explicit satement. He assigns, through technique and style, the resolution of his themes to the reader, and thus provokes from him the imaginative act that becomes one with the apprehension and resolution of his narrative as myth. His detachment and impersonality do not lie in the cold, inhuman manner, but in the fact that his encyclopedic range is the way to the mythical contemplation of the book's actions. One example from "Ithaca" will have to suffice here. In two separate sets of question and encylopedic reply Joyce juxtaposes Bloom's reflections as he gets ready for bed against a mythical dimension in the baldest way. Yet where these two passages "coincide" imaginatively in our apprehension we shall have a perfect equation between "jewgreek" and "greekjew"; and that "coincidence," again, is what establishes the quality of balance between opposites that gives us the Joycean myth of Bloom-Ulysses.

> Would the departed never nowhere nohow reappear?

> Ever he would wander, selfcompelled, to the extreme limit of his cometary orbit, beyond the fixed stars and variable suns and telescopic planets, astronomical waifs and strays, to the extreme boundary of space, passing from land to land, among peoples, amid events. Somewhere imperceptibly he would hear and somehow reluctantly, suncompelled, obey the summons of recall. Whence, disappearing from the constellation of the Northern Crown he would somehow reappear reborn above delta in the constellation of Cassiopeia and after incalculable eons of peregrination return an estranged avenger, a wreaker of justice on malefactors, a dark crusader, a sleeper awakened, with financial resources (by supposition) surpassing those of Rothschild or of the silver king. *U* 727–28/688

> What past consecutive causes, before rising preapprehended, of accumulated fatigue did Bloom, before rising, silently recapitulate?

> The preparation of breakfast (burnt offering): intestinal congestion and premeditative defecation (holy of holies): the bath (rite of John): the funeral (rite of Sam-

uel): the advertisement of Alexander Keyes (Urim and
Thummin): the unsubstantial lunch (rite of Melchizedek):
the visit to museum and national library (holy place): the
bookhunt along Bedford row, Merchants' Arch, Welling-
ton Quay (Simchath Torah): the music in the Ormond
Hotel (Shira Shirim): the altercation with a truculent
troglodyte in Bernard Kiernan's premises (holocaust): a
blank period of time including a cardrive, a visit to a
house of mourning, a leavetaking (wilderness): the eroti-
cism produced by feminine exhibitionism (rite of Onan):
the prolonged delivery of Mrs Mina Purefoy (heave offering): the visit to the disorderly house of Mrs Bella
Cohen, 82 Tyrone street, lower, and subsequent brawl
and chance medley in Beaver street (Armageddon): noc-
turnal perambulation to and from the cabman's shelter,
Butt Bridge (atonement). *U* 728-29/689

It seems to me futile to insist that Joyce's intentions are
ironical and his effect only comical, and to conclude that the
naturalistic and symbolical elements of his juxtapositions so
negate and cancel each other out that "comedy" is the only
sense by which we can accept the episode as the affirmation of
any meaning.[49] What deserves to be fully apprehended here is
the situation in technique and narrative determining the
quality of his irony. In the first place, that irony is not really
"critical," because no distinct object of a distinct criticism is
evident. Bloom is not being exposed as a paltry individual,
unworthy of the symbolic parallels, but as a representative,
universalized "Joycean" male. Nor is the course of life in
Dublin on June 16–17, 1904, the object of a "corrosive" or
nihilistic exposure. What we have as irony is really the
achieved balance of what Goldberg calls "moral attitudes,"
and is the Joycean intimacy being conveyed. For our purpose
we need to go a little further and speak of a *stasis*, or balance of
tensions, achieved between two opposite directions of inference. The first direction is the universalizing of naturalistic

events as mythical occurrences, and the other direction involves the particularization of certain myths in the events of
Bloom's day as naturalistic events. The quality of Joyce's irony
is derivable from this balance of tensions, the result of an
intended equivalence between what is being represented by
the narrative and the mode by which we are obliged to apprehend it. By this *stasis*, or balance of tensions, we are made
aware that the intimate insights of James Joyce, the familiarity
of his literary world, is accessible to us as an act of objectified,
impersonalized, apprehension, and that *what* he expresses as a
permanent condition of humanity is inseparable from *how* he
does so—from his means; and, finally, that the quality of the
responses instigated by his irony actualizes the concrete ends
of his art. And these ends, as we have seen, are to disclose, as
the act of apprehension adequate to what is thereby apprehended imaginatively, the mythical perspectives to the actions
of everyday life.[50]

Our discussion of *Ulysses* will not presume to go beyond
these general statements, our concern thus far having been to
trace the workings of Joycean irony in the works leading up to
*Finnegans Wake*. We have indicated that the ironical dimension
in Joyce's books is less interesting for the content of what is
ironized than for the quality emerging from the way the ironization is carried out. That quality can be specified from several
directions. It can be described from the critical consideration of what is objectified by it, that is, by analyzing the
content of Joyce's books (the usual approach taken by his
critics). But this approach excludes much that is important,
and does not really do justice to the intricacies of artifice or
craft Joyce lavished on *A Portrait* and *Ulysses*. "Style" had for
Joyce a more deliberate and precise meaning than for most
novelists. Style was a means to objectivity and impersonality
in works inspired, and impelled to their strange elaboration,
by a powerful self-exorcism.[51] Style, in the most restricted as in
the most comprehensive sense, was a means to the complete

self-apprehension on the part of its author that the work of art must possess in its Joycean completeness.

I am not proposing, of course, anything so untenable as that every detail about Joyce's use of symbolic correspondences and analogues, that his every trick of technique and artifice, must necessarily have an objectifying function and value. I am proposing that since style and artifice were indispensable to an unprecedented degree for Joyce, they are indispensable for us to a significant degree at almost every point in his works because they are intended to arrest our powers of apprehension and to establish the imaginative meaning of his books. We need, as a counterweight to Hugh Kenner's proposals, an interpretative study of Joyce's use of parody as a technique of objectification. Such a study would bring together the raw material Joyce worked from, the often calamitous, fatuous, "strident and absurd,"[52] stuff he seems to have delighted in, and would attempt to fix the signposts by which his imagination and verbal virtuosity set out to enlarge and universalize that material by elaborating an equivalence (as artifice and technique) between *what* of the human condition the narrative reveals and *how* to the apprehending mind and receptive senses of his readers.

Joyce possessed a view of life and an understanding of the moral values that make civilization possible that one may call the view of life of the literary artist. What we have termed here the equivalence between form and content of his books and between the mode of presentation of his narratives and the mode of their apprehension is perforce only a convenience by which to approach the very sensitive question of "style" as the expression of that view of life. But of course Joyce's "style," from 1904 to 1921 and after, underwent a continuous evolution that, from our point of vantage, appears to have developed with the necessity of a complex and highly differentiated organism. The narrative stylization of *A Portrait* developed into the multiple styles and techniques of *Ulysses*, and these into the all-encompassing and reconciliating night language of *Finnegans Wake*.

This equivalence pertains to Joyce's works of prose narration. Thus the play *Exiles*, about which I could add very little to what Joyceans have said about it, stands apart and outside my range and purpose.[53] The Joycean idea of a "dramatic" work of literature is one of engagement of the apprehension of the onlooker through the dramatic presentation of a narrative, and in the play all that can be represented is the activity of the (three) characters, not the activity of the apprehending author (S. L. Goldberg's "fourth" character in *Ulysses*),[54] forming the center of gravity for the indirection of technique and style. In this respect Joyce is quite unlike Ibsen, in spite of some similarities (a play about three characters). More decisive are the similarities between Joyce's "dramatic" techniques in narrative prose and Wagnerian music-drama.[55] Wagner's elaborate and "simultaneous" correspondences between action, theme, myth, and music is another kind of equivalence brought forth by an artistic mind determined to create a universe of its own.

We shall need to press, at this point, the notion of a "simultaneous" expression of multiple themes and meanings in Joyce beyond the discreet limits of a rhetorical use. Simultaneous expression of this kind instigates two sets of problems. The first set is usually dealt with by analysis of the multiple components and their relations (motifs, correspondences, identities, levels of narrative and narrative events, etc.). The other set is more peculiar: how to deal with the unitive and total sense that the effect of a simultaneous whole is attempting to produce and convey. It is with respect to this kind of problem that the writing of "Ithaca" in 1921 proved to be a turning point in Joyce's art of narrative and verbal techniques. It settled in his mind the "style" for resolving the action of *Ulysses*. It also launched the techniques of parody onto new levels of objective statement and impersonalized narrative.

Most decisively, it showed that these bounds had moved undisguisedly out onto the level of myth and the mythical. Thereafter, in *Work in Progress*, the unitive sense produced by the effect of simultaneity would be mythical, and Joycean irony and its quality would become likewise mythical. The "howness" of his art would now coincide implicitly with its *whatness*. And his irony, resulting from parody as a technique of objectification, was now potentially an objectifying means of access from the subjective concerns of the artist Joyce to the impersonality and universality of myth. This much is neither surprising nor difficult to grasp. But when we move on to consider that the simultaneity of effect reveals or releases the mythical through a catalytic operation of irony in the time-interval of our apprehension, and thus becomes a question involving various notions of time, we move to less familiar ground.

Myth and the mythical are intimately related to temporal concepts precisely because they are "timeless," because they are in a manner of speaking a "resolution" of time. Their universality, impersonality and objectivity are beneath or beyond the currents of historical and personal time. To reach out to myth and the mythical is, in some measure, to "resolve" time, to experience an objectifying, imaginative act "resolving" time. We may say, therefore, that as irony comes into play as a means for producing the unitive sense of Joyce's multiples, the effect of simultaneity upon our perceptions becomes an operation suspending, dislocating, or displacing the historical, particular, or contingent context at hand and revealing or activating the mythical, the timeless beneath or beyond. This is why it is relevant to speak (as an effort on the part of a critic to designate the limits of Joyce's naturalism)[56] of "coincidence" in Joyce's view of life and his techniques of representing it.

The present essay, for reasons needing no special emphasis, is not the occasion for considering what constitutes myth and the mythical in a literary, anthropological, psychological, or philosophical frame of meaning or experience. The very fact that in our critical endeavor we find irony the activator and stipulator of myth is reason enough to discourage the impulse to define myth and the mythical in the contemporary and restrictive terms of any of these disciplines, even those of literary theory.[57] In fact, the interesting state of affairs is that irony, parody, and humor are exclusive and necessary means of access to the manifestations of myth and the mythical in two twentieth-century authors like Joyce and Thomas Mann. Irony, parody, and humor belong to our twentieth-century sense of the relativity of values, the relativity of time, and the relativity of historical change, of morals and cultures, and perhaps even of the relativity of scientific concepts; whereas myth pertains to our conceptions of the absolute and unchanging, the archetypal, archaic, and primitive, the ontological, the prehistorical and infra-historical. An irony providing accesses and "contexts" to myth and the mythical receives by that very fact its resultant quality from the reality and the coherence which its intervention resolves or establishes in works of literature. What follows is an attempt to specify this quality in a book notorious for its ambitiousness as the ultimate understanding of life of the artist, and for its obscurity as the expression of that view.

# JOYCE 4

*How paisibly eirenical*     FW 14.30

*Finnegans Wake* is clearly an ironic treatment of mythical themes, but one so comprehensive in some respects and so restrictive in others that it may be said the book characterizes its own kind of irony as it does its own kind of myth. The quality of that irony we may specify as arising from the equivalence which Joyce's *vis comica* explored (as early as some portions of *Ulysses*) and then exploited, decidedly after 1927, between the ironical potential of a naturalistic situation transposed as a mythical theme and the verbal enactment of that transposition, an equivalence between thematic content, orthographic form, and total structure.[58] Joyce reached that equivalence by surmounting all manner of obstacles to the fusion of his encyclopedic materials, but once accomplished the fusion established the ironical potential as one arising from distensions between opposed meanings. The structure of *Ulysses* offers an opposition between a naturalistic action and mythical parallels which, because it is entirely outside the consciousness of the characters whose lives are represented, forcibly maintains for the reader the requisite tensions for separating the dramatic action from its resolution as a symbolical meaning. In the *Wake* we have a structure of cyclical recurrence in which a naturalistic fiction is explicitly resolved and fused into its mythical and epical schema within the representation of a dream. We do not have an opposition between myth and naturalistic action, but a fusion or "reconciliation."[59] One way then of accounting for the difference between the structure of *Ulysses* and the cyclic dream structure of the *Wake* is to consider that Joyce after 1922 turned from an art representing a dramatic situation between characters to one in which the tensions arising from an oppositeness of meanings were confined almost entirely to the surface structure of words and their relationships.

The *Wake*, among other things, is a narrative of a dream; the more inconclusive it is as a narrative of any action in the real sense, the greater the suggestive power that its stylistic innovations impart to the thematic content. But the dream narrative of the Earwicker family alludes to and evokes an action that gathers the sense of any real action into the sweep of an all-embracing figurative and circular action ("fall →  resurrection"), and in its potential to do just this it is the verbal enactment and "night image" of the universal, "unholy" family, and of human society and its history as Joyce came to see them. Hence the action of the dream narrative, as we are told continuously in the process of reading it, is the verbal enactment of a naturalistic fiction resolved inwardly as a mythical situation and hence with a corresponding outward resolution which is potential rather than actual until the total sense of the book becomes apparent to the reader.

A way a lone a last a loved a long the     FW 628.15

riverrun, past Eve and Adam's, from swerve of shore to bend of bay, brings us by a commodius vicus of recirculation back to Howth Castle and Environs.     FW 3.1

They laid him brawdawn alanglast bed. With a bockalips of finisky fore his feet. And a barrowload of guenesis hoer his head. Tee the tootal of the fluid hang the twoddle of the fuddled, O!     FW 6.26

Hence when the clouds roll by, jamey, a proudseye view is enjoyable of our mounding's mass, now Wallinstone national museum, with, in some greenish distance, the charmful waterloose country and the two quitewhite villagettes who hear show of themselves so gigglesomes minxt the follyages, the prettilees!     FW 7.36

The verbal distortions appear anarchical but comic even to the uninitiated eye, ear, and mind because they indicate and convey some deliberate meaning showing forth mockingly through the arbitrary concealment. To the initiate, of course, it is immediately very clear that the verbal distortions proceed from a naturalistic basis (the dreaming consciousness) and are directed with clever control to their resolution within a monolithic myth. The multi-sense puns strike the mind as fortuitous and spontaneous, as good puns should, but because their meaning, when traced inwardly toward an invisible, hypothetical center where all Joyce's meanings converge, is not incidental or autonomous, they are not puns in the ordinary sense of a "play on words of the same sound but different meanings"; their sense and "play" are neither fortuitous nor dependent on the reader's frame of mind, but deliberated and dependent on Joyce's purpose in distorting language in order to level all meanings involved to a common and communal denominator. "Guenesis," for example, when considered as a pun, is really a pun only in Joyce's sense because he intends a context of identity ("fall-resurrection"), and hence a distension, between Genesis and Guinness's, a simultaneity between and a resolution of the meanings inherent in their "fortuitous" opposition. Thus "guenesis" puns self-parodically on the structure of the *Wake,* since it "opposes" and "resolves" in the effect of simultaneity the drunken state of the book's language and one of its major themes—creation, or Genesis. In the landscape description quoted above we have an instance of the simultaneity of the recurring total sense within apparently coincidental details. The description, a verbal surface, enacts the themes of exhibitionism, temptation, and incest. This verbal enactment, among other things, resolves a "meaning" conveyed orally and an "action" into an "image."

By way of the barest premise we may say, then, that the action of the *Wake* is the occurring of its involuted meanings as the recurrence of a total meaning, which is established to a large degree by a suspending effect of dis-tension, due to the simultaneity and equivalence rather than the oppositeness to one another of Joyce's levels of meaning.

I propose to mark our guidelines into the workings of

irony in the *Wake* first, in this chapter, by way of a theoretical discussion of the difficulties presented by its cyclical form and distorted language. My aim is to provide here, in somewhat capsulated form, the indispensable briefing for the exegetical tasks reserved for the following chapter. The two chapters cover the same ground, this one with a theoretical schema the next retraces with textual aids.

2

The verbal enactment of a dream, even a cosmic one, does not necessarily involve the literary conventions and techniques of narrative, but Joyce's concept of both dream and narrative presupposes a dreamer and the conventions of a narrator, both all-inclusive, mythical but stereotypal.[60] Joyce himself is neither the dreamer nor the narrator except insofar as his individual life and personality are seen merging into his all-inclusive configurations. The "ideal" date of his naturalistic plot is probably the Friday night of the year in the twentieth century in which the occurrence of the vernal equinox on a Friday night coincides with a symbolical significance like that of the year 1932,[61] and the place is of course the pub in Chapelizod. While it is possible to fix in our minds the actions and movements of the Earwickers through the night, and conceive them as the plot of the book, these actions and movements take place at different levels of wakefulness, clouded, so to speak, by the mists and mystery of night, so that they are not more "real" in the suspension of their enactment as mythical actions than the figurative actions of the multitudinous dream figures. The thematic substance of the dream and its total sense are "timeless," comprising the "monomythical" action and the family situation, which have recurred continuously throughout history in particular events and situations, and which we apprehend as immanent in the cycles within cycles of individual life as in the cycles within cycles of the day and night, of the week and the solar year, of the centuries and aeons, and so on, to the all-encompassing arc of the great cycle, the "great recurrence" of Joyce's notebook.

> dream thoughts are wake thoughts of centuries ago: unconscious memory: great recurrence: race memorial: repressions: fixations . . . [62]

HCE is replaced by his sons in the course of the dream, but in another sense their struggles ensure his regeneration. This cyclical, "monomythical" action is recurring continuously in the occurrence of particular events and situations in the lives and figures of legend, history, and fiction, but the structural relation between occurrence and recurrence is not continuity but simultaneity. Continuity is a thematic relation, susceptible of, and accessible through, extended paraphrase of Joyce's text.

Northrop Frye, who discusses the *Wake* as an ironic treatment in the twentieth century of the epic quest,[63] more or less defines the initial difficulties as well as the ultimate consequences imposed on Joyce's readers by his cyclical form and "cyclical" language. In the ironic view of the quest of the hero, which in Joyce's case, one might add, is ironical because comical, "the quest is seen inside an inevitably and perpetually recurring cycle, where everything that is done, however heroic, has sooner or later to be done over again." The cyclical form contains the quest, and from this there follows another major point about the book. The entire treatment of the heroic quest is ironical because the central figure is not the hero but the female figure, Anna Livia, who is, he says, "the kind of being who makes a quest possible." It is evident that Frye is thinking of Anna Livia as Joyce's central symbol of reconciliation and as corresponding to the book's total form. But if the immediate result of the ironic treatment of the epic quest of HCE is the enlargement of ALP into the central symbol of the book, there remains for the reader to draw the inevitable

consequences from this transposition: that the inner sense of
the book as a work of reconciliation has its counterpart in the
total experience of the reader who assimilates the inner sense.
It is not only a question of perceiving that Joyce treats mythological and religious themes ironically, but that he refers to the
reader the meaning of his work in the quality of the perceptions which he is to make in order to possess its "total" meaning. Eventually it must dawn on the reader that the figure who
achieves the quest is not a son-figure, not Shem or Shaun, nor
a father-figure, not HCE or Finnegan, but the reader of Joyce.
"Eventually it dawns on us that it is the *reader* who achieves
the quest, the reader who, to the extent that he masters the
book of Doublends Jined, is in a position to look down on
its rotation, and see its total form as something more than
rotation."

It may be of very slight comfort to the reader to know this,
or that *Finnegans Wake* is a great work of literature for this or
that reason, in the face of the extreme length and difficulty of
the text and the extreme obscurity to which Joyce consigned
his ultimate designs. How to read it is an easy matter, relatively speaking, compared with the question of what sense
one is to make of the whole of what one reads; that is, resolve
the sense of what one reads as a qualitative whole.

A quarter of a century after its publication,[64] for the ex-
perts as for nonexperts, it becomes increasingly evident that a
full appreciation of how the text should be read and assimilated can only come about by a breakthrough into how its
particulars (motifs, correspondences, identities, the dream
structure, and the naturalistic fiction of the Earwicker family,
and so on) are to be resolved at any given point as an instance
of the monolithic unity of its encyclopedic contents. My own
view is that, although a diversity of response is exacted from
us, the decisive line of focus should be on the qualitative
resolution of Joyce's multiple levels of narrative and meaning.
This may well be the most difficult and perhaps even a ques-

tionable approach, considering the incomplete understanding of the book as a whole by Joycean scholarship, but the critical perils to which it becomes vulnerable are unavoidable, for we cannot pretend to the perception of irony or the ironical if we do not have at least a tentative notion of what constitutes the "literal" or "direct" side of Joyce's text. Northrop Frye has gone as far as anyone toward an understanding of the ironical basis of the book, yet his vantage point is only a good foothold on what I shall call the second, objective and outer direction of resolution of Joyce's meanings. Clive Hart is in the same vicinity when he speaks of characters who "once again . . . must suffer the heartbreaking cancellation of all their effort which is the most tragic thing in Joyce's great tragi-comedy."[65] This is exclusively an outer vision of what goes on in the book. The reconciliatory basis of the book, along with its comic-ironic potential, must be construed as turning inward within its involuted meanings, toward an innermost point of reference and resolution. The book has equally an outer resolution, but it is dependent on the inward. When the inward sense allows the outer to become manifest, the reader is in a position to link the two end points of the book of Doublends Jined (20.15), resolving and, therefore, objectivizing its form and content into a "resurrection myth." And this comes about, not in spite, but as the effect, the complete experience, of its obscurity.

### 3

The *Wake* is not only a difficult and obscure book, inaccessible to the normal reader without the extensive use of critical notes, the *Census, Skeleton Key, Concordance,* and the assorted commentaries, exegeses, and paraphrases which have become standard, yet call unremittingly for the erudition James S. Atherton, John Kelleher, Clive Hart, and a few others possess, but once the voluminous "pony" literature has been assimilated to the reader's capacities, the text itself must be labored over with cunning and intelligence, the patterns of language related constantly to the patterns of meaning. Yet all this is preliminary to reading discreetly and pleasurably, comprehending and absorbing the minute particulars. One of many paradoxes in it is that the narrative is the private content of the sleeper's dream, but the symbolic significance of the dream is public and universal. To assimilate the book in the privacy of one's thoughts is to read it in the way that probably best enacts that "invasion" of privacy. To hear a performance of the text by a choir of voices would amplify the public context. Somewhere between these two extremes there is a way of assimilating the text that combines visual concentration on the printed page and an audio presentation.

Now it is a question whether one or the other, the visual or the aural concentration, or a "synthesis" of the two, will give us a more "literal" version of the text. It is usual to comment that when we hear Joyce's recorded reading of Anna Livia Plurabelle (213.11–216) we get a "clearer" and resolved version of the music-like text, which I presume means we get a sustained line of denotative meaning and reference, whereas the printed text impedes our concentrating on any one of the several levels of meaning and the establishing of a denotative primacy for any one of several packed into a phrase or a single word. A performance of the text through controlled choral speaking by a small group, Clive Hart contends,[66] would bring out not only the hidden pattern of cyclical counterpoint, but accents, intonations, rhythms, and mimicry on which a "maximum" apprehension of a given passage depends. What Clive Hart proposes is very nearly a reading of *Finnegans Wake* that will correspond to the "condition of music" the text presumably aspires to.

Here is a fragment from Anna Livia's final monologue, where one assumes that one voice only is to be "heard." It is not a difficult point in the text, but still as removed from the monologues of *Ulysses* as anything else in the *Wake*.

And stand up tall! Straight. I want to see you looking
fine for me. With your brandnew big green belt and all.
Blooming in the very lotust and second to nill, Budd!
When you're in the buckly shuit Rosensharonals
near did for you. Fiftyseven and three, cosh, with the
bulge.      *FW* 620.1

Now in order to render vocally the exact (denotative-connota-
tive) meanings of "the buckly shuit Rosensharonals near did
for you" wouldn't two voices, two simultaneous pronuncia-
tions, be needed? We would need to hear the opposition con-
noted between the scatology and, shall we say, eschatology of
the phrase *and* their implied resolution in the same interval. In
this choral rendition the "simultaneity" of the two voices would
produce a merging of the opposed meanings which our apperception would then resolve into their unitive sense, because the phrase is a distortion reverberating with the major
motifs of fall and resurrection. No one has seriously claimed
that Molly Bloom's monologue aspires to "the condition of
music." One good reason why is that there Joyce's text is
nearly completely objectified in what it denotes about his
character and his novel; there are no meanings, cloacal or
otherwise, turned inward to resolve, and all his (or Molly's)
contexts face outward.

    If the language of *Finnegans Wake* can be enjoyed as "mu-
sic," the reason is that the denotative and connotative possibilities of his verbal techniques are structured and controlled
with the purpose of producing an effect of simultaneity that
"resolves" them into an imaginative whole. A prolonged
familiarity with this effect brings into play both precise, denotative reference and connotative imprecision because Joyce
imposed on his materials a verbal form and a literary structure
facing both outward and inward, and the reader or listener
who expects to bring them together with any kind of result
must do so consciously and even laboriously, with acute concentration of mind, eye, and ear. The analogy to music is
helpful so far as it reveals that Joyce's verbal form must be

resolved as if it were a kind of music, because its denotative potential is enclosed within a "night" language which must be made apprehensible through logical analysis and rational deliberation by the "day" mind. Though the omniscient Joycean dreamer never does wake up, the entire sense of the book is directed to his counterpart: an omniscient mind, quick and awake, not only extremely perceptive in logical analysis but equally sensitive and receptive to the instantaneous equivalences between verbal structure and themes.

Although the thematic content of the *Wake* is encyclopedic, the form which the total sense of the cyclical structure imposes upon that content is unitary and monolithic. We are provoked into a continual confrontation with a myriad of themes and their associative meanings, but the sum total of that multiplicity is always less than the monolithic total significance alluded to by their simultaneity. To the initiate it is evident that this simultaneity is the full, immediate, and comical sense of the enactment taking place at a given point. A portrait of the artist as a babe asleep: "What a teething wretch! How his book of craven images! Here are posthumious tears on his intimelle. And he has pipettishly bespilled himself from his foundingpen as illspent from inkinghorn (563.3)." The effect on the "day" mind is instantly comical because a bed-wetting is being transposed anagogically into a macrocosmic "night" image of literary prophecy. Shem-Jerry's mini-portrait is aiming at a simultaneity of expression outlasting whole pages of *A Portrait*, which by comparison seem like paraphrase.

4

If, as John Kelleher says,[67] Joyce attained an unprecedented economy in condensing themes of history, mythology, and religion through a revolutionary use and conception of language, that economy offers a proportionate return to the reader

only if he can experience for himself the simultaneity of the
*Wake's* contents in the "right form." Otherwise, he is assimilating the text purely on the level of an extended, voluminous
paraphrase of its themes many times over the length of the
book. It is unlikely it will ever dawn on such a reader that he
has accomplished anything like an "epic quest" because he
will not come close to mastering the book of Doublends Jined.
Mastery of the book is not a knowledge of its thematic content,
whether in digested, portable, or paraphrastic form, but the
experiental assimilation of the simultaneity of verbal structure
and thematic content.

Here is a passage where Joyce is most literally "splitting"
the form and meaning of words while reconstituting them into
a "new perception" of "cosmic" man; the interval in the Mutt
and Taff episode interrupting the skit at the moment Butt tells
how (he or) Buckley fired the shot that killed the Russian
general. It is the moment of the shot, yet of both silence and
explosion. The interval enacts the shot verbally, but the noise
of the shot is clearly the "splitting" of the atom of physical
matter, the digestive fission of HCE, and the fission-fusion of
the "etym" of Joyce's night language.

> [BUTT] . . . Prronto! I gave one dobblenotch and I ups
> with my crozzier. Mirrdo! With my how on armer and
> hits leg an arrow cockshock rockrogn. Sparro!

> [*The abnihilisation of the etym by the grisning of the
> grosning of the grinder of the grunder of the first lord of
> Hurtreford expolodotonates through Parsuralia with an
> ivanmorinthorrorumble    fragoromboassity    amidwhiches
> general uttermosts confussion are perceivable moletons
> skaping with mulicules while coventry plumpkins fairly-
> gosmotherthemselves in the Landaunelegants of Pinka-
> dindy. Similar scenatas are projectilised from Hullulullu,
> Bawlawayo, empyreal Raum and mordern Atems. They
> were precisely the twelves of clocks, noon minutes, none*

> *seconds. At someseat of Oldanelang's Konguerrig, by dawny-*
> *break in Aira.]*    FW 353.19

The multiple levels of "twelves of clocks," of the time and the meaning of the shot, its cause and effect as an event, are apparent from an outward direction: a historical moment in twentieth-century history and science, the clock-time of the shot in the dream narrative, the encounter with the Cad, the familial and psychical time of HCE's replacement by his sons. But the distorted syntax of the last sentences almost plainly reveals that the time the shot takes place is mythical and "timeless," "precisely the twelves of clocks, no minutes, no seconds"; both "sunset" and "dawn"; "at sunset in Old England's kingdom, by the break of dawn in Eire."[68] The passage is replete with motifs of leveling and renewal. The allusions to the alchemy of his night language are accompanied by others that remind us that guilt, evacuation, and literary creation were related for Joyce in a way both psychical and "cosmic." The noisy "detonations-denotations" and the silent connotations are pointing inwardly toward the "moment of silence" on which the entire "vicociclometer" pivots. But to assimilate all the components of the event as a qualitative whole we need to experience the effect of the simultaneity of noise–silence, the equivalence of sunset–sunrise at "twelve o'clock," by equating the three notions of temporal movement, *occurrence*, *continuity*, and *recurrence*, into their "monomythical" projection; that is, by resolving the verbal occurrence of the shot as the recurrence of an inward meaning that points HCE's "fall" toward an impending "resurrection." The "right form" is thus this effect of simultaneity that, while resolving the mystico-scientific time schemes, will provoke and thus release into the reader's apprehension the sense of the total cyclical form (of the book as a whole) as an experiental and qualitative resolution of all the components he has before him.

Quite literally here the "tensions" of this etymic

fission–fusion are resolved on the verbal surface into the dis-tensions of the impending reconstitution. These are the same dis-tensions of the book's peculiar irony, which is structural and qualitative in its functions, its verbal particularity qualified and resolved by the cyclical form. I do not, however, wish to pursue this point here, but to emphasize that assimilation of the text in our "right form" depends almost exclusively on the reader's ability to resolve the purely quantitative elaboration of Joyce's verbal structure and it thematic dichotomies into a qualitative apprehension of his insights into fundamental human realities. It is the qualitative effect of Joyce's complexity of techniques which gives us *Joyce's* theme and myth, *his* conception of the great themes of the Fall, creation, death, and resurrection.[69]

Thus, while probing into the smallest details of his text in a sustained period of visual-aural concentration, we are activating a concatenation of microcosmic effects of which each, ideally if not in our rudimentary practice, is aiming at the arrestment of those cycling and reiterative details into their monolithic whole. Here we intuit that the "opposite" senses of a given unit of meaning are moving away from a "dialectical" state of opposition and toward a central point of reference and unity which we conceive as hidden in the involuted cycles.

As I see it, reading the "collideorscape" (143.28) exacts from us a focus, or equivalence, of a verbal "action" into a verbal "image," a resolution of the narrative and descriptive contexts of a variety of patterns and organizations of sense into their monolithic unity which is centered structurally in the "eternal now" of Book IV. We approximate to this focus, or equivalence, when our visual and auditory concentration on the text becomes "simultaneous" with our cognitive grasp of the enactment taking place. At this moment of "maximum apprehension" the simultaneity of our sensory and intellective responses will confirm the simultaneity of Joyce's meanings, and his effect becomes a fact of our sensations and perceptive

impulses, of our experience. The omniscient, "ideal" insom-
niac (120.13) might be in a state to sustain that act of apprehension for the length of the book, but would his be an act of
cognition, proceeding from "analysis" to "resynthesis"?

5

Now, whether the Joycean effect gives us a "cosmic 'style'
in action,"[70] or "a new way of feeling, of perceiving"[71] is a
matter of critical and personal emphasis, but we are justified
in speaking of *Finnegans Wake* in this way only if we acknowledge that an immediate simultaneity of his meanings
within the cyclical form imposes on us the necessity of apprehending that simultaneity as the esthetic integrity of the work
itself, as *that something itself*[72] it purports to be. The first part of
my proposal, that Joycean irony in the *Wake* is indissolubly
linked to this effect and to the most intricate as well as the
comprehensive questions of style and form, leads to the second: the quality of that irony arises from an equivalence between *what* is treated ironically and *how*, between *what* is
ironized and *how* it is ironized, between thematic and structural aspects.

Beyond this point I propose to illustrate and sum up our
discussion of the *Wake* by recourse to a diagram. Brancusi's
"Symbol of Joyce"[73] is a spiral suggesting visual as well as
aural contexts of the labyrinth. It is not unlikely that it has
struck others for its possibilities as an exegetical device for
Joyce's book; even for precisely what follows. My purpose in
resorting to it is strictly exegetical, however fanciful my use of
it may seem. The spiral, a single line in four involutions, is a
"stylized" Archimedean spiral that provides the illusion of
continuous motion in two opposite directions, one counter-
clockwise toward the center, the other clockwise, toward an
outer and indefinite projection. It also provides the illusion of
a potential release of force from within, corresponding to a

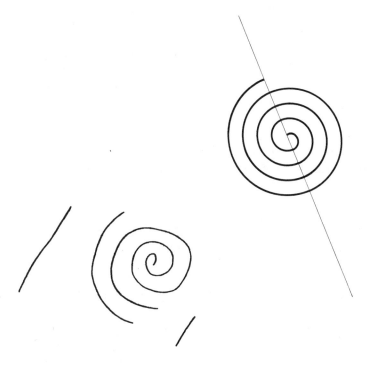

*O* please *trun over! Of course it's not all sideways like that but those are the lines and it's signed and called Symbol of J. J. [Joyce's sketch of Brancusi's drawing in a letter to Harriet Shaw Weaver, 27 May 1929, L 279. Reproduced by permission of the Society of Authors, London.]*

> *Sometimes he [Joyce] would tell picaresque tales of his father's wit, and the last one I remember was one that concerned his father's reaction in Dublin to a minuscule sketch of Joyce made by Brancusi. It was merely a geometrical spiral study symbolizing the ear. "Well, Jim hasn't changed much," said his father on seeing the portrait.*
>
> Eugene Jolas, "My Friend James Joyce"[74]

potential expansion without, the outermost point suggesting a projection into the relativity of infinite space (and time). The geometrical symmetry of the symbol is such that the single line can be construed as "beginning" or "ending" at either of its ends, but the end points themselves "denote" opposite approximations to infinity. At its center the spiral "begins" or "ends" at a fixed point, which remains the geometrical center of the entire series of turns and is clearly no particular point in space (or time); it is a finite point "poised," let us say, at the brink of infinity. At the other end, the symbol "denotes" the possibility of extending the line outward in an infinite series of similarly spaced turns. The two directions of movement, then, can be seen as spiraling simultaneously from a finite point out to an infinite expansion and from a possible infinite expansion inward to a finite point. The symmetry of the figure will also "denote" that a balance or equilibrium between these two movements is the structural principle sustaining the whole.

I propose now that we look at it as a symbol representing our apprehension of a "total form" for *Finnegans Wake.* All leg-pulling aside, Irish and otherwise, let us proceed to impose on this symbol a diagrammatic explanation of that interval of our "maximum apprehension" spoken of above.

We have before us a cyclical structure of themes and planes of meaning, voices, and multilingual locutions, revolving outward to a projection of coherent statement and intellective resolution which must yet be referred back through the counter-rotation to the central point of obscurity, concealing the "etym" of Joyce's dream language. By its paradoxical nature as a "finite" point, differing in no way from any other in the spiral, and yet the one point on which the entire structure pivots, our central point becomes the gravitational center of Joyce's obscurity and transpositions—hence a "mythical" and "mystical" point, containing in embryo the entire spiralling motion and a resolution of all contexts relative to one another;

the point of monolithic unity where all planes of meaning will ultimately converge, where all characters will coalesce, and all identities coincide into "equals of opposites" (92.8), into "one stable somebody" (107.30).

In the interval of our reactions to Joyce's effects we are aiming constantly at resolving and arresting those cycling planes of meaning by attempting to equate the terminal points; that is, by equating and bringing to an equilibrium their "opposite" senses as they occur in the verbal enactment of the dream. But we do this, of course, by directing our perceptions first to the inner point of reference because it forms the basis for reconciling to the "night image" our "day world" of conscious will, rational purpose, and intellective clarity. That inner sense of reconciliation will then in turn permit the outward projections of expansible contexts, intended to encompass the range of our sensory and experiental references, to complete and resolve themselves into a cognitive resolution. In this process the comic-ironical potential of a given unit of meaning is activated, resolved by our sensory and intellective grasp of it, and then reflected back to that center of monolithic unity. If we react instantly, the qualitative effect is one exacting from our sensory-intellective reflexes a resolution of the duality of being, the reconciliation of opposites or contrarieties, the reversibility of time, and an "eternal now" of time, containing the entire past and future of the human race.

Perhaps now my reader has seen through to my justification for using Brancusi's spiral. Its four involutions can also be seen as a diagram of the total cyclical form of the *Wake*'s four-part enactment of historical ages and the phases of personal life. Each involution may be thought of as a complete cycle of three ages and a *ricorso*, returning to a point exactly opposite and parallel to the point at which the cycle begins; or the entire figure may be thought of as one cycle, beginning from either end. We can imagine, then, that we are looking at a diagrammatic representation of our act of apprehension resolving the opposite approximations to infinity into the "timeless moment" of their equilibrium. Hence the "point of maximum apprehension" of our reading must be referred and correspond, as an approximation to the book's total sense, to that "timeless moment" in the narrative on which the entire structure of equilibrated cycles-within-cycles pivots, the "moment of silence" represented by Book IV, the Book of Waking. The reader who finds the whole idea turgid, misspent, or simply an idle esoterism, will profit from Clive Hart's clarification of Joyce's cyclic form in *Structure and Motif in "Finnegans Wake."*[75] This "timeless moment" is of course the "eternal now" of Book IV, proclaimed at its opening ("Sandhyas! Sandhyas! Sandhyas! 593.1). But it does not actually "occur" on the level of the naturalistic fiction until immediately after Anna Livia's final *the* — that is to say, in the interval between the book's close and its beginning. Here then the two end points of the book of Doublends Jined are held apart, in hiatus, in an interval of mystical silence, before they join again, at a re-beginning. It is likewise the moment when the reader is obliged to suspend and resolve the entire contents of the dream, or, as Northrop Frye puts it, "to reforge the broken links between myth and consciousness."[76]

Now, since the final "moment of silence" occurs within the cyclical narrative and outside it, it may be represented in our figure by drawing a straight line that connects the two opposite end points, across the spirals at the point of "silence" between cycles. Hence we may say that what we accomplish by thus equating the two opposite approximations to infinity is the projection of Finnegan's wakening poised as imminent in the "eternal now," in eternity. The sense of the entire book, then, as deducible from our "total symbol," is this resolution of its structure equilibrated or pointed in static expectancy toward the moment of Finnegan's wakening. The Irish cosmic dream embraces centuries and even aeons, but it has occurred in one night and can occur any night; in fact, as an equivalence of myth and naturalistic fiction, it occurs each and every night, and each dawn of our lives enacts the "myth of resurrection."

The dis-tensions of this structure in which our irony becomes operative are to be referred ultimately, therefore, to the sense of an impending wakening or reconstitution of the dreamer's spiritual forces from the depths of the dream. This irony owes its condition of an "opposition of contrarieties" to the kinetic movement of the verbal enactment, and its condition of "reconciled contrarieties" to the equivalence of "action" into "image"; that is to say, to the effect of simultaneity. It arises from tensions within the verbal-acoustical surface, from the connections between words and their phonetic deformations and reconstitution, but its quality proceeds from the comprehensive dis-tensions between themes and planes of meanings, and between the outermost range of intellective apprehension and the elusive inner depth of obscurity and bafflement of rational distinctions. Joyce himself gave it a name at once as equivocal and precise as its functions, and expressive of his ire and love, attraction and repulsion for things Irish in the years of his maturity. Through "Bryonic Jaun" of the Second Watch he called it "Iereny."

# JOYCE 5

*Iereny allover irelands*     FW 455.8

"The time had come for him to set out on his journey westward. Yes, the newspapers were right: snow was general all over Ireland," *D* 242/174. The tragic overtones of the symbol of the snow at the close of "The Dead" and the comic overtones at the expense of a self-inflicted parody describe, in their opposition, the ground traversed by Joyce in the direction of the conciliatory overview of Irish life and history, of which that journey "westward" is perhaps an anticipation, and of his life as father and artist that *Finnegans Wake* was meant to enact: from a symbolic shrouding of the living dead of *Dubliners* to the cock's *Cocorico!* (584.27) of ironic humor projecting the mythical resurrection of all Finnegans. The sentimental, evocative charge of the symbol of falling snow, indicative of the temper of his craft in his twenty-sixth year, proved an irresistible opportunity to display a brilliant bit of self-parody, emphatic of the resolve to be, at all costs and to the very end, the artist constantly outdistancing himself.

The self-parodic dimension of the *Wake in Progress* is at once so comprehensive and outrageous that on one "literal" level of meaning it makes sense only as a clue to the way we are to read the "negative" of itself the book provides.

> (Stoop) if you are abcedminded, to this claybook, what curios of signs (please stoop), in this allaphbed! Can you rede (since We and Thou had it out already) its world? *FW* 18.17

That the *Wake* should parody itself as well as Joyce's other works is not more surprising than its many other odd features carried out perversely and brilliantly; yet the idea and its practice, and even more, its significance, must have evolved slowly in Joyce's mind and must have evolved from the inspiration to press the massive use of parody toward the achievement of a total indirection of meaning unlike anything in *Ulysses*. However we may interpret the parodies in *Ulysses*, we cannot say that they betray a self-consciousness about their

use and purpose. An aspect of Joyce's comic self-consciousness
in the *Wake* about the resort to parody is that the techniques of
indirection are constantly attempting, all too transparently, to
keep the narrative developing at several levels by avoiding the
explicit formation of a single level of denoted meaning in the
verbal and syntactical form of the text. Between 1923 and 1927
Joyce discovered that the massive use of parodic styles, or
"imitative form,"[77] provided more than freedom from commitment to direct expression; he discovered that it provided,
even for him, a novel and positive approach to the task of
organizing, controlling, and sustaining a narrative. The result,
the effect of a simultaneous expression of multiple themes and
their counter-themes, is that for the reader of the *Wake* the
verbal form itself, the surface of orthographic and syntactical
form, considered purely as an artificial surface or artifice, takes
on all the charge or tension that a writer usually packs into the
significance of direct statement, while the indirectness with
which Joyce compels him to resolve the interacting levels of
meaning could accomplish its purpose only in a vast neutral
area of what we have called dis-tensions.

For the purposes of the present exposition we may consider that the lengthy text of 628 pages in Four Books divided
into seventeen sections tells a narrative in two sequences: the
first, the temporal sequence of verbal occurrence which enacts
the dream as it occurs on a naturalistic level; the second, the
sequence of total recurrence, or total meaning, which is the
recurring sense of the first but whose concretion is independent of the first since it does not involve narrative development
but the resolution of the narrative. The effect of simultaneity
occasioned by the recurring verbal motifs, correspondences,
allusions, or the tone and voices, or identities, at any point in
the first sequence is "denoting" the resolution of the narrative
into its total recurrence, or total sense, of the second. When we
say, then, that the verbal surface is enacting a naturalistic

fiction as a mythical situation, and that this is the "action" of the *Wake*, we are indicating that by our relative and approximate apprehension of Joyce's indirect methods of organizing and controlling the narrative we have read correctly the denoted content of the book by resolving or equating the two sequences into an "image." Looking at the book in this fashion allows us to determine that the context by which we are to resolve the simultaneous occurrence of multiple themes and motifs of the verbal enactment is the context of their inward resolution, unity, and reconciliation, but a context not accessible to us until we can assimilate the text at a level of apprehension that, in the diagrammatic explanation of the preceding chapter, would correspond to drawing the line connecting the two opposite ends of Brancusi's "Symbol of Joyce." What I now propose to explain is that in arriving at this level of apprehension we discard whatever negative value we have assigned to Joyce's use of parody and suspend the ironical opposition confronting us; and that contingent on this we activate at this level itself the myth-making potential of the *Wake* that is the source of the quality of Joyce's irony, but which, paradoxically, would not be there without the use of irony or parody, and is not to be confused with the presence or use of mythological themes in the book.

My intention in what follows, then, is to specify, in the barest outline, how the ironical relates to the mythmaking potential, since I see the functional value of Joyce's ironic qualitativeness in a resolution of the narrative as a contemporary "myth of resurrection." I offer no apology for failing to provide an exhaustive exegesis of the passages I chose to cite.[78] My intention is simple and *Finnegans Wake* is a complex book. If the length and roundabout abstractness of my discussion have appeared out of proportion to the declared simplicity of my aims, I can only offer the apology that, considering the ground to be covered, no other means more practical were

available than to traverse it from various angles in the expectation that their intended convergence at the center would be
manifest.

2

The expedient point at which to begin to probe this qualitative equivalence between what is ironized and how would
seem to be the opening passage of the Ballad section of Book I
with which Joyce actually began, in the autumn of 1923, the
narrative enlargement of a character of naturalistic fiction into
a representative father-figure of the third, democratic or human Viconian age. In the passage 30.1–34.29 it is the tone
of the narrator proceeding from a self-conscious parody
of the style of historical reportage which almost exclusively
establishes and releases the ironical potential of the configuration of the pubkeeper of Chapelizod as "Here Comes
Everybody."

> And while he was only and long and always good Dook
> Umphrey for the hungerlean spalpeens of Lucalizod and
> Chimbers to his cronies it was equally certainly a pleas-
> ant turn of the populace which gave him as sense of
> those normative letters the nickname Here Comes Every-
> body. An imposing everybody he always indeed
> looked, constantly the same as and equal to himself
> and magnificently well worthy of any and all such
> universalisation. . .      FW 32.14

The objective of the narrative is the enlargement of the pubkeeper into the "folksforefather," and the theme, purportedly
the "genesis" of HCE's "occupational agnomen," is the guilt
complex of the male. The base for the dream configuration and
universalization is then Earwicker's fall and guilt ironically
provoked as that of a god-hero, king-father figure. Joyce left
portions of the passage as published in 1925 almost un-

changed, and these permit us to perceive the ironic indirection released by the tone of the narrator in a manner deceptive to a degree as a conveyer of a single level of meaning.

> A baser meaning has been read into these characters the literal sense of which decency can safely scarcely hint. It has been blurtingly bruited by certain wisecrackers . . . that he suffered from a vile disease.    FW 33.14

In tone and manner the draft version of the passage published in 1925[79] resembles the four earlier pieces written in 1923,[80] but differs significantly as to subject and hence as to objective or intention. The earlier pieces give us a parody of chronicle modes while narrating an episode from Irish legend or history. Our passage represents the first effort in an inverse direction, from a naturalistic character and situation to a mythic-heroic enlargement, and hence the parody takes on a tone of self-consciousness not only about the parody but about the circumvolutory enlargement itself about an innocent man victimized by public slander. In the following the changes and additions to the 1925 text appear in brackets.

> To such a suggestion the one selfrespecting answer is to affirm that there are certain statements which ought not to be, and one should like [to hope] to be able to add, ought not to be allowed to be made. Nor have his detractors, who, an imperfectly warmblooded race, apparently conceive him as a great white caterpillar capable of any and every enormity in the calendar recorded to the discredit of the Juke and Kellikek families, mended their case by insinuating that, alternatively [alternately], he lay at one time under the ludicrous imputation of annoying Welsh fusiliers in the people's park. [Hay, hay, hay! Hoq, hoq, hoq! Faun and Flora on the lea love that little old joq.] To anyone who knew and loved the christlikeness of the big cleanminded giant H. C. Earwicker throughout his [excellency] long [vicefreegal] existence the mere

suggestion of him as a lustsleuth nosing for trouble in a boobytrap rings particularly preposterous.[81]    *FW* 33.18

In the parody of direct statement the tone of explication is countered by the ambiguity of what is actually stated, the result being a discursive inconclusiveness that allows the expansion of dream associations on the most tenuous of threads, the pubkeeper's disturbed feelings of guilt. It is this discursive tone and its inconclusiveness maintaining the equivalence of verbal form to theme that allows us to perceive the equivalence between what is being ironized—the disturbed mind and feelings of the pubkeeper, projected as the archetypal guilt of the god-hero, king-father figure; and how—by a discursive reiteration permitting dire imputations in public talk about a sexual transgression. These, even as imputations, involve nothing more than the merest suspicion of homosexuality, voyeurism, incest, and exhibitionism, but conveyed in denotative statements about his reputation, they insinuate a defamatory collective opinion about his character. Their ironical potential thus releases the sum total of these statements as the collective guilt of male society, as borne on the conscience of one man.

The statements are all about Earwicker's good reputation, defensive protestations of his innocence, but as such they are countered by the discursive turning back and reiterating that there is a basis in fact for his feelings of guilt. The parodic inconclusiveness of just what is stated about the pubkeeper's supposed transgression forces our attention on the antithesis projected between the monstrous imputations and the inconsequence of the act on the verbal artifice itself. The "tensions" proceeding from the narrator's account are dis-tensions between the naturalistic situation and the mythic-heroic enlargement, and between guilt and innocency, as the inconclusiveness of the statements and the inconsequence of the act make clear.

"Christlikeness" and "vicefreegal" release any number of denotative possibilities. These will end up inevitably in the reader's mind balanced between the polarity of guilt-innocence of HCE as a sacrificial victim and the cyclical opposition of *fall* to *resurrection*. At this point of balance, or equilibrium, the ironic potential is evidently suspended in the emergence of the myth-provoking potential of the disclosure. Our grasp of Earwicker's "original sin" is qualified by the simultaneous intuition that out of sin, fall, and guilt there come renewal and resurrection. The two incidents giving rise to his feelings of guilt occurred, as we are told, in the case of the first in "the people's park," that is, in Phoenix Park, Joyce's analogue for the Garden of Eden, and "Phoenix," e.g., "foenix" (23.16), "Pynix" (534.12), is the simplest of all the portmanteau-words, after the title of the book itself, for the *Wake's* circular "action" of *fall-resurrection*.

In the final sentence of our passage the single "woodward or regarder" of the 1925 version has been substituted by three men who, in the course of the night's narrative, become identified with the Welsh fusiliers and are the three males who, with the two temptresses, form the symbolic group appearing repeatedly in the action-image of the father's guilt. In the 1925 version "with ongentilmensky immodus" reads "in an ungentlemanly manner." The change introduced a reverberation of the Russian general episode and theme and hence added to the implications of guilt that Earwicker had exposed himself in the act of defecating. As an action-image, then, the guilt complex implies an exposure of the male while defecating and observing the two temptresses in the act of micturating.

> Slander, let it lie its flattest, has never been able to convict our good and great and no ordinary Southron Earwicker, that homogenius man, as a pious author called him, of any graver impropriety than that, advanced by some woodwards or regarders, who did not dare deny,

the shomers, that they had, chin Ted, chin Tam, chinchin Taffyd, that day consumed their soul of the corn, of having behaved with ongentilmensky immodus opposite a pair of dainty maidservants in the swoolth of the rushy hollow whither, or so the two gown and pinners pleaded, dame nature in all innocency had spontaneously and about the same hour of the eventide sent them both but whose published combinations of silkinlaine testimonies are, where not dubiously pure, visibly divergent, as wapt from wept, on minor points touching the intimate nature of this, a first offence in vert or venison which was admittedly an incautious but, at its wildest, a partial exposure with such attenuating circumstances (garthen gaddeth green hwere sokeman brideth girling) as an abnormal Saint Swithin's summer and, (Jesses Rosasharon!) a ripe occasion to provoke it.     *FW* 34.12

Now, since the ironical potential of the transposition of the pubkeeper's reputation as the archetypal father's is resolvable by the myth-making potential when the verbal artifice claims our entire apprehension, it is essential to note just how the discursive inconclusiveness of the parodied chronicle style has managed to convey the structural simultaneity by means of the syntax of a sentence apparently conveying but one level of denoted meaning. The dis-tension between guilt and innocence arises from the fact that Earwicker's feelings and the public talk are as ineradicable as the evidence which gives rise to them is inconclusive. This is of course a structural characteristic of the theme of original sin and evasion of guilt throughout the book. In the sentence above, beginning "Slander . . . ," we have an "antithesis" of movements which forces its resolution on the reader and hence compels him to concentrate on the ulterior and symbolic meaning of the syntactical development of the sentence itself. The antithesis is that between the syntactical unity and rhythm of a sentence protesting Earwicker's innocence and the repetitive interpolations which break that rhythm and unity; and these are to be construed as semi-accusations counterpointing his innocence, and stemming from an ineradicable and inscrutable sense of guilt in the sleeping mind of the dreamer. We may interpret the sentence, then, as the maximum that the dreamer's unconscious mind is willing to permit to come to the surface about the transgression and about the identity of the men and the young girls involved; that is, the maximum disclosure permissible at this point in the dream about the nature of Earwicker's feelings toward his wife and children.

A complete exegesis of the passage, or even of the last sentence, will inevitably trace and reduce the verbal components to the basic situation of identities and relations between Earwicker and his wife, daughter and twin sons, down to a recurrence of Joyce's monomythic nucleus. The two temptresses are a configuration combining his feelings toward the two aspects of his daughter and his wife as a young bride. The three soldiers are a configuration of the twin sons plus the father's own identity, which is related to the shame that sunders them from one another and from the father, as well as to the divided male unity they will each constitute as a father figure in the future. The acts of defecation and micturition are in their Joycean sense "acts of creation" which give us secretory parallels to the two major symbols for male and female, the mountain and the river.

3

The dis-tensions between levels of meaning permit an ironical indirection to operate, in our apprehension, in two directions: inward to the irreducible situation of Joyce's "monomyth," and outward to an intellective resolution. A thorough acquaintance with the total sense of the book is of course essential for resolving the ironical potential released from a given passage. But the greater our insight into the structural interconnections of Joyce's themes, identities, motifs, and correspondences, the greater the accuracy with which the effect of simultaneity will impose on our receptiveness the total sense of the book. We have indicated, in an abstract and theoretical way, that at the point of maximum apprehension the reader of the *Wake* is obliged to equate and hold in balance the two extremes of whatever contexts or planes of meaning engage his attention, and that in doing so he is reconstructing, in the main, the basic intuition of Joyce's comic-ironic enactment of a naturalistic situation as a mythical projection. This moment of equating opposites, we said at the close of the preceding chapter, corresponded practically to equating the two opposite approximations to infinity as drawn on our spiral. Since this maximal point is a relative one, and contingent on the reader's grasp of the unity of contexts to be arrived at by means totally indirect, we shall continue to think of it also as the moment or interval when the effect of simultaneity becomes easeful and tangible for Joyce's reader, and decisive for revealing Joyce's intentions and accomplishment.

Now, again, and considering the matter in a hypothetical way, I propose that it is at this moment, when an "opposition" of contexts is equated in our apprehension, that we attain an equilibrium between opposed levels of meaning and the verbal enactment of Joyce's text communicates its total possibilities as a *possible* equilibrium of all its denotative components; and, farther, that this equilibrium, in practice unstable but in expectation precise and illuminating, is what allows us to reconstitute Joyce's themes through their verbal form as myth. I repeat that this sort of experience can only be described in a theoretical way, but I am convinced that it is one shared by many readers of the *Wake*. There is ample testimony to it in a significant portion of critical discussion on Joyce, but we lack the critical concepts with which to specify what we think and feel when we have come to know the book well, and to see life in our contemporary society through its cyclical design.

To those readers of *Finnegans Wake* to whom it offers that cardinal difference, that *more* of human experience than they bring to it, and that *more* of what literature is all about, and to whom this difference comes about precisely by virtue of the esthetic unity that the book's disparate elements constitute, it becomes evident that its total possibilities of denotative reference have a coherence that, however unstable and imprecise in our relative approximations to it, possesses the absoluteness, permanency, and authenticity of myth. To speak, then, of a level of resolution arrived at by means totally indirect and constituting a myth will indicate, I think, but of course not explain, why the book's denotative possibilities must remain in our intellective apprehension as something less than the total monolithic unity to which we are obliged to refer them by an exertion of our imagination as well as our intelligence.

Of the various concepts of *myth* at the disposal of the literary critic, I am basing my arguments primarily on the concept that a myth manifests by its existential functions an acquiescence of belief (or an anticipation of that acquiescence) or an organization or projection of value beneath and impenetrable, in a final analysis, to an intellective reduction of the matter. Hence, if we recognize that in assimilating the contexts of *Finnegans Wake* we are compelled to suspend, relate, and equate into an imaginative unity and coherence what the verbal surface is enacting, in the spirit of comedy, at the levels of the primitive, subliminal, or archaic, of the trivial, incidental and symbolic, of the physiological and psychical, of the sacred and ritualistic, of the sensory and the intellective, and so on, we acknowledge perforce, because of the effect the unity produces on our responses, that what Joyce accomplished in his book provokes the effect of myth, that it possesses unmistakable attributes of myth, and this from all directions, since it provokes its apprehension as *that myth itself which it enacts* (to rehabilitate the phrase used by Samuel Beckett).[82]

My specification of this complex and delicate process will

remain very rough and abstract throughout my discussion. I have found a head-on approach to it unavoidable if I am to get on with my proposal that what we have issuing from our resolution of Joyce's ironical oppositions is the myth-making potential derived from the unity he imposed on his materials. To take an example of the simplest order: when we hear Anna Livia, in her final monologue, say, "Away! Rise up, man of the hooths, you have slept so long!" (619.25), we respond to the discord between the levels of meaning which give us Earwicker a sleeping pubkeeper of the naturalistic fiction ("man of the house") and Earwicker the sleeping giant of mythical and heroic proportions interred in the landscape ("man of the hill," i.e., "Howth") by balancing or equating their opposition and thereby arriving at their reconciliation and unity. When we attempt to specify what makes that unity possible we find that it comes about by the effect of the suspending dis-tension between two opposite levels of meaning. The effect, concentrated in the precise oral-audio rendering-reception of "hooths," is of course comic, because we perceive that an ironical opposition neutralizes itself in order to produce the effect of its reconciliation. And when we discern that we equilibrate the opposite levels of meaning according to a context of their reconciliation, disclosable from within Joyce's nuclear involutions, we are obliged to recognize that this unity of opposites makes sense only if we are provoked into accepting the outcome arrived at by such indirect means as myth-making.

By now it should be apparent that whatever our approach to the difficulties of Joyce's text we come back to the question of dis-tensions between opposed and interacting levels of meaning, which is in fact the question of their structural unity contrived by Joyce's techniques of indirection and conveyed to us in the effect of simultaneity. As I see it, the function of the ironical opposition is to neutralize itself by provoking not a sense of opposition but of the unity of opposites. In other words, the comic-ironical indirectness has the effect of a unity of opposites because it neutralizes itself while activating that context in which all the levels of meaning released from, or denoted by the verbal surface, are to be reconstituted in our perceptions as myth.

4

When we attempt to explain how an ironical operation neutralizes itself, we find, even where we have the closest thing to a single level of meaning, that the matter is an intriguing composite of interactions. Joyce's indirectness is actually the result of two processes of ironization meeting and neutralizing each other. In one he is ironizing a naturalistic fiction by projecting it as a mythical situation. This projection alone, of course, is not what I designate as the myth-making unity and equivalence of the verbal structure to his themes. In the other he is ironizing mythological themes or elements by provoking their displacement by the naturalistic fiction about the family in Chapelizod. The equilibrium between levels of our apprehension, exacting from us a resolution of the four contrarieties and the two processes, constitutes the one level at which Joyce's humor, despite all excesses, is nearly always sustained because it is at this level that we perceive the verbal enactment of his themes to be identical to the comic enactment of their structural reconciliation. The sustained effect of comedy in the *Wake*, then, bears a direct causal relation to this self-neutralizing of its ironical potential.

It is no novelty of course to declare that in *Finnegans Wake* we have mythical themes treated ironically. It is something else, however, to propose that out of an ironical indirection that neutralizes itself to produce a comic effect in an equivalence between what is ironized and how, we have issuing a context of myth altogether different from the mythological elements with which we started. There exists, therefore, a direct relation between Joyce's self-neutralizing irony and the issue of his myth, and between the conciliatory contexts of his comedy and the fact that his monomyth, as archaic as it is supra-logical, is a *resurrection* myth.

Our configuration, *fall (guilt-innocence)* →*resurrection*, is a convenient way of expressing the basic oppositions which emerge from their "timeless" Joycean reconciliation as myth. We found it useful above in explaining the basic unity of the themes enacting Earwicker's evasions of guilt as the original guilt of an archetypal father-figure. We can expand it to include the other major themes and arrive at an ideogrammatic symbol of the meanings packed into the thunderword: *fall (guilt-innocence) (stuttering-language) (defecation-creation)* → *resurrection*. In order to follow the ironical indirectness enacting these themes, we are obliged to resolve, in the act of sustaining the apprehension that HCE's guilt is that of one man and of the human race and the Joycean equation of the One and the Many, the interacting symbolical oppositions according to the operative sense, provided by Joyce, for neutralizing them.

The most obvious sense is that Earwicker's indiscretion in Phoenix Park involved a symbolic three other men. In the passage we looked at above, the three men were called "woodwards or regarders," and their names, "Chin Ted, chin Tom, chinchin Taffyd" (see L 250, 254)[83] are a cryptic formation of a divided (two)three in one, which also suggests the four elders when young, if they were ever young. The symbolic Joycean male trinity is a *division in unity*, whereas his symbolic female duality is a *unity in division*. On this level of symbolism human society is constituted by a schismatic male guilt and the dual role of the female as temptress, or daughter-wife, and mother-wife. The female symbols are forms of water, river, rain, cloud, and, most significantly, the rainbow.

At the inquest of HCE (III.3) the three soldiers are identified with the twin sons, "*Shem and Shaun and the Shame that*

*sunders em.''* In the context of the total recurrence what these
two revelations "denote" together is that "three soldiers"
represent HCE's guilt as it relates to the guilt of collective male
society. That the three soldiers were drunk at the time of the
indiscretion is an iterative detailing of the resurrective powers
in the "soul of the corn" (34.18). In order to avoid a repetitious
explanation I shall resort to a diagrammatic representation of
the two processes of ironization as they relate to the themes
and identities enacting the guilt complex of HCE, but, for the
sake of brevity, omitting details about the encounter with the
Cad or the shooting of the Russian general.

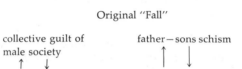

IRONIZATION 1                    IRONIZATION 2

Original "Fall"

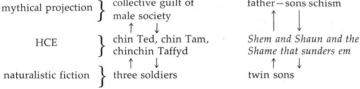

mythical projection } collective guilt of        father — sons schism
                      male society

HCE                 } chin Ted, chin Tam,        *Shem and Shaun and the*
                      chinchin Taffyd            *Shame that sunders em*

naturalistic fiction } three soldiers            twin sons

Joyce intends that we should see a qualitative parallel between
this configuration of male guilt and the persons of the Trinity,
a parallel as convincing or suggestive as the comic enactment
of his themes can convey it in the interval of our reactions.
Perhaps nowhere in the book is he more successful than in the
all-but-incredible conceit in III.3: "Dodgfather, Dodgson and
Coo" (482.1), which gives us one version of the division in
unity of the archetypal father's feelings of schism and guilt.
The explicit revelation occurs some pages later, toward the end
of the questions of the four old men. The passage provides a
good example of the Joycean equivalence between what is
ironized and how, of the qualitativeness of his verbal enactment of a unity of opposites. Each of the multiply occurring
motifs enacts the context of its unity and reconciliation with

its opposite by neutralizing the sense of an opposition. The questions and answers concern the attempt by the sons to catch the father-fish, *"Our Human Conger Eel"* (525.26). In Joyce's timeless context of myth they will "land him" on "lif- feybank" and replace the father even as they have already replaced him.

> —Do you say they will?
> —I bet you they will.
> —Among the shivering sedges so? Weedy waving.
> —Or tulipbeds of Rush below.
> —Where you take your mugs to wash after dark?
> —To my lead, Toomey lout, Tommy lad.
> —Besides the bubblye waters of, babblyebubblye wa- ters of?
> —Right.
> —Grenadiers. And tell me now. Were these anglers or angelers coexistent and compresent with or without their *tertium quid?*
> —*Three in one, one and three.*
> *Shem and Shaun and the shame that sunders em.*
> *Wisdom's son, folly's brother.*     FW 526.3–13

The verbal enactment consists of both a structural and a thematic equivalence of opposites, or "equals of opposites" (92.8), since we have, thematically, the father and the sons identified as a timeless "one," and an enactment of the sleep- ing Earwicker's obsessive fear of being replaced by his sons. The voice of the questioner parodies the rhythm of the closing motif of the Anna Livia section (I.8) because it is here equated to the theme of micturating by the young female. The sound of her passing water is both a temptation and a promise of her motherly reconciliation, and therefore the parody includes not only the sense and rhythm of "hitherandthithering waters of" (216.4) but also of "as she bibs us, by the waters of babalong" (103.10), their equivalence being the denoted sense of "Where you take your mugs to wash after dark?" Since the Joycean

"equals of opposites" also includes, structurally and thematically, the merger of the sexes,[84] we find "tulipbeds" equating
the flowers of the Quinet sentence (15.1) and the sleeping
twins upstairs in their bed ("tummlipplads" 570.4). "Rush
below" (I construe the capital *R* as the clue) equates a reference
to the father's act of defecating and the female pole of the
merger of the sexes ("Rosasharon" 34.29). "Toomey lout,
Tommy lad" recalls the naming process of the three soldiers,
whose anonymity is equal to their identity as Earwicker's sons
and to his feelings of self-division.

The questions and answers down to "Right" oppose and
therefore convey as an "image" the father's fall and the
mother's reconciling efficacy and power. The questions are
denoting that image from the direction of the female motifs
and rhythms, and the replies from the direction of the male's
original fall, and together they accomplish an equation between them that is one and the same with the "image" behind
Joyce's myth. "Tell me now" reminds us that the voices are
echoing the opposition between the washerwomen of I.8 who
are Shem and Shaun in female form.

When the voice of HCE in "Haveth Childers Everywhere"
speaks we have an instance where the basic opposition between guilt-fall and innocence-resurrection, indicated by the
correspondence between the color green and the male's stut-
tering, is resolvable in the context of the rejuvenescence of the
father through the incestuous identification of his wife when
young to his daughter Issy, with himself as a young Shaun.
We can reconstitute the elements of the opposition apparent in
the self-exculpation as an equivalence or unitiveness of a
mythical context by virtue of the structural dis-tensiveness
between the multiple correspondences which the time-
schemes of the dream narrative permit.

On my verawife I never was nor can afford to be guilty
of crim crig con of malfeasance trespass against parson

with the person of a youthful gigirl frifrif friend chirped Apples, acted by Miss Dashe, and with Any of my cousines in Kissilov's Slutsgartern or Gigglotte's Hill, when I would touch to her dot and feel most greenily of her unripe ones as it should prove most anniece and far too bahad, nieceless to say, to my reputation on Babbyl Malket for daughters-in-trade being lightly clad.    *FW*   532.18

5

It should be more than evident by now that what we have termed *dis-tensions* between multiple levels of meaning, permitting the resolution of those meanings into a monolithic unity, bear a close relationship to a universal attribute of mythical thought as explained by contemporary philosophy and anthropology, namely, a conception of man and his natural surroundings in which everything is potentially identical to everything else. "With myth," on the one hand, says a contemporary anthropologist,[85] who proceeds to postulate from the evident contradiction a basic structure of myth, "everything becomes possible. But on the other hand, this apparent arbitrariness is belied by the astounding similarity between myths collected in widely different regions." In myth "by a sudden metamorphosis," says a contemporary philosopher, who finds the basic structure of primitive myth expressing a belief in the indestructible unity of life, "everything may be turned into everything."[86] We could not begin to explain this close relationship by simply assuming that because Joyce employs a vast and varied amount of mythological material his work as a matter of course will resemble the archaism of myth in this way.

The *dis-tensions* of *Finnegans Wake* are most apparent to us as a qualitative equivalence between a multiplicity of levels of meaning and expansible contexts facing outward and an inner monolithic unity which always appears to be greater than the sum total of that multiplicity. This equivalence can be traced to various structural aspects of the *Wake*, of which two have been the concern of several of Joyce's commentators, who ascribe them to a literary source and think of them as ideas or concepts employed by Joyce but not as thematic-structural attributes closely related to the techniques of indirection and to the effect of simultaneity: the equivalence or simultaneity of past, present, and future time and the reconciliation or coincidence of contrarieties. It is usual to point out precedents for these in the philosophies of Vico, Bruno, and Nicholas of Cusa. What is often overlooked is that Joyce, in the use to which he bends their ideas, indirectly reveals the mythological elements in the philosophies of these writers, elements which go back to Plato and beyond.

We have indicated summarily that the guilt of HCE, enacted on the interacting symbolic levels of twin sons, three soldiers, and four old men, is apprehendable in its diverse contexts as a narrative "action" but that once we resolve this "action" within the conceptual framework of Joyce's monomyth we can see that the male figures of the book are all reiterating the inscrutable divisiveness of the archetypal father's "fall." The Shem-Shaun polarity, a structural-thematic movement toward and away from a point of unity or coincidence, is resolvable within the father–son polarity, which is in turn resolvable in the future, as in the past, instance in which the sons take over the father's role and replace him. What we find, then, establishing the qualitative resolution of male division in unity is that we are always proceeding from an enactment of strife, rivalry, and opposition toward the monolithic oneness of the mythical projection.

For its proper apprehension the twin-sons polarity depends on the release of an ironical potential which neutralizes the sense of the occurring opposition of Shem and Shaun by referring their contrariety to the context of their eventual reunion in the role of Earwicker, the sleeping father-giant. It is a psychological polarity which becomes a cosmic one by virtue of the simultaneity of past and future time in the presentness of the occurring dream. Joyce seems to have worked out in the Shem—Shaun polarity more or less a complete mystical and cyclical representation of Bruno's doctrine of the unity of contrarieties. It was Bruno's idea that opposed contrarieties, good and evil, light and darkness, underwent a dialectical movement toward and away from their poles of opposition and the central point of unity, the oppositeness or contradiction between them being greater at the polar extremes. Clive Hart has demonstrated how the Shem–Shaun polarity can be construed as that of the motion of two orbits around the globe meeting at opposite points, at Ireland (Dublin) and Australia.

> . . . when their orbits are in close proximity they war with each other and—at a moment of exact equilibrium—even manage to amalgamate, while at the other extreme there is total incomprehension and a failure to communicate, symbolised by the point of farthest separation of the orbits. The two structural meeting-points are at the coincident beginning and end, I.1 and IV, and at the centre, II.3—that is, diametrically opposed on the sphere of development. The strands spread out from the initial point of contact—the conversation of Mutt and Jeff, who have just met—widen throughout Book I and converge until they meet once more during the Butt and Taff episode, at the end of which they momentarily fuse, only to cross over and separate again during Book III before the final meeting (identical with the first) when Muta and Juva converse. 'Mutt and Jeff' and 'Muta and Juva' are the same event looked at from opposite sides; the book begins and ends at one of the two nodal points, while, when Joyce has cut the circles and stretched them out flat, the other nodal point falls exactly in the centre of the fabric. Represented in this way, the basic structure of *Finnegans Wake* thus looks rather like a figure 8 on its side, which forms the 'zeroic couplet' (284.11) $\infty$, or the symbol for 'infinity.'[87]

The Shem–Shaun thematic-structural coincidences are relatively accessible to Joyce's readers at those precise points where they occur in the dream narrative (18.15, 349.6, 563). Yet they are not in themselves the best instances for ascertaining the qualitative equivalence between the occuring brother–pair contrariety and its resolution within the total recurrence of the father's fall–resurrection. As a more revealing instance we can consider a sentence from III.2, which is likely to be well known to Joyce's readers by reason of the extended study David Hayman has made of its content and structure through the thirteen-odd stages of its development.[88] In III.2 Shaun, as Hayman explains, is a child-like Adam-Christ-Buddha figure undergoing the trials of a "dark night" while sermonizing to his sister and her companions. From the direction of a naturalistic basis of the dream narrative Joyce is ironizing the trials of the barrel–postman–son figure "travelling backwards" as those of a savior and sacrificial god. Shaun, as Christ, is executing a *via crucis*. There are numerous other parodic or imitative correspondences of superstructure I shall not go into. The chimes at 449.25, as Clive Hart tells us, have just struck two a.m., and this naturalistic fact provokes our sentence, in which Jaun dwells upon a desirable prolongation of the present moment of inaction. On a bare naturalistic level, we have the barrel on its side against a log. This is the sentence:

> I could sit on safe side till the bark of Saint Grouseus for hoopoe's hours, till heoll's hoerrisings, laughing lazy at the sheep's lightning and turn a widamost ear dreamily to the drummling of snipers, hearing the wireless harps of sweet old Aerial and the mails across the nightrives (peepet! peepet!) and whippoor willy in the woody (moor park! moor park!) as peacefed as a philopotamus, and crekking jugs at the grenoulls, leaving tealeaves for the trout and belleeks for the wary till I'd followed through my upfielded neviewscope the rugaby moon cumuliously godrolling himself westasleep amuckst the cloudscrums

> for to watch how carefully my nocturnal goosemother
> would lay her new golden sheegg for me down under in
> the shy orient.      *FW* 449.26

For us the remarkable unity and consistency of this sentence lies in the completeness with which each of the sets of
contrarieties, potentially ironical, neutralize their opposition
by denoting their resolution in the context of an impending
dawn, or resurrection. This unity becomes operative on the
level of our apprehension which finds, and sustains throughout its interval, the equilibrium established by the thematic-
structural equivalence of time and the identity of opposites
between the occurring themes of the twin-brother rivalry and
coincidence   and   the   recurring   theme   of   Earwicker's
fall – resurrection. This unity is made possible by the suspending dis-tension between a complex of multiple meanings,
each of which denotes in the effect of simultaneity the equivalence of their ironic opposition to their comic resolution. The
sum total of their equivalence thus indirectly established
becomes, therefore, indicative of the total sense of the narrative, and this total sense in turn reflects or reconstitutes the
occurring "action" of the sentence as an "image" of the total
recurrence.

The present moment Jaun would like to prolong is a
mythical and hence timeless suspension, and therefore an
equation, between sunset and sunrise—here the poles of the
interacting themes of the twin-brother, light-darkness, rivalry.
The recurring themes of Earwicker's guilt are clearest in the
parenthetical sounds "peepet" and "moor park", which convey both a divisive and a unitive sense, for Swift in the *Wake*,
as a paradigm of the godhead, combines the roles of Shem and
Shaun.[89] But the recurring theme of the archetypal father's
guilt is subtlest in the phrase describing the indulgent feasts
of the child-like Adam in a paradisiac garden, "leaving tea-

leaves for the trout and belleeks for the wary." The sense of
who is to watch the goosemother lay the egg, whether Jaun or
the rugaby moon, here the surrogate of Shem, is purposely
dis-tensive, because the impending moment of birth and
sunrise will be coincident to the coincidence of the two orbits
of the twin brothers at the pole opposite Ireland, that is,
"down under" in Australia. Thus the plural coincidences occur
at, or rather they constitute, the timeless moment of HCE's
awakening and resurrection.

The entire denotative potential of our sentence, down to
the smallest detail, is resolvable entirely within the total denotative possibilities of what we called above the sequence of
total recurrence, which is to say that a full comprehension of
the sentence reveals how it enacts, in the interval of the occurrence of its themes, the total recurrence of the theme of the
archetypal father's fall–resurrection. What I wish to stress is
that the more thorough the reader's effort to break down the
sentence to its smallest denotative particles, the more clearly
stands out the reiterative and unitive total sense they constitute. The ironical potential neutralizing itself in dis-tensions is
also to be referred to this unitive qualitativeness between the
part and the whole, to the sense of an opposition of meanings
resolved by the sense of a monolithic unity of opposites. My
particular concern does not go beyond the proposal that Joyce,
by ironizing the mythological in the direction of the naturalistic, and the naturalistic in the direction of the mythological,
pressed toward a "new way"[90] of telling the story of his Chapelizod family which was new only to the extent that it sought
to equate from every direction a naturalistic narrative into its
mythic projection. We may think of his techniques as new, or
nearly so, but he pursued them to the point where they are
nearly indistinguishable from the universal ends and ways of
mythical thought and imagination.

David Hayman has worked out a nearly complete sketch

of the mythological materials in the sentence. Thus, by comparing these materials with the resultant unity Joyce labored to impose on them over a period of fourteen years, we can measure the difference between the presence of the mythological, as such, and the effect that these materials, in the various contexts in which they appear, will produce on our perceptions as a unified, simultaneous whole. The effect is immediate, and the difference cardinal, because the cohesion of these contexts (the physiological, ritualistic, esoteric, symbolical, and so on) is now the consistency of myth, made new.

Our sentence is only a small unit of a complex book, but it is the small scale that permits us to determine in what way an ironical reading is provoked in order that the total denotative possibilities of the sentence may result, in the Joycean effect of simultaneity, as myth. The sentence opposes a recumbent barrel-son to the father's impending resurrection, but this opposition is equilibrated in the reiterated *till*, denoting the structural-thematic equilibrium by which we are to suspend the present moment as the containment of past and future time and therefore equate and resolve the sunset-death-apocalypse motifs to and with those of sunrise-genesis-resurrection, a resolution very precisely denoted in the goosemother's "new golden sheegg." Now this dis-tensive "timelessness" is something we expect in the least disarming myth as a matter of course, but we do not expect, outside the covers of *Finnegans Wake*, that it is to be dependent on an operative irony expending its intellective potential to convey an indirect meaning by neutralizing the sense of oppositeness in the very opposition it is intended to convey. Irony and myth, since at least the time of Socrates, have been such incompatibles that the outcome of their direct encounter has been the intellective reduction by irony of myth. Even the Romantic tradition of the nineteenth century, with which Joyce is sometimes identified, would have found strange the notion that irony was susceptible of a mythic qualitativeness.

6

Once we become aware of its presence, we can detect the dis-tensive qualitativeness of Joyce's indirection in its operative exposure of unitiveness at the most sensitive points of the verbal surface. We can, in fact, go one step further and decide that the verbal artifice is itself that function which equates, unifies, and reconciles the sense of occurring oppositions and contrarieties which excite, attract, and neutralize our intellective responses. A description of the babe Shaun-Kevin asleep in III.4: "Do not you waken him! . . . like the blissed angel he looks so like and his mou is semiope as though he were blow-delling on a bugigle" (562.23) The effect on us of a neutralized composite of ironical oppositions is of course comical, but the qualitativeness of the effect is as much a result of the operation taking place as of the substance of what is ironized. An action purportedly realistic and narrated in a parodistic or mock-literal manner is one that is potentially reducible almost completely by means of irony into the intellective terms that irony is meant to establish. This is what usually happens in Swiftian irony, where the outcome is called satire. On the surface it would appear that myth, or a mythical action, is the easiest thing to reduce into its comic opposite by means of irony, but the truth of the matter is that the substance and workings of myth are impenetrable to either comedy or irony. What irony in a comical operation can dispel and reduce are the circumstantial manifestations of the mythical, the social, and the literary conventions in which it may appear. The qualitativeness of Joyce's ironical indirection in *Finnegans Wake* pertains to the mythical unitiveness of the verbal artifice. It pertains then to that which an ironical reading cannot really affect or reduce to intellective terms; it pertains to what in fact compels the neutralizing of the ironical reading, which can only be maintained in our apprehension by the sense of an intended opposition between what is said and how it is said. But we have already indicated that the level of narrative Joyce attempts to sustain is that level at which our apprehensions are obliged to reconstitute a multiplicity of meanings and contexts as a mythic and a myth-making unity. Our equivalence, then, between what is ironized and how is both required and fulfilled by this end to which Joyce has pushed his techniques of indirection.

Structurally and thematically the act of coition in III.4, as a union or conjunction of the sexes, is so clearly exposable as a mythical action that one finds it difficult to explain the currency it has as a realistic event taking place on the most literal level of narrative. It is, however, understandable that this erroneous view should also construe the parent's copulation as infertile or unsuccessful. Such a reading of pages 584–85 is, to say the least, unsophisticated in a book about fertility and generation.

Clive Hart's recent reinterpretation of the action in III.4 should go a long way toward an understanding of the complexities of this section that shall do justice to its importance in the narrative.[91] In "Shaun d", following Clive Hart's arguments, Joyce's narrative descends to the deepest level of the cosmic dream and the corresponding revelations about the father figure. We should also expect a corresponding depth with regard to the temporal simultaneity between past and future events. Shaun is the narrator of this section, but Shaun is dreaming, and his dream unfolds at the deepest level of the cyclic rejuvenescence of HCE. The structural simultaneity of past and future time corresponds to the thematic identity of the son who is father to the man and of the son begotten by the father, a four-part equivalence amounting to a structural-thematic mythical timelessness, a time dimension in which events are conceived as taking place simultaneously in their presentness in the occurring dream.

The simplest matter we can solve by a reference to this level of apprehension is a discrepancy in the ages of both

parents and offspring. We are confused by a situation which
gives us an aged pair attempting intercourse downstairs and a
trio of babes upstairs, because we are working with only two
elements of the equivalence. The aging parents go with the
lusty Shaun who is dreaming, as the sleeping babes correspond to parents in possession of their procreative vigor. If we
work these elements down to their point of convergence the
act of copulation on pages 584–85 turns out to be the act of
conception for Shaun and his twin. Joyce's parody of dream
mechanics could not allow the exposure of such a "coincidence" in anything like a direct manner. Shaun, who is being
rejuvenated in Book III, moves backward toward the dawn of
creation of Book IV. His birth is described on pages 589–90;
he reappears briefly as a newborn babe on pages 605–6 and
then disappears into his mother's womb.[92] The Joycean reader
who is prepared to read the *Wake* backward will read through
the natural growth and development of Shaun from the end of
Book III to its beginning, but since he has to account for the
moment of conception, he will be obliged to conclude, like
ourselves, that it takes place, for any number of tortuous
reasons, at the deepest level of the dream.

It is not incumbent on us to determine the difference,
similarity, or relation here between myth and dream. Both
interpretations designate an objective mode of apprehending
Joyce's narrative. But whereas the dream interpretation obliges
us to keep identities, meanings, and events separate in order
to apprehend the narrative from without, the myth interpretation obliges us to bring them together, to attempt to apprehend
them in the simultaneity with which they occur in the verbal
artifice.

Once we free ourselves from a restrictive view confining
us to the realistic level of a literal action we can consider a
level of apprehension for pages 584–85 at which Joyce is attempting a structural-thematic equivalence of fertility – sterility,
conception – guilt, and life – death. At this level we should be

able to equate, these opposites: the exalted sense of a conception at the mythical hour of the Annunciation and the purely mechanical and carnal pleasures of a sterilized act of coition, the Annunciation-cricket match dichotomy of "kicksolock in the morm" (584.3); the derisive sense of the cock's crow and its three reverberations and its obvious sense of the fertilizing of the young hen's egg by the cock; and a literal or physiological context to the act of "annastomoses" (585.22) and a symbolical one. The dreaming HCE, through the dream of the son, is evidently re-enacting more than one night on the bed of marriage; he is, in the mythical sense, enacting all of his sexual and procreative trials on the bed of fertility, which is also the bed of guilt, birth, death, and a grave. In any case, a successful union of the parents is being derided by the mock-Gabriel son in a comical obeisance to the material objects permitting the mechanical pleasures of intercourse. We have the son begotten deriding the parents for their crime against the unconceived of his seed and her womb, as indicated by the parody of Matthew 11:28 at 585.14. Who else, in this equivalence of identities and time, is to indict the father in the name of the unconceived sons but the son begotten, who here announces their "virgin" conception and union to his twin ("How blame us?/ Cocorico!" 584.26) as an exposure of their parents united "in bonds of schismacy" (585.25) in their bed of fallen humanity? What abusive Shaun is apparently saying by the allusion to a birth preventative, as a counterpoint to the reverberations of the cock's crow, is that its use permits the fertilizing of his mother's womb by the "word," here to be read as the contrariety of "contraception."

Since no commentator has ventured to explain the I-you-thee, he-she identities throughout the passage, I propose that we have Shaun describing the parent's intercourse to Shem, as a counterpart to II.2, referring to the parents as the third persons, "he," "she," "Humperfeldt," "Anunska," and parodying or mimicking the exchanges he imputes to them. By this explanation the close to the commentary: "Withdraw your member! . . . Humbo, lock your kekkle up! Anny, blow your wickle out! Tuck away the tablesheet! You never wet the tea!" is not a reproach of the spouse on a nearly realistic level of narrative, as many readers suppose, but a derisive oedipal mimicry of the boy-angel speaking in the tone of adolescent sport and good, clean fun. At the deepest level of the dream we get, by means of an irony intended to blunt and disperse our intellective preparedness, a transparent revelation of the origin of our hero-as-boy sprung from the oneness of the body of Anna Livia, his mother earth. At this point in our discussion it seems unnecessary to insist that the ironical potential of the passage is released and apprehended as self-neutralizing in the effect of a comic simultaneity between the verbal artifice and the qualitative total sense we reconstitute as mythical. What we may proceed to consider presently, as part of our conclusion, is a correlation between Joyce's resurrection myth and the operative sense of his irony on one hand, and the structure of mythical thought which conceives death as an impossibility on the other; that is to say, a correlation between the *Wake*'s dis-tensive irony and the substance of universal myth which amounts to a declarative denial of death.

7

Sandhyas! Sandhyas! Sandhyas!
Calling all downs. Calling all downs to dayne.
Array! Surrection! Eireweeker to the wohld bludyn world.
O rally, O rally, O rally! Phlenxty, O rally!     *FW* 593.1

The mythical moment of resurrection is 6 a.m. The entire narrative of Book IV is to be thought of as occurring in the eternal presentness of this moment which, because it is both here and imminent, belongs to time and is yet out of time. This is the dimension of time suspending our apprehension of the cycles of the *Wake*: the twenty-four-hour cycle of day and night projected toward its simultaneous end and beginning at sunrise; the cycle of the seven days of the week projected toward its simultaneous end and beginning at sunrise on Sunday; the cycle of the year projected toward its simultaneous end and beginning at the vernal equinox, and because of simultaneity of beginning and end, paradigmatic of the cosmos itself arrested in all its movement at a point poised at the brink of infinity. It is by this dimension of time that looking back into the book or forward to its beginning, we apprehend how all its episodes occur and its characters exist at a level of time which is the presentness, the permanent now, of myth.

Looking now into the Earwicker bedroom in Chapelizod as this cosmic event is both about to take place and taking place, we are expected to believe that at the close of the Joycean dream-night this particular Dubliner, by enacting in his sleeping consciousness certain repressed wishes and fantasies concerning his children, has experienced a rejuvenescence of his declining powers, and, stirring at the clarion call of eternity, is about to undergo a resurrection that is still impending when the narrative of the bed scene drops off with Anna Livia's final *the*. Our belief, or disbelief, rests inevitably upon the loaded query: resurrection in what sense? A physiological or a psychological context, which is to say, one acceptable to a scientific view and corresponding to the level of a naturalistic fiction? Or resurrection in a religious, or spiritual, context, giving us the trials of one man seen in a dream vision as an allegory of the history of mankind from a primordial fall to redemption? The proper, and I daresay loaded, reply is that the proper context is the context of myth. By the mythical I mean that context by which we are to suspend, equate, relate or refer all others, the one context by which all other possible contexts are relevant or applicable.

Our discussion has attempted to show how this mythical context becomes actualized in the Joycean effect of a simultaneity of meanings by a dis-tensive and self-neutralizing irony. We have noted that this irony, by its operative sense of equating and reconciling opposed meanings, becomes the intellective catalyst, so to speak, precipitating in our apprehension a multiplicity of interacting contexts into a monolithic unity of myth. Its qualitativeness arises from the dis-tensive accord between a seemingly infinite variation and repetition and the unitiveness of all the materials Joyce sought to include in his book. Further, the operative sense and value of this irony are what makes possible the situation in which disparate, antagonistic or unpropitious allusions, symbols or contexts will neither contradict nor negate one another, but on the contrary and by reason of the esthetic purpose to which they are bent, will constitute the intended unity at that level of our apprehension where, as we noted, the verbal surface communicates its total possibilities as a *possible* equilibrium of all its denotative components.

"Array! Surrection! Eireweeker to the wohld bludyn world." The metaphorical relation between the stirring pub-keeper and the rising sun is only one facet of the equivalence between numerous meanings suspending the one context in which we can accept the publican as sun-god, fertility-god, and solar hero and hence as the sun itself, as an archaic mentality might if ever it found itself in the improbable act of reading *Finnegans Wake*, and this because we have neutralized our very understandable impulse to do so in an ironical sense, to pursue the nuance of "weak" along with "week" and "wake." The irony is still there in the operation, magnetizing our response to the verbal surface, but it is there to support our belief and, by fermenting and releasing our imaginative potency, to dispel our disbelief. The denotative possibilities of the single word "Eireweeker" may serve to illustrate our point that the all but unsustainable equilibrium between our apprehension and the possibilities emitted from the verbal surface becomes sustainable precisely to the degree that this equilibrium posed by the entire unit before us becomes one and the same with the comic effect of Joyce's techniques of indirection and transposition. We get the maximum effect by balancing our responses between the domestic and the cosmic sense of the awakening day. In the dis-tensiveness between these opposites we apprehend cosmic dimensions of terrifying political and social convulsions, of cataclysmic prophecies and eschatologies in "Surrection!"—which likewise denotes forces of renewal and re-genesis out of the ruins of shattered civilizations; but, in the other direction, we cannot be unaware that these cosmic proportions to the scene correspond rather explicitly to the state of the pubkeeper's male member at this fearful hour of the morning. The comic effect eroding away our dis-belief—some would say our sense of literary propriety—is simply another approach to the recognition that we approximate to that equilibrium of denoted components by a detachment greater or less according to the number of contexts we have been able to assimilate and gather to a focus.

> Well, we simply like their demb cheeks, the Rathgarries, wagging here about around the rhythms in me amphybed and he being as bothered that he pausably could by the fallth of hampty damp. Certified reformed peoples, we may add to this stage, are proptably saying to quite agreeable deef. Here gives your answer, pigs and scuts! Hence we've lived in two worlds. He is another he what stays under the himp of holth. The herewaker of our hamefame is his real namesame who will get himself up and erect, confident and heroic when but, young as of old, for my daily comfreshenall, a wee one woos.
> Alma Luvia, Pollabella
> P.S. Soldier Rollo's sweetheart. And she's about fetted up now with nonsery reams. And rigs out in regal rooms with the ritzies. Rags! Worns out. But she's still her deckhuman amber too.    *FW* 619.6

The letter's close tells us how Earwicker will rise into the impending day, but insofar as the restoration of his heroic prowess is due to his return to the young female, the new day will be but a repetition of the cycles of the past. I think that any attempt on the part of an assiduous Joycean to break down the foregoing passage into the number of contexts of which it is susceptible, from the symbolical to the scatological, for the "Post Script" is a flow of urine of the young female-rivulet,[93] will reveal that (although the meaning of the passage is to be determined by referring back, or ahead, to the other three Books) in order to apprehend the exact manner in which the occurring sense equates to the total sense of the complete book, the hypothetical reader will have to bring the multiple contexts together and will have to make the effort to equate them. In doing so he will recognize that, as a total meaning, they possess a qualitativeness disclosable in the effect of simultaneity and proceeding from a mythic dimension of time — that is to say, the notion of time as a permanent or timeless now, a constant presentness. He will confirm the fact that when those multiple contexts combine together as a simultaneous expression of multiple meanings, their unity is actualized as a mythic temporal simultaneity which bestows a qualitativeness on those contexts which are purely quantitative at the other extreme.

Lying alongside each other in the bed that is also a grave, the Earwickers are archetypes of father and mother; he, the giant Finn interred in the landscape, a mountain, a building, a solar god; she, a lunar goddess, the conciliating mother and providress, the river Liffey flowing past Dublin to the sea. They are this body and that thing, they are symbols of day and night, they are realistic characters at the same time that they are symbolic characters by virtue of the unity Joyce sought to impose upon his materials, from the smallest particle to the scale of the whole. We approximate to that unity when our responses are most complete; when they are engaged with the qualitativeness of his effects as a result of a detachment indicating that we have subsumed and assimilated any number of contexts. Joyce's book is a resurrection myth, that is to say, a

positive and affirmative book, in part by reason of its potential of a dis-tensive irony. A proper approach to what it
affirms should offer an explanation for the structural as well
as thematic necessity which critics call Joyce's repetitiousness,
ornamentation, and excessive detail, his obsession for all-
inclusiveness, and to which almost unanimously they deny the
value it evidently possessed for him. The wife awakening—
whose "Bussoftlhee, mememormee!" (628.14), echoing the plea
of the fading ghost of the father-king to Hamlet ("But soft
. . . Adieu, adieu! Hamlet, remember me" (Act I.4),[94] contains a hidden last word to his readers and his son as well as a
leavetaking to his own youth as artist; Anna Livia, the mater-
nal voice of night dying away with the sunrise, the river Liffey
flowing past the Dublin quays, cannot be the river Liffey, even
for Joyce, from within the monolithic nucleus of his myth,
unless the identity and the equation between the wife-mother
and her voice and her bodily functions with all the rivers of
the earth assert the identity and equation with the irresistible
immediateness the myth must possess by virtue of its accomplishment from within by the artist and its apprehension from
without by the intelligent participant.

We may conclude then that the dis-tensiveness of this
irony we have described serves to establish the absoluteness
of Joyce's myth in relation to the relativeness of our means of
access to it, and that this is the reason that explains why irony
and the ironical appear in the *Wake* primarily as functional
and subsequently as qualitative. By its function it actualizes
that irreducibleness which is myth and the mythical and, to
put it directly, may be said to be one and the same with the
affirmation that the regenerative powers of natural life and of
the life of the spirit are impervious to death and overcome it.

Whether we approach it from the direction of the anthropologist, psychologist, religious thinker, or the myth-maker
himself, the substance of myth is in one way or another immortality. That scientific methods and speculation and reli-

gious thought should have rediscovered the mythical for our scientific age in the very period in which Joyce lived and wrote is an extremely interesting social and literary phenomenon the study of which, however, lies outside Joyce's works themselves. That Joyce, like his contemporary Thomas Mann, should have devised irony and humor as a necessary approach to the mythical, corresponding to the skepticism and relativity of religious beliefs and scientific tenets of our century, is a question which, to my mind, will be appreciated in far better perspective within a half-century or so. But before this can come about, even to a degree, we shall have had to acquire an insight into Joyce's mind, techniques, and idiosyncrasies, at once more rigorous and detached and more delicate and sensitive than we now possess. Joyce rejected the religious faith that was his by education if not by temperament as he rejected the social institutions of a nation that was his by temperament if by nothing else. Yet he devised, and in a way that places Ireland and Roman Catholicism in the center of his works as no believer or Irishman would have been compelled by faith or nationality, two great books of our literature where the positive relation of structure to substance is that of myth: *Ulysses,* "the great myth of everyday life," and the *Wake,* which we might call, for the sake of a witticism, the great myth of every night; or, rather, the great myth of reconciliation between the world of night and the world of day, the myth of their cosmic oneness.

# JORGE LUIS BORGES

*The Ways of Irony in the Labyrinth of Consciousness*

*ANALYSES OF "THE GARDEN OF FORKING PATHS"*
*"DEATH AND THE COMPASS"     "EMMA ZUNZ"*
*"THE GOD'S SCRIPT"     "THE IMMORTAL"*

# BORGES 1

*It behooves us to suspect that reality does not belong to any literary genre; it is as risky to decide that our life is a novel as to conclude that it is a colophon or an acrostic.*[1]

The first impression Borges' stories make on his readers is most often a sense of uneasy but profound discovery. In many cases a reader may be unable to say what he discovers. In others the sense of a new thing confronted is so immediate that impressions and reactions are attributed to techniques and brilliant intellectual play. But Borges' short narratives are highly representative literary phenomena of the mid-twentieth century for reasons that go deeper than questions of style and techniques. They are ironical in structure in a way a critic might have predicted fifty or more years ago because they are evolved, with great artistic skill, which is, however, their own, from those tendencies in Western literature that have exploited irony as a mode of apprehension.

On the surface Borges does not make nearly the same demands that Joyce does. Like Joyce, but not in such marked stages, he has undergone over a period of years an intensification and refinement of certain features, propensities, and themes, never betraying, however, a disposition for distorting the structure and meaning of words. Borges disintegrates not words but ideas and the beliefs behind them, their orthodoxy, value, and logic. Like Joyce, he possesses an organizing instinct for relating concrete details to an abstract pattern, and an erudition that seems monstrous because it is so consistent in what it knows and obsessed with how it knows it. The interval of some fifteen years between his early poetry and the first success in the short narrative, roughly the years 1923–39, served as a period for defining, in the course of an essay, a lecture or book review, his own unorthodox approach to a rather eccentric selection of problems and questions of a philosophical, religious, esthetic, and moral nature; an approach the subsequent twenty-year period of productivity in the short story was to see refined into something like the perspective of a heretic within the walls of an indiscriminating twentieth century.

The expanse of themes traversed by Borges resembles

Joyce's in many ways, but where Joyce found the horizon of his world a conciliating dis-tension between the personal and the archetypal, Borges has created a world sustained by an irresolvable conflict between the same antagonists. Borges provides a dialectical art, subjecting the primordial and the esoteric into new and perplexing forms, while reducing the innovational and the concrete into hallucinatory ghosts without a resting place in either present or past. He offers the reader a form of highly stylized and intellectualized fiction which tolerates equally the categories and hypotheses of ethics, mathematics, and metaphysics, the postulates of mysticism, the incantations of magic, and the fantastic. Detached and noncommittal, he offers an art attempting oecumenical ends by adopting the means of any expedient, attractive heresy. On the surface of his short stories the most venerable literary orthodoxy is reflected. On the surface an imperturbable clarity and an impeccable precision govern. Unlike the *Wake*, here the directions for losing one's way in the labyrinth of symbols and allusions, paradox and irony, are clearly printed. Furthermore, the stories are elaborated precisely, even painfully, within the standard and traditional norms of the short story or the detective story. Yet the surface effect is a concision of style and a compactness of ideas and themes pressed to a nearly intolerable degree. The amusing disavowal of any but a fictional purport provides the humorous but solitary note of relief.

An art conveying its sense through the tensions of contradiction, parody, and paradox is intrinsically an art aligning and subjecting to the pressures of interaction contraries the content of which is reasonably well established in the reader's mind. It is the predicament forcing conflict on the contraries which assumes importance. In the case of Borges we recognize that the traditional meanings of the contraries are being subjected to the pressures of a conjecture pursuing a course beyond the probable and possible. The conjecture shaping up the predicament, we also recognize, is not the work of a purely intellectual impulse; the obvious drift of the speculation toward the imaginative and fantastic exposes the original impulse, a poetic intuition. The peculiar quality of this intuition is that it needs to set up an analytical apparatus and impel it as an intellectual conjecture on a trajectory bearing toward the symbolical and fantastic. The conjecture will maintain a tension shaping the narrative in the interval of our heightened awareness of just what ideas and their orthodox values, and of our personal attachments to them, are being subjected and "annihilated" in the process of dissent. The dialectical drama will differ, to be sure, from a demonstration of, say, a problem in metaphysics, or a mathematical demonstration or "amusement," where our absorption is never more than cogitative.

The success of Borges' method, judged by his more original efforts, depends on that problematical degree to which the reader is impelled by the fiction to commit his resources and impulses, and yet react to his alacrity. The "objectivity" of the narrative is coherent with reciprocal, subjective reaction in the reader bringing about the activation and dislocation of its symbolic potential. The imagination, as well as the intelligence, of the author has anticipated the potential responses as a structural element. To exhaust the possibilities of both subject matter and style, to arouse and displace the tensions enforced by contraries compressed and "annihilated," is to anticipate an exhausting of the reader's potential responses. The displacement, the vacuum of the enigma, follows inevitably. To insure that this response is to be that disengaging compulsion toward ironical displacement becomes decisive in the minute ordering of details, from stylistic manner to the ideational or intellectual point of the story.

2

A dialectial art attempting transport in such fragile conveyance evolves, necessarily, from the isolation and the reiterative compression of subject matter, themes, conflicts, and ideas. Borges' stories are woven with the threads and designs of situations and ideas unwoven or unravelled in his obsessive, personal need for the experience of analytical reading. In fact the attitude of his critical essays may be taken as an example of the sort of close critical reduction a reader should impart to his stories. On one occasion he listed some of his reading subjects: Schopenhauer, De Quincey, Stevenson, Mauthner, Shaw, Chesterton, and Léon Bloy.[2] One could add: Poe, Kafka, Coleridge, Valéry, and Henry James; the Cabalists, medieval philosophers, and recent metaphysical speculators; but a complete list of authors to whom he is specifically indebted would be lengthy. The need behind his predilections is other than an enthusiasm for erudite knowledge or universal literature. The predilections he feels compelled to mention would seem to indicate that his imagination has found release more readily in elaborating stories derived from the stories of others than in attempts at outright invention.[3] It would seem that his imagination, once prompted, could only get under way when faced with the task of relating and re-elaborating the assimilated literary products of others. The seven biographies of *The Universal History of Infamy* (1933–34), owe their stylistic brilliance to the labored preoccupation with certain intellectual and philosophical themes and their effects. In retrospect, the biographies do not evidence an "intellectual" style of narrative quite as much as an imagination feeling out its communicative possibilities. In 1954 that style is termed "baroque." "I would say baroque is that style which deliberately exhausts (or aspires to exhaust) its possibilities and borders on a caricature of itself."[4] All intellectual endeavor, according to Shaw, he says, is humoristic, and the baroque is an intellectual propensity in which humorism is voluntary or involuntary. What he means by reiterating Shaw is that the intellectual propensity equips itself with an introspective faculty into its own deficiencies. No one, no thinking subject, can possess the whole truth of a given question. To stretch intellectual capabilities to the point where they conceal ostensible deficiencies is to expose, humorously, a kind of deferential, gratuitous reiteration. The humor of Borges' art is centered in the contradictory attempt of intellectual conjecture to detonize and to contain, simultaneously, its own exhaustion. It invites the tautology that somehow a story is to displace its own displacement. Erudition, humor, the re-elaboration of ideas and stories, conducted as a gratuitous metaphysical sport, all involve a large measure of repetition and, invariably, of its counterpart, inversion.

We can turn to Borges' numerous essays and articles and find ideas, situations, or conjectures corresponding to the compressed elaborations of the stories. We find also that same dialectical rhythm of the mind tracing out a conjecture to its displacement. Two essays in particular, "The History of Eternity" (1936)[5] and "A New Refutation of Time" (1944, 1946),[6] are indispensable to an understanding of several basic ideas elaborated in the stories; they are also important for their indirect revelation of subjective concern, a poet's concern, for the concepts of time, eternity, universe, archetype, and personality. Both essays lead the reader to a reconsideration of a personal experience recorded in 1928.[7] The substance of that "experience of eternity" in a shabby section of Buenos Aires, on a street of the "elemental clay of America," recurs in the phrase: "I felt myself dead, I felt myself an abstract perceiver of the world."[8] My purpose here excludes an appraisal of the extent to which the articles and essays comprise an experimental or rehearsal room for the dialectical dramas of the narratives. An outline of a story is tentative occasionally in even the briefest of them, and not infrequently a single sentence suggests or even projects a future story, or recapitulates one already written. The advanced state of a group of articles following *The Universal History of Infamy*, and preceding "The Garden of Forking Paths" (1941), brings them perceptively to the threshold of narrative form. These works are now grouped with "The Garden" as the first part of *Ficciones*. "The

Approach to Al-Mu'tasim" (1935), "Tlön, Uqbar, Orbis Tertius" (1940), are "fantastic" conjectures taking the form of "notes on imaginary books."[9] What these "fantastic" conjectures lack, and others like "Pierre Menard, Author of *Don Quixote*" (1939), is the full mounting on imaginative terms. Without it even the intricately devised conjecture of "Tlön," a fantastic utopian realm displacing our real world, cannot elicit the sense of compulsion inveterate in the stories. However similar the attitude of the essayist and narrator in their ambiguous detachment, a real distinction applies to their esthetic products. Now, considering the product, at what hypothetical point in the Borgian creative process the essayist becomes a narrator and an essay begins to assume the shape of a narrative is decided, I would presume, by the immediacy with which the creative powers can respond to a poetic intuition demanding a dialectical conflict shaped by plot, action, and character. I would say "The Circular Ruins" and "The Library of Babel," published in 1941 with "The Garden," are decidedly fantastic conjectures taking the form of a narrative. The first devises, in imaginary place and time, a magician's hallucinatory exertions to dream and create the real existence of a man, a son, only to discover that his own existence is the dream of another man. "The Library of Babel" conjures up the horror of the universe seen as a classified collection of human knowledge, with all man's enthusiasms and follies nightmarishly catalogued, and God as the Great Librarian. Both narratives involve a minor degree of displacement because they involve, through characterization, a minor alignment of contraries imparting a narrative tension. The fact that their structure is that of a "nightmare" would indicate their execution obeyed an intuition differing discernibly from the one-sided lucubration of "Tlön." They demonstrate, also, that in the case of Borges, and perhaps contrary to what one would expect in so intellectualized a writer, imagination is a more resourceful factor in the compressing and displacing of contraries by exposure to irony than an analytical intelligence.

3

The valid distinction, then, between a conjecture taking a narrative form and one that does not is that the content of the contraries is referred to us in a conflict of antithetical forces. Again, it is the predicament forcing conflict on the contraries, resulting in the energized charge of the content, which assumes importance. Now, since the tensions activated by that predicament acquire and maintain their intensity due to the compression enforced on the contraries, the Borgian narrative actually assumes its shape and directional sense from the form of iterative compression of the content. The reader, provoked into fathoming the hermetical isolation of plot, characters, and events, ascertains that form initially as a forcible disengagement from reality, a gravitational pull toward the unreal or fantastic. The characteristic form of iterative compression, for its insularity and its suspension of reality, is the dream or a state of consciousness of similar attributes and possibilities: hallucination, revelation, obsessive recalling, incantations and magical spells. The iterative form is automatic in the process reproducing a story within a story, or a dream within a dream, and so on, or a conjecture within a conjecture, etc., in endless progression, as in a game of shifting mirrors or Chinese puzzles. The process arises automatically from the structure of the narrative, which presumably attempts to anticipate its own displacement *ad infinitum*.

This structure producing the effect of a compulsive engagement of our responses pertains to a mode of apprehending the predicament or antagony of Borges' contraries, and as a structure it is a unity of the substance of his stories and the functions inherent in the apprehension of that substance and its themes. Thus, if the substance before us is a dialectical drama in which certain states of consciousness are being represented by means of an encounter between reality and unreality, the way into and through this structure of consciousness is by means of the functional or operative inductions of irony. It is this connection between the ideational and cognitive content of the contraries and the mode of their apprehension that gives rise to the compulsive aspect of Borges' effects. What appears to be primarily thematic in the stories—the states of consciousness—is really substantive and structural, and for this reason we shall find it more appropriate to speak of dimensions of human consciousness—personal will, being, and desire, understanding and memory—when it occurs within dimensions of time, than to speak of intellective concepts like reality and unreality, or even some conceptual notions of time and causality. As we shall see, the motives of some of his characters and the exertions of others correspond to motives and exertions to foresee and control events and their causes. The apperception of causality of events in the story is related structurally to the actions and perceptions of his characters, so that what the reader has before him as he goes through a narrative in the first person is a representation, a polarized account, of the occurring consciousness of the character.

In the dialectical drama of some of the more intricate stories the "unreal" states of consciousness invoke and compel their displacement by "reality." An antithesis of dream and reality invariably infers an alignment of contraries involving the concepts of time, infinity, eternity, memory, concepts of the real and the mythical, the personal and the archetypal. A "realistic" Borges narrative like "The Dead Man" ("*El muerto*"), by inverse direction to the apparent significance of its events, will imply the mythical, the universal. The real in conflict with the mythical, the particular with the universal, indicate that the directional sense of the narrative is toward a forcible conversion of the content of the contraries into symbol. That is, the aroused perceptions of the reader are forced to construe the predicament of the states of consciousness represented on the level of a symbolical meaning. The communicative mechanics of this dialectical art involve, again in the stories of more consummate structure like "The God's Script" and "The Immortal," the inference of an absolute symbolical value in the content predisposing its complete and total displacement. The compressed reiteration of the content, we shall see, has the reverbative effect of symbols activated and disintegrated in the process of our perception and displacements. We shall call this process and its effect the Borgian representation of consciousness through the displacement of symbols.

The foregoing may seem to some rather overcritical and to others not really discriminate, since many kinds of literature are susceptible to the same critical exposure. Again, my argument is that the deliberate compression of Borges' stories acts as a charge upon the content and imparts a symbolical meaning. The stories have their peculiar structure, compelling an "inevitable" symbolical interpretation — and this besides the fact that the content itself is already invested with traditional and even esoteric overtones. In an essay on H. G. Wells, to cite but one occasion, we find Borges revealing not only his own conception of what the writer of fantastic fiction does but his own subjective and inferential reactions to it. Speaking of the early scientific romances, which he admires as the best of Well's work, he explains that their superiority over the rest of the literature of scientific fiction is their depth of symbolical possibilities. Take, for instance, *The Island of Dr. Moreau* and *The Invisible Man*:

> What they narrate is not ingenious only; it is symbolical also of processes in some way inherent to all human destinies. The harassed invisible man who has to sleep somewhat with his eyes open because his eyelids do not exclude light is our solitude and our terror; the seated assembly of monsters, jabbering in their night a servile credo, is the Vatican and is Lhasa. A durable work of literature is always capable of an infinite and plastic ambiguity; it is everything for everybody, like the Apostle; it is a mirror proclaiming the reader's features and it

is also a map of the world. Moreover, all this must come
about in an evanescent and modest way, almost in spite
of the author, who must appear to be ignorant of any and
all symbolism.[10]

In passing, it can be said that Borges has come a long way
from the kind of fantastic fiction original with Wells *circa* 1900,
that he has quite a different concept of its purpose and
method, even in a piece like "Tlön, Uqbar, Orbius Tertius."
The simplest difference is the brevity of Borges' stories, and
this brevity, corresponding to deliberate compression, is a
propensity of mind and feeling to convert literary expression
to something like a cabalistic symbol or a hieroglyph. It never
becomes these because the same mind and intuition, by inverse direction, has construed the critique and displacement
of its own creation. Borges compels the reader to respond to
his symbolism by activating, as a function of his irony, the
impulse to displace it, and thus uncover and experience the
"inevitability" of all symbolism. The more inevitable and
compelling the displacement and its effect, the more audacious
the congruity, *ex more ironico*, of his symbols.

   This, from a certain angle, will explain the "compelling"
and "inevitable" nature of his stories, which is a quality
Borges strives for as other writers strive for realism or veri-
similitude, and which accounts for a large share of the reader's
initial reactions of distress or discovery. Now, then, the sequential succession of events in a Borges story, a purely contrived or imagined order of events, acquires the inevitability
of temporal succession as experienced by personal consciousness. The sense of inevitability is the axiomatic result of the
compact and compressed organization of events and calculated
disclosures. The predicament forcing conflict on the contraries
is sensed by the reader to correspond to the inevitable, irreversible, and total movement of the narrative. The sense of
inevitability communicated in the succession of events and
actions of the protagonists arises, discernibly, from the "total-

ity of compulsion" generated by the structure of consciousness of the narrative. The directional sense of the narrative as a whole is a total compulsion, bringing about the displacement of symbols by the counteraction of irony. The narrative forcibly creates an elusive, illusory "vacuum," and our reaction to a vacuum, real or illusory, is not to tolerate it but to fill it.

The peculiar distillation of this process is that the reader is prevented from resolving the conflict of antithetical forces because his impulses have been directed, engaged, and expended in the activation and displacement of the symbolical charge of the content. I am describing in an abstract, general way what Borges has accomplished in the most skillful of his stories, some of which I shall treat in particular further along. But the reader can verify from his own experience much of what I say here and later. An aspect of some of these stories demands a more detailed analysis than I can provide in this essay: the contrast they offer between the sportive attitude inspiring the conjecture and the seriousness of the ideas involved. The sportive attitude is what appeals initially to our intelligence because its effect is to disengage the imagination from an egocentric concern. The reader is thus attracted by and induced to become involved in the conjecture much as he feels a pleasurable involvement of his imagination and ingenuity in the solution of a mystery, mathematical puzzle, game, or theorem. However, the tensions of which the reader is aware are not the playful tensions of an intellectual game, but the committing tensions of an involvement in the "totality of compulsion." It is true that his disinterestedness corresponds in a meaningful way to the speculative and abstract beauty of the pattern of ideas in the problem, but this is only one side of the process. Actually, the very seriousness of these ideas is antithetical to an attitude of "disinterested play," a thing not true of a detective mystery or a *jeu d'esprit*. The reader becomes involved in Borges' stories as he cannot become involved in the solution of a detective mystery or a chess problem or a theorem of higher mathematics because the conjecture is about radical questions of human existence, time, personal will, consciousness, and destiny. To appraise them as *jeux d'esprit* is as injudicious as reading Shakespeare's tragedies as exercises in imagination. Borges' stories have been compared by critics to mathematical games and puzzles, such as problems of chess, but unless such a comparison is qualified, it betrays a most unfortunate misunderstanding. As G. H. Hardy said, chess problems, however intricate and ingenious, are "trivial" mathematics; they are *unimportant* because their mathematical ideas are unimportant. Borges' stories should be compared to what Hardy called *serious* mathematical theorems because in his dialectical dramas the predicaments forcing conflict on the contraries are, as problems of life, as serious to the writer and the critic as the significant ideas of the best mathematics are to mathematicians. And only in this sense can the critic claim for Borges' stories an abstract beauty or elegance comparable to the beauty of mathematics.

4

Our approach to Borges' art from the angle of how it communicates its meaning is a way of emphasizing the correlation between what it says or means and how it says it. In other words, a way of emphasizing the extent to which the initial impulse shaping the content has determined also the compulsive nature of the communicative mechanism. The objection that I have overworked the notion of inevitability and compulsion would certainly be in line if the question were not one of the irreducible nexus between form and content in Borges' stories. I am well aware that they are, after all, quite apart from the seriousness of their contents, stories like other stories. Futhermore, regardless of the demands Borges imposes on the reader, there is little justification, or need, to consider what he has to say as more compelling in itself than the content of the books of other authors.

The art of Borges conveys its sense through compelling reiteration because it assumes as the axis of its meaning and form a radical predicament of consciousness. Borges' own view of man and his being is a conception of fallible powers compelled to attempt infinite or transcendental ends. In human consciousness, for Borges, this fatal opposition is nuclear. In consciousness, as if in mirrors juxtaposed a single image were doubled, then tripled, and so on, we have the reiterated awareness of awareness, experiencing its fallibility as a protracted, inexorable awareness of itself. Every effort to break out of the radical predicament becomes its reiterated persistence. Every attempt by man at transcendental action will find its betrayal in the roots of consciousness. Consciousness knows itself most profoundly in anguish and anxiety, the effects of past failures enduring as presentiments of future ones. But despair and anxiety and other aspects of the existential condition may be thought of as a means of survival of individual consciousness, confronted not only with the knowledge but immersed in the experience of its own integration and disintegration in time. The approximation to human consciousness we find in Borges is an antithetical structure subjecting the fragility of symbols to the inexorable disintegration of time. Yet the integration of symbols obeys the same inexorability on a cosmic scale that man experiences as temporal succession. The gestation of symbols signifies the annihilation of others: "... *all novelty is but oblivion,*" we read in the Baconian epigraph to "The Immortal." This antithetical sense of the structure of consciousness is conveyed in the predicament of individual man who finds himself (or who may not find himself so, but is) *a fallible being compelled to will and attempt actions presupposing an infallible doer.* The first part of this antithesis (enforced by the verb "compel") is the context in which irony intervenes in the reading or interpretation of the stories, and the second is the context of the action invested, variously from story to story, with symbolical value.

The total inevitability of displacement which I stress,

then, is a structural consequence of Borges' intellectual and fantastic conjectures, doomed by an inexorable law to trace their trajectories within the motions of consciousness. We find the most radical (because the most subjective) formulation of this inconsolate knowledge in the personal "failure" to refute time, in the finality of despair and resignation of the phrases: *El mundo, desgraciadamente, es real; yo, desgraciadamente, soy Borges.* The final passage of "A New Refutation of Time," a contradictory effort in more than one sense, may serve here as a transition to the analyses of the stories.

> *And yet, and yet* . . . To deny temporal succession, to deny the self, to deny the astronomical universe, are visible despairs and secret consolations. Our individual destiny (unlike Swedenborg's inferno and the inferno of Tibetan mythology) is not terrifying because it is unreal; it is terrifying because it is irreversible and of iron. Time is the substance I am made of. Time is a river wresting me away, but I am the river. Time is a tiger crushing me in its jaws, but I am the tiger. Time is a fire consuming me, but I am the fire. The world, unfortunately, is real; I, unfortunately, am Borges.[11]

# BORGES 2

*Determinists deny there can be a single possible event in the cosmos, id est, an event which could or could not have occurred. William James conjectures that the universe has a general plan, but the minutiae in the execution of that plan are left to the actors. For God—it behooves us to ask—which are the minutiae? Physical pain, individual destinies, ethics?*[12]

"The Garden of Forking Paths," published in 1941,[13] is Borges' first completely successful story and in several respects an unsurpassed effort. For the first time Borges executed a complete imaginative structure compressing action, or plot, character and ideas, and fusing them as a dialectical conflict into a "totality of compulsion." The fact that it is a spy and murder story, involving intrigue, violence, and sensational elements of the mystery thriller, indicates that the success of the story is due to the original effects attained by the displacement of these ingredients by a Borgian structure of consciousness. In other words, the elements of the thriller have been the instigators of a conjecture and dialectical conflict which determines the destiny of the protagonist. A murder mystery, literary and conventional, is expected to have a so-called inevitable solution, based on deducible, natural—not supernatural —causes, explaining that the crime happened as it had to happen, given the motives and circumstances. It is just this solution that is parodied in "The Garden." Here, on recognizing it, we shall see that it corresponds to the "inevitability" of Borges' structure. The motives or compulsion for murder correspond, likewise, to the Borgian "totality of compulsion." My analysis will be an almost point-by-point elucidation, with no apology for its length or detail. Since we shall need to explicate and expand where Borges has compressed, we have no alternative but to deliberate at length the content of his antitheses.

"The Garden," Borges says, is a detective or crime fiction (*pieza . . . policial*);[14] the detective in the story, however, plays a minor part. He is actually outwitted, but then the murder would not have occurred if he had not been outwitted. The story is in the form of a statement of the murderer confessing to the crime. The "detective" in this case, the "detector," is actually the reader, who must deduce not only the motives leading to the crime, but beyond these motives, the infinite, "insoluble" mystery of crime. This would explain why Borges has contrived a crime fiction in which the narrator-criminal re-enacts the crime, an atrocious nihilistic act of violence, so that the detector-reader sees the crime as it was committed by the murderer; or, more accurately, as it is now impressed forcibly upon the consciousness of the killer. The narrative gives us a sequence of actions and perceptions of the killer leading to the crime, but that sequence is being directed to the reader as a re-enactment of the crime. Accordingly, the character refers the cause and significance of events to one set of explanations displaceable, in turn, by the reader, who is to refer those actions, and the character's perceptions of cause and effect, to the "inevitable" set of explanations comprising the total symbolism and total irony of the story. There is then no murder or detective mystery in a conventional sense. The reader "knows" as much about the motives for the murder as the criminal himself. But the detector-reader, like the criminal, is confronted at the close with a metaphysical enigma. There are other features of a detective story which Borges conventiently exploits, but these I shall point out as we proceed through the story.

A nihilistic act of violence, narrated as a radical predicament of consciousness, emphasizes once more Borges' predilection for exposing and subjecting themes of horror and violence to the displacements of an ironical comprehension. In "The Garden" the displacements receive their initial charge from the antithetical tensions in the murderer's revelatory account. The state of consciousness represented in the account, a statement dictated and signed by the spy-killer, Doctor Yu Tsun, who has been sentenced to die by hanging, re-enacts the crime through retrospection and introspection, and, consequently, the feelings of hate, fear, and terror which accompanied the act of violence are re-experienced in the accounting of it as an unresolved anxiety, humiliation, and regret.

A brief explanation introduces the account. The reader is referred to page 252 in Liddell Hart's *A History of the World*

*War, 1914–1918*, where the historian states that an offensive of thirteen British divisions had been planned for the 24th of July [*sic*] against the line Serre-Montauban, but was postponed because of heavy rains until the morning of the 29th. We are invited to compare this explanation for the postponement with the account dictated and signed by Doctor Yu Tsun, a former professor of English in the *Hochschule* of Ts'ingtao.

The reference is more than slightly misleading.[15] It sounds genuine but it is patently a combination of distorted fact and ingenious fiction. Its function, or purpose, in the story, however, is part of Borges' symbolism, and the key to this is the combination "Serre-Montauban," and the number thirteen. The two villages, Serre and Montauban, in the vicinity of Albert, were just inside the German defense line prior to the British attack of July 1, 1916. Like Albert, Serre ("grip" or "claw" or possibly "closed") and Montauban ("white or inviolate mountain"), we shall see, have both an ideogrammatic purpose and a symbolical meaning in Borges' story, coincidental but "inevitable" to its structure.

The ostensible purpose for making the spy's deposition known has been to furnish a more plausible reason for the five-day delay on the Somme front. The introductory explanation provides the initial pointer to an objective or exterior frame of meaning to the subjective disclosures which follow. This frame of meaning is a struggle of world dimensions between races, empires, and nationalities, and the war of 1914-18 remains throughout the story an objective or exterior point of reference by which the reader's perceptions activate the symbolical potential of the spy's narrative. Ts'ingtao, the Shantung port seized from the disintegrating Chinese empire by Germany in 1897, had been in Allied (Japanese-British) hands since November 1914. Presumably Doctor Yu Tsun had been recruited by German intelligence to work in England because of his knowledge of German and English. The first two pages of the deposition are conveniently missing. In another neat parody of such devices we are obliged to begin the account *in medias res*, with the reverbative "I hung."

> . . . and I hung up the receiver. As soon as I had done so, I recognized the voice which had answered in German. It was the voice of Captain Richard Madden.

Madden, the police or detective figure, is an Irishman working for British counter-intelligence; his presence in the apartment of the fellow German agent Viktor Runeberg means that Runeberg has been arrested and Madden has found the trail leading to Doctor Yu Tsun's hideout.

> Madden's presence in Viktor Runeberg's apartment meant the finish of our efforts and—but this seemed very secondary, *or should have seemed so to me*—likewise the end of our lives. It meant that Runeberg had been arrested or murdered. Before the sun should set this day, I would incur the same fate.

The principals of a spy tale present us with the earliest motif of compulsion: flight or escape. From the moment Doctor Yu Tsun hung up the receiver, his existence resolved itself into a predicament of a fugitive who must expend his freedom in order to make an escape. This situation may seem only paradoxical, not ironical. It can be thought of as paradoxical, however, only in an isolated context unrelated to the structure of the story. Paradoxical elements will be evident at every point in the story, but their function is that of a fuse, or detonating device, for the irony. To recognize an isolated paradox is simply to recognize a disparity contingent on certain beliefs, arguments, sentiments, or opinions. To proceed to contemplate a cumulative series of such disparities is to become involved emotionally, intellectually, in the contemplation of a depth of multiple causes and effects determining the events of the story and their interpretations. This process compels us, to the extent of our capabilities, to a more or less complete detachment from the events of the story and from the initial substance of the isolated paradoxes. The process will complete itself when the total ironies of the story reveal that the paradoxical elements have had their origin in the irresolvability of the dilemma of consciousness of the protagonist.

Madden's pursuit is being reiterated by the fugitive's search for a way out. Once our attention is fixed on this "dialectical" opposition between the spy and his pursuer we become aware that the compression of the story corresponds to the predicament that is forcing the contraries into dialectical conflict. At the close of the long first paragraph in the spy's account the compulsion to flee from Madden will have resolved itself in his perceptions as the necessity to find "Albert."

> Madden was implacable. Better said, he was obliged to be implacable. An Irishman in the service of England, a man accused of equivocal feelings and perhaps even of treason, Madden would not fail to welcome eagerly and thankfully this miraculous opportunity: the uncovering, capture and perhaps the death of two agents of the German Empire.

The Chinese and the Irishman represent two nationalities not involved directly in the hostilities on the Somme; but the feelings, on a scale of world history, of both inferiority and arrogance of Ireland toward Britain and of China toward Germany and the Occident provide a historical context for the personal motives of the two agents. The personal rivalry between them, the ambiguous "psychological" motives and moral instigations for espionage reiterate the historical rivalries of 1914–18 in the game of power. The reader, reacting to the glaring ambiguity of several of Yu Tsun's phrases, is thereby warned to detect the incongruity of moral considerations and personal honor at stake in the ethical vacuum in which the antagonists move one against the other as agents of alien nationalities.

> I went up to my room; there, absurdly, I turned the key in the lock and lay down on the narrow bed of iron. Through the window I could see the usual roof tops and the clouded, pale sun of six o'clock. It seemed incredible that this day without premonitions or symbols should be the day of my implacable death.

This last statement designates the metaphysical void into which the events of this evening will be compressed, and should be understood as a paradigmatic reiteration of the structure of consciousness in the story. At one extreme we have the objective, outward point of reference to the spy's disclosures and at the other this centripetal and subjective point of reference, a centripetal polarizer, so to speak, fixing our apprehension. The perceptions experienced by the spy on the "bed of iron," like the act of hanging up the receiver, were actions occurring in an irreversible sequence of events. They were "inevitable" because they are perceived, now in the present re-enactment as the "content" of their particular moment of time in the irreversible sequence. The symbolical potential of the disclosure, as the statement portends obliquely, is related to this "content" of time.

Thus the first phrase, ". . . and I hung up the receiver," (. . . *y colgué el tubo*), stands for the initial action and its "content" in a series of irreversible events. Yu Tsun has been sentenced to die by hanging. The initial act, he perceives, was a premonition of his end. The connection between "hanging up" the receiver and "death by hanging," if symbolical for the Borgian character, is all but parodistic for the Borgian reader, and self-parodistic for Borges. This is the oblique way the Borgian reiterative process chooses to work. By forcing on us a parody of itself it expects to ensure that we shall read correctly the symbolism it exposes. Hence we should be prepared to displace the subjective symbolical content of the spy's disclosures with an ironical context, provoked by the parody, which is insinuating itself as a counterpoint to the confessional disclosures. But the ironical context cannot be fully operative until we complete the story — that is, until the "inevitability" of the content becomes "total" and activates the counterpoint of ironical meaning as likewise "inevitable." We shall then be in the position to apprehend the spy's deposition not alone as a narrative of events but as a representation of the very process by which these events acquire their symbolical significance in the consciousness of the protagonist and, reciprocally, in the mind and feelings of the Borgian reader.

The initial action of hanging up the receiver, the interval on the bed of iron, the pale afternoon sky, were indeed premonitions and symbols, but of something other than his death alone. They were intimations of the ineluctable mystery behind all symbolism.

> Was I going to die now, in spite of my father having died, in spite of having been a child in a symmetrical garden of Hai Feng? Then I realized that all things happen to us precisely, precisely now. Centuries and centuries and events occur only in the present; endless numbers of men in the air, on the land and on the sea, and all which happens happens to me.

These thoughts are passing through the mind of the Chinese spy in the interval of time that shall prove to be the enigmatical center of this evening's confrontation with destiny. They are the perceptions of an Oriental mind, conceived, as Borges never allows us to forget, by a writer of the Occident. Hence, following the direction of his conjecturing, we are to apprehend that Yu Tsun's anxiety arises from his attempt to perceive a transcendental significance not in events themselves but in what they symbolize when referred to his present predicament. On one level the Oriental's perceptions are reiterating the space-time equation of the symbolical garden-labyrinth; on another they describe his predicament as the moral isolation of the perceiving subject of Berkeleyean idealism. This first group of disclosures introduces a plurality of correspondences which we shall find marvelously compressed in a passage analyzed below in section 5: the decline of day (a quotidian yet cosmic event), the (moral) decline of civilizations and empires, the death of a father figure, a symmetrical (that is, labyrinthine) garden.

The spy secret of our story, a scrap of information reducible to the cryptic brevity of code, is a circumstantial instance illustrating the meshed interconnection of human lives, intrigue, motives, and objectives in the struggle for power within the ethical vacuum of war. The secret Doctor Yu Tsun considers so important, the location (Albert) of the new British artillery park on the Ancre, the little tributary of the Somme, is the military secret which the events of this evening will disclose (solely to him and to us) as the unfathomable metaphysical Secret concealed beneath the ontological secrets we can decipher and apprehend. The next stage in the spy's perceptions delineates his predicament as a countermove of strategy: how can he transmit the name of the site to German intelligence in Berlin before he is killed or captured? He must evade capture long enough to transmit the information. The only means of communication he can employ or rely on are British news dispatches. His Chief in Berlin, a sick and hateful man despised by the Oriental, knows only that he and Runeberg are somewhere in Staffordshire. The Chief reads through newspapers and dispatches "endlessly." A plan begins to form in Yu Tsun's mind when he searches his pockets and takes out a revolver "with one bullet" and hefts it, absurdly, "in an attempt to gain courage."

> I had the vague thought that a shot can be heard a great
> distance away. Ten minutes later I had thought out my

plan completely. The telephone directory gave me the name of the only person capable of transmitting the information: he lived in a suburb of Fenton, less than half an hour away by train.

At this point (the close of the long first paragraph) we are provided with the clue to the detective mystery. The oblique disclosure is that this "only person" is "capable" because his name is the same as the location of the artillery park. By killing him the spy can transmit, secretly, the meaning of the name "Albert" to his Chief. The spy secret, the detective mystery, and the metaphysical enigma of Yu Tsun's destiny, are all contained in the "totality" of the name of his victim. We shall arrive at that "totality" by displacing the military secret and the detective mystery with the total implications of the metaphysical Secret. But the necessary displacement comes about here when the reader infers that the person is "capable" because his life and identity are expendable. Thus, as we shall find, between the one compulsion to escape from Madden and the other, to find and kill "Albert," the "quantity" to be expended is "Albert" as the freedom of Yu Tsun.

## 2

Yu Tsun's plan is to make the journey to the suburb of Fenton and, before Madden can arrest him, kill the person bearing the all-important name. Madden does not know the military secret and cannot prevent public knowledge and reporting of the murder. But his plan and intrigue are not made evident until the very end of the story. They are not disclosed until the entire design of time, places, and identities is made evident and one and the same with the intention on Borges' part for withholding the spy's reason for killing that one person with the name Albert listed in the telephone directory. The clue to all this has been supplied, however, according to the requirements of the detective story, with the first suggestion of murder. The account continues.

I am a coward. Now I admit this, now that I have carried out a plan that no one can fail to recognize as daring.
I know its execution was terrible. I did not do it for Germany, no. A barbarous country, a country that has forced
upon me the abject life of a spy, means nothing to me.
Besides, I know of a man of England—a modest man
—who is for me no less great than Goethe. I did not speak
with him for more than an hour, but during that hour he
was Goethe . . . I did it because I felt the Chief held in
scorn those of my race, the innumerable ancestors whose
confluence I am. I wished to prove to him that a man of
yellow skin could save his armies. Moreover, I had to
elude Captain Madden. At any moment his hands and
his voice could knock and threaten at my door.

The "psychological" motives are stated as the most compelling, but their counterpoint is the metaphysical ones alluded
to in the abstruse description of his victim. The modest Englishman is his victim in that final hour: "Stephen Albert," a learned
sinologist and, on the plane of the story's symbolism, an archetype of the Goethean faculties of Western man. Again, to be
clearly seen, the antitheses have to be referred to the "totality"
of the name Albert. The Goethean archetype, the antithesis to
the Chief, is embodied not in a German but in an Englishman
because, as Borges notes in one of his essays, the English mind,
unlike the German mind, conceives reality in terms of concrete
individuals and not in terms of abstract concepts . . .[16]
The metaphysical motivation which will displace the
psychological is an intricate confluence and conflict of time or
times, of personal wills and identities, of history and geneal-
ogy, alluding to causality on a cosmic scale. Doctor Yu Tsun is
able to avoid arrest for something like four hours. Since the
metaphysical enigma is one of the "contents" of time, it is
important to account for every turn in the events of this summer eve in Staffordshire. Reconstructing the events according

to a time-schedule on which the trains operate and to which the intrigue of the spy tale and the detective mystery are confined, we have the following: Yu Tsun went downstairs to call Runeberg's apartment at six o'clock. Back in his room, the interval of digressive introspection on the "bed of iron" up to the moments the plan took shape in his mind amounted to nearly an hour. The fugitive left his hideout sometime after eight o'clock and arrived at the station about eight-thirty. He bought a ticket for a station beyond his destination, as a stratagem. His train left the station at eight-fifty. Madden was on his trail but failed to catch the train. The next train left at nine-thirty. The journey to Ashgrove, "the suburb of Fenton," took less than half an hour. The walk from the station to Albert's home probably took another half-hour. It was nine-thirty, we conjecture, when Yu Tsun, seated in Albert's library, looked up at the clock and computed that Madden would not show up for another hour. He had succeeded, with a stroke of luck and the ticket stratagem, in eluding Madden in the twilight of the Midlands countryside for something like an hour. The irony in this particular turn in events is that this hour of destiny, which can be seen either as a fortuitous escape from Madden or a fatal encounter with Albert, deferred the murder of Albert for the length of the conversation. The enigma is simultaneously disclosed and concealed in the displaceable "content" of this hour, disclosed as "inevitable" and concealed as "infinite."

The final hour of Albert's life and the final hour of Doctor Yu Tsun's freedom are acquiring "other dimensions of time" as Madden tracks down the fugitive and approaches Albert's home; as the substance of the conversation and the act of murder round out, fulfill, and displace the profane span of sixty minutes. In short, the final hour is a symbolical and enigmatical period of time — time in a metaphysical sense. But this period is enclosed within the meaning of the other period of time, the hour's journey from the station to Albert's home.

At the point of climax, Madden appears outside the library and Yu Tsun, consummating his plan, draws the revolver and kills Albert. This is the close of the story:

> I had the revolver ready. I fired with utmost care: Albert fell without a sound, instantly. I swear his death was instantaneous; a flash.
>
> The rest is unreal, insignificant. Madden burst in and arrested me. I have been sentenced to die by hanging. I have triumphed abominably: I have transmitted to Berlin the secret name of the city the Germans should attack. They bombed it yesterday; I read this in the same newspapers that reported to the English public the enigma of the murder of the learned sinologue Stephen Albert by a stranger, Yu Tsun. The Chief has deciphered that enigma. He knew my problem was to transmit (above the crash of war) the name of the city called Albert, and that I had no recourse but to kill a person by that name. He does not know (no one can know) my infinite contrition, my infinite weariness.

The actual firing of the shot that kills Albert is a matter of timing which, when dislodged from the structure of the story, can only be understood as an outrageous intellectual parody of such scenes in detective or mystery fiction. But once we displace that timing with the ironical meaning, and then refer back to the structure, we are in a position to displace the detective mystery with the metaphysical enigma. We have to see the success of the parody in order to get the sense of the final passage, which in turn leads us to Borges' inner purposes.

The parodistic effect is the result of the sustained compression and suspense. Not until the closing passage do we discover that a murder has been committed—the usual starting point for the reader of an orthodox detective story. We are witnesses to the killing, and, therefore, no detective mystery remains for us to solve. We watch the murderer proceed step by step—so closely, in fact, that the whole process is hallucinatory rather than deductive and real. The victim himself seems unreal, and he dissipates like an apparition. Moreover, the killer is arrested immediately after by the counter agent, who has also seen the crime but does not know the circumstances, cannot detect either the motive or meaning of the crime, and therefore cannot hinder the killer's secret design. It is the killer who reveals his own strategy and motives, but does so because the killing has turned out "meaningless." All this the reader discovers or detects almost simultaneously at the point in the account in which the inevitability and irreversibility of Yu Tsun's actions become "total" activating the counterpoints of irony as likewise "inevitable."

Now we shall go back and take up the story at the moment Yu Tsun leaves his hideout and undertake an explanation of the crime equating the totality of the enigma of "Albert" and Yu Tsun's destiny to the "meaning" of the story as arrived at through the analysis of its ironical structure.

3

I dressed silently, bade myself farewell in my mirror, went down the stairs, surveyed the peaceful street, and left the house. The station was a short distance away, but I decided it was preferable to take a cab. I argued that I ran less risk of being recognized; the fact is I felt visible and vulnerable to an infinite degree on that deserted street. I remember I told the cabman to stop a little before the main entrance. I got out with a voluntary and almost painful slowness; I was going to the village of Ashgrove but bought a ticket for a more distant station. The train was leaving in a very few minutes, at eight-fifty. I hurried; the next train would leave at nine-thirty. The platform was almost deserted. I went through the coaches; I remember a few working men, a woman in mourning, a young man reading fervently the *Annals* of Tacitus, and a soldier, wounded and blissful.

If we reduce the directional sense of the story to the fewest words possible, we can say that Borges is conjecturing the metaphysical isolation of an individual perceiving the total implications of a deed that is to decide the meaning of his personal existence. That deed has been consummated, but the individual is evoking the events leading to its consummation; hence these events in the present re-enactment of them are not only premonitions of the act but also symbols of its irrevocability. Every action and event, every detail of his movements, is charged now with a symbolical "content" within this double reference of retrospection and presentiment. That "content," moreover, is perceived by him subjectively and by us objectively as inevitable because it is fixed now in his experience as part of an irrevocable and irreversible sequence of actions. The first phase of this isolation, corresponding to the interval of the train journey, gives us the ethical ground on which Yu Tsun acts. The reader's initial task is to apprehend that ethical ground as an ethical vacuum.

The effect Borges strives to maintain is that of an irresolvable opposition between the two conflicting interpretations of the actions, movements, and perceptions of his protagonist as either autonomous and spontaneous or the result of compelling circumstance and necessity. To maintain such a conflict in our apprehension is to carry out the elaboration of his themes while reiterating their structural interconnections. The symbolical potential of the details fixed in memory of the hurried passage through the train is evidently dependent upon our perceiving the ironical coincidence of their adventitious and obsessionary character with the reiterated coincidence of the story's themes. The ironical context, however, is one of structure because behind the coincidence of time and

circumstance reiterating the story's themes there is operative
the decisive coincidence of Borges' conjecturing and revelatory
techniques and our apprehension, and the effect is really the
consequence of this.

The images of recall are the result of a private and exonerating dialectic which is reiterating and coinciding with the
pervasive dialectical conflict of the story, suggesting to our
outward observation both a certain futility and fatality of a
man's consciousness isolated in attempts to perceive depth in
images and movements. To his consciousness each of the
images of recall is charged with a meaning that is either a
parallel or an antithetical reiteration of his predicament, and
the allusion to Tacitus is revelatory in this sense. The *Annals,*
keeping in mind Borges' purpose in alluding to them, give us
an indelible perspective on an epoch of violence and moral
degradation, at the disintegrating center of an empire. But the
inner, compelling sense of the allusion for the Borgian hero is
the sense of the inevitable reiteration, and this is perceptible
only under the stress of a heightened consciousness, or exertion of consciousness, to put it less mildly. The young man
reading fervently is absorbed in an account reiterating (reflecting) the moral state of the Chinese stranger who presses
by him, absorbed with his predicament.

Now, the man who is compelled and who compels himself
to perceive his actions "totally" undergoes a metaphysical
ordeal in which he is both the willing subject of his actions
and the perceiver of their total implications. He is, and the
term is all but inevitable by now, the hero of consciousness,
compelled to perceive his actions to their ultimate ethical and
even metaphysical consequences. But this· same compulsion
makes it inevitable that these consequences can have their
"total" effect only upon that consciousness of the hero. His
ordeal is to increase, intensify, and survive the compelling
exertions of consciousness as a reality of consciousness itself;
hence his radical isolation. Yu Tsun, as a Borgian hero of

consciousness, is compelled to execute and to perceive the execution of an irrevocable act of destiny, and his perception of that act as an act of absolute self-consciousness is its "total" execution. Now, for this very reason the antithesis to the totality in this Borgian dialectical design is a vacuum, and the hero of consciousness is a nihilist.

> The coaches jerked forward at last. A man I recognized ran to the end of the platform in a vain effort to catch the train. It was Captain Richard Madden. Annihilated, fearful, I huddled into the far corner of the seat, away from the perilous glass.
> I passed from my feeling of annihilation to a state of almost abject happiness. I told myself that my ordeal had begun and that I had won the first round when I fended off my adversary's blow, even if for only forty minutes, even if only by a stroke of chance. I argued that this scant victory prefigured total victory. I argued that it was not insignificant; since but for this precious difference presented to me by the timetable I should now be imprisoned or dead. I reasoned (no less fallaciously) that my cowardly happiness proved I was a man capable of carrying the audacious plan to a successful close. From my weakness I gathered a strength that did not abandon me.

This interaction of emotion and logic, this dialectical confronting of "psychological" motivations (like the motives of individuals who attempt to make history and shape its course by applying nihilistic means in order to attain "historical" goals, Borges reminds us), is occurring in a moral vacuum. Morality is replaced by the inner, centripetal dialectic. Here, under dialectical pressure (despair and anxiety), a statement predicates its antithesis, with the result that each statement entails a conflict of dichotomies. We are obliged to displace the dichotomies (victory—annihilation, courage —cowardice, terror—happiness), not by reconciling them, for they are occurring in a moral vacuum, but by annuling or cancelling them; that is, by reiterating the context of vacuum in which they occur.

Nonetheless, our alignment of counterpoints is compelled to follow Borges' conjecture, which is superimposing the executor of a nihilistic action upon the perceiving subject of that action and forcing their identity. Thereupon, by our own displacing, we are obliged into the irony that the perception of an action arising from a "will to power" which is also a will to "nothingness" cannot impregnate that action with moral significance even in the case of the ideal dialectical identity of both the willing and acting and the perceiving subject. Having committed himself to the atrocious deed, Yu Tsun pressed on under the illusion that his motives and actions corresponded to an exonerating ethic of heroic exertion. The "content" of the interval on the moving train (again the space – time reiteration) is the ethical commitment of his will and freedom to the execution of the irrevocable deed.

> I foresee the time when man will resign himself to attempt enterprises each day more atrocious; soon there will be only warriors and bandits; I give them this advice: *the executor of an atrocious enterprise must imagine that he has already carried it out; he ought to impose upon himself a future that is irrevocable like the past.* That is how I proceeded, while the passing flow of that day that was perhaps the last and the slow diffusion of night were registered in my eyes of a man already dead.

That an Oriental should profess the methods of Western nihilists and revolutionaries in betraying a Western power at war with another that the Oriental despises, in order to prove (in a moral vacuum) his indispensability and autonomy as an agent, is the kind of involuted irony to which the reader of Borges becomes accustomed as a matter of course. These involucra begin with the inverted connotations of the prognostic "I foresee." Yu Tsun assumes, retrospectively, the detached point of view (a chiliastic tension sustained here in the void of his dialectic) of the Western "prophet" of history who denounces the present but projects, as an imperative, the consequences of its evils into the future. Only in the despair and anxiety of this Nietzschean-like paraphrase could the irreversibility of the future serve as an instigation to him and offer deliverance. Only in the negation of being of this moral vacuum could the self-imposition of a guilt-ridden, irreversible future assume the nature of a just instigation and of a test of "moral" qualities, courage, will, and power. The real victim of this self-imposed irreversibility and violence, the tensions of irony forewarn us, can only be the executor of the atrocity. The annihilation of "Stephen Albert," a person bearing a secret name, implied and impelled, in the moral twilight of the vacuum of world war, the annihilation of the city of Albert, of anonymous armies, and of the Doctor himself, this bleak reflector on violence. To attempt to break out of a present anxiety by committing the "will to power" to an irrevocable future, thereby displacing the freedom of personal will with the irreversibility of time, was an attempt of nihilistic despair to impregnate a present "nothingness" with the "totality" of a compelling, inexorable destiny. Only in the consciousness of the Borgian hero compelled to this commitment can such a horror have assumed a reality of meaning, and then only by the isolation and paralysis of personal freedom—the value on whose inviolateness the European nihilist of the early twentieth century, the destroyer of all values and negator of being, precipitates "history." It is a "twilight" morality, productive of an infinite despair.

An entire ideological landscape is thus evoked by the correspondences between the thoughts of the train passenger, his re-enactment of the interval, the oppressive atmosphere of war, and the movement of the train itself. The effect also provides a parallel to the strategic importance of the railways in waging war in 1914–18. The intention is to prompt our reactions to invoke the "crepuscular" atmosphere of July 1916, the violence and slaughter of the Somme front, the roaring guns, the brutal encounter of flesh and steel, as the background to this sequence of perceptions disclosed to the immobile perceiver in the compartment of the moving train as the sequence of his own ethical motions. Thus our reactions to his disclosures are being pressed to polarize about the opposite points of reference, the inner and subjective and the outer and objective. This process imposes itself upon us as necessary to the apprehension of the story because we are reacting to the antithetical tensions of a predicament of consciousness whose sense cannot be conveyed other than as a conflict of a personal will and its forcible objectivization in time.

The developing sense of Yu Tsun's disclosures corresponds, then, to the sequential stages of his journey. Each stage consists of an internal movement corresponding to the "form" in which he expresses his perceptions and describes his actions. The train journey gives us the ethical ground on which he is moving, and through the counterpoints of irony we secure the metaphysical isolation of the microcosm he represents. The internal and subjective movements are fixed and therefore appear as symbolic movements, determinations of personal will in time as perceived in his own consciousness by the hero.

The fugitive's going forth in search of the man with the secret name and his pursuit by Madden is a design of movement and countermovement suggesting the multiple personal identities and multiple ramifications of the labyrinth motif.[17] The flight has become a symbolic quest and encounter with the self, a drama of consciousness. The symmetrical demands of Borges' dialectical design will require that this encounter with the self become "an encounter with Goethe," the archetypal figure of the Occident embodied in an enemy of Caesarian Germany.

4

The train journeyed sweetly, through rows of ash trees. It came to a stop almost, it seemed, in the middle of the countryside. No one called out the name of the station. *Ashgrove?* I asked some children on the platform. *Ashgrove,* they replied. I got off.

A lamp cast its light over the platform, but the children's faces were hidden in the shadow beyond the rim of light. One of them questioned me: *Are you going to the house of Doctor Stephen Albert?* Without waiting for a reply, another said: *It's quite a long way to the house, but you won't get lost if you take that road to the left and turn to the left at each crossroads.*

The next alignment of counterpoints is more easily inferred from the outcome of the story than the preceding. The first point is that "Albert," "the only person capable of transmitting the information," turns out to be Doctor Stephen Albert, a noted sinologue. This explains why the children can so obviously direct an Oriental alighting from a train in the lonely twilight to his home. Where, but to the home of Doctor Stephen Albert, would an Oriental stranger be going in Ashgrove? Even a child knows.

I tossed them a coin (my last), went down some stone steps and came out on the solitary road. The road sloped down gently. It was of elemental earth. Above me the branches crossed confusedly, and the low and circular moon seemed to accompany me.

For a moment the thought crossed my mind that Richard Madden had in some way seen through my desperate purpose. I realized very quickly that this was impossible. The instructions to turn always to the left reminded me that just such was the common procedure for reaching the central court of certain labyrinths.

The second point to be inferred is that Albert has prepared the approaches to his home, perhaps even to make it
easier for strangers to find their way, in the form of a labyrinth
passage. Here the coincidence becomes inevitable. Concur-
rently, as one point of irony is reiterated by the next, the activated elements release the inner meaning of the disclosure.
The first point indicated a surprising coincidence; the second
displaces the requirements of certain detective plots that isolate the victim in a distant, lonely place. The crime has not
been committed yet, but Albert is already the inevitable victim
of "such and such" designs, since he has made it inevitable
that his killer will find the way to his home. The metaphysical
enigma has displaced the detective mystery at still another
point. Albert has laid out the approaches to his home as an
eccentric but by no means improbable repetition (a spatial
reiteration) of *The Garden of Forking Paths*, the enigmatic Chinese novel he has laboriously studied and deciphered.

> I know something of labyrinths: not in vain am I a
> great-grandson of the Ts'ui Pên who was governor of
> Yunnan and who renounced worldly power to write a
> novel that would be even more populous than the *Hung
> Lou Meng* and to build a labyrinth in which all men
> would lose their way. Thirteen years he devoted to these
> ill-assorted labors, but the hand of a stranger killed him,
> and his novel was incoherent and no one ever found the
> labyrinth. Beneath English trees I meditated on that lost
> labyrinth. . .

The third point of irony is that this novel by Ts' ui Pên is
*The Garden of Forking Paths*, conceived and "lost" in an interior
province of China and deciphered in a Midlands county (and
the geographical heart) of England. This third point is charged
with other ironies whose consequences are revealed later. The
movement through the labyrinth approach to Albert's home (a

movement his pursuer reiterates) is simultaneously a flight or escape from Madden and an approach to and search for Albert, giving us a fugitive in search of his victim, who, moreover, *is* expecting a stranger and an Oriental. The fourth point is that the fugitive's awareness of his movements through the labyrinth reiterates the actual situation. However removed from reality his imagination, however improbable the situation, he *is* moving through a labyrinth among the woods and meadows of Staffordshire.

The inference by irony is one way the reader is obliged to detect the directional sense of the story, and as each point of irony inferred is a further projection of the sense, each recapitulates as it reiterates. It is convenient to stress this matter here, where the situation in the story is relatively simple. Borges' conjecturing will have produced its effect when the isolated points of irony have provoked in our perceptions a sense of infinite possibilities emitting from an alignment of inferences, or even from an isolated one. The directional sense is a predicament of consciousness disclosed as an increasingly irresolvable one as each of the events of the story becomes fixed in the irreversible sequence. Yu Tsun, meditating beneath English trees on the "lost labyrinth," is about to expend, in killing Albert, his own freedom as the price exacted from within his own determination to experience himself as the perceiving subject of his own actions while expending that very freedom. This commitment of his freedom is the act of destiny which is irresolvable in consciousness and irreversible in time.

Destiny, in the Borgian design, is the commitment of freedom, and therefore, the "total act." It is a commitment of will in time, and a commitment, thereby, which remains for all time irreversible, and, in retrospect, irresolvable and hence "inevitable." That is, once the act is consummated, for the consciousness of the hero the irreversibility of that act becomes the "total content" of any given moment of his existence leading to the event and leading away from it. The "content" of the isolated past events which led to its execution is now a premonition and a symbol of the inevitability of that act, and the action itself constitutes a total, impersonal compulsion annihilating personal will. Once personal freedom is committed and expended in the act of destiny its loss is thereafter perceptible to the hero's consciousness only as the sequent of an impersonal compulsion. Personal will is a totality of freedom, an individual will actually or potentially free; but to the consciousness of the Borgian hero who has survived the self-annihilation of freedom its loss is only perceptible as the result of a total compulsion.

We may now proceed to "detect" the workings of this inner and directional sense in the story's structure of consciousness. Our detection must necessarily attempt, over and above the critical, a metaphysical investigation of the crime. We should be able to trace Borges' conjecture to a final explanation of why, the crime having been committed, Yu Tsun must be the inevitable killer. Yu Tsun is approaching Albert's home and meditating on the "lost labyrinth" of his ancestor. This is a convenient point to "temporize" on the labyrinthine structure in which he is to "lose his way."

The potential "content" of any given moment in the hero's existence, once the act has been executed and his freedom expended in the act, is a reiteration of his present predicament, of which the final sentence in the story—"He does not know (no one can know) my infinite contrition, my infinite weariness"—is only the initial disclosure. The despair and anxiety of his predicament is the consequence of a man compelled to live in a truncated present, condemned to die, but already dead. For him there cannot exist a real future, because a real future is possible only as a potential of freedom available to an individual will and consciousness, a freedom as yet inviolate and still to be disposed. The "content" of a real future is an uncommitted freedom. The act of destiny is the central act of a man's existence, one moment in the temporal succession constituting his identity. It is only one moment, but that one moment discloses to the Borgian protagonist *who he is*. It is the moment consummating all the moments of his life, and therefore "total." His perception of the meaning of a given moment leading to the decisive act (on account of the antithetical tensions of his anxiety, the void resulting from the loss of freedom and the impossibility of a future) is this continuum of a present anxiety.

To evoke in anxiety a past action or event leading to the central and decisive act is to perceive and prefigure the premonitional "content" of that past action or event. The "content" is thus discerned as a symbol of his destiny. Since the act of destiny is already total and irreversible, the symbol becomes an "inevitable" disclosure. Like the act of destiny it reiterates, the symbol expresses a clash between freedom and compulsion, between a personal will and an impersonal power. In order to see this clearly the detecting reader is obliged to conjecture the "content" of a symbol pointing to a real future: that symbol would express a still inviolate freedom. But the "content" of the symbols of Yu Tsun's consciousness reiterates a total anxiety which has come to fill the void left by the annihilation of freedom.

As symbols of his destiny their "content" is constantly disclosing a "total" potential of freedom effaced and replaced by a "totality of compulsion." The ultimate charge of a symbol in the consciousness of the hero is the imminent disposal of his freedom. A symbol of destiny is then this "content" of a given moment in the temporal succession constituting the hero's existence and prefiguring the disposal of his freedom. When the symbol releases its meaning under the tensions of anxiety, the "content" discloses the commitment and effacement of the hero's personal freedom as "inevitable" within the temporal succession of events leading to the decisive act. The total meaning or direction to which these symbols are pointing in the consciousness of Yu Tsun is an intensified awareness of his fallible powers. The commitment of his freedom is the total act of a man's life, and the complete exposure of his fallibility and his precarious existence in time, marking the center of the labyrinth in which, simultaneously, he finds himself (that is, discovers the meaning of his personal existence) and perishes.

If poetic and metaphysical symbols could be treated as if they were mathematical symbols, we could state Borges' conjecture and the mystery of the story in the form of an equation demonstrating how the "totality of compulsion" is derived from the "totality of freedom." Thus, according to our poetic and metaphysical equation, only a "totality of freedom" could give us a "totality of compulsion"; the compulsion is a displacement of freedom and derivable only from the displacement. Now, just this metaphysical and poetic equation is what we encountered in the opening sentence of the story, in the guise of a description of the battleline on the Somme front, "Serre-Montauban," "compulsion-freedom," in the order of the final displacement. Borges' purpose, then, in mentioning the battleline, was to indicate the structural or "inevitable" coincidence between the inner, metaphysical conflict of the condemned spy and the outer, historical conflict analyzed in Liddell Hart's *History*.

## 5

The approach to Albert's home from the railway station is our second phase in the isolation of Yu Tsun, and the interval providing the metaphysical ground on which the Borgian hero is moving toward the center of the labyrinth. In "The Garden," as in the stories we shall analyze in the following two chapters, the representation of consciousness is a labyrinthine structure equating and, in its fusion of form and sense, expressing the simultaneity of time, place, and personal identity. *The Garden of Forking Paths*, as we are to learn presently, is a "labyrinth of symbols," that is to say, a structure representing our perception of a symbolical order in time, events, and personal destinies. So complete is the fusion of form and content in this Borgian structure that the music heard by Yu Tsun on approaching the gate to Albert's garden is its veritable symbol.

The approach is the central passage of the story, connecting the interval of the train journey with the revelations taking place in Albert's library, and the most carefully constructed fusion of antithetical elements, the most decisive of which are *motion* and the *still* perception of that motion, and the present moment as *either* a unique moment of time *or* a recurrence of a past event. The approach is accomplished in four movements corresponding to four "moments." The Chinese music heard by Yu Tsun is the climactic occurrence of his approach, itself a total fusion of forms and meanings. It is important to keep in mind that a tradition also exists in Chinese literature and historiography in which "form" and "sense" are stated simultaneously.[18]

The first movement began with the phrase "I know something of labyrinths . . ." of the passage quoted above. Incidentally, Yu Tsun is the name of the young man in the opening episode of the *Hung Lou Meng* (trans., *The Dream of the Red Chamber*). The "content" of this particular "moment" of temporal succession appears first as an unconscious association with the ancestral past, set in motion by the directions given by the boys playing on the platform. The directions appear to have instigated the "inevitable" association of the present moment with the efforts of the great-grandfather "to build a labyrinth in which all men would lose their way." The obscure suggestion is that a past event is being repeated in the events of this evening. The "content," then, takes on the aspect of a compulsive recurrence of the past. We shall see presently that this particular disclosure, when displaced, exposes the open way to the inscrutable enigma. A foreigner, or stranger (*foras-*

*tero*), killed Ts'ui Pên, and a foreigner kills Stephen Albert, who deciphers the novel and discovers the labyrinth and the novel are one and the same.

The tensions of the account arise here from the irresoluble "content" of the present moment as either a recurrence of the past, or a "unique" moment in itself. According to our "equation" stated above, the uniqueness of a specific moment or event in time is greater or less as it denotes a commitment of a free will. A personal, inimitable freedom is the "unique content" of a moment occurring within the flow of temporal succession. In retrospect, the "content" of this moment of transit is "irresoluble" because Yu Tsun, by committing his freedom irrevocably, attempted to impose on temporal succession an "inevitable" direction and meaning, to precipitate and to "fill" time with personal will. But this deed is possible only if the future remains an "open way," a real and inviolate future. By his irrevocable determination Yu Tsun has already severed himself from the possibility of such a future. His predicament is an ethical dilemma enclosed in a metaphysical enigma. The disposal of individual freedom is the decisive, indeterminate element of time, which is occurring in an ireversible succession of moments. Yu Tsun could not have "lost his way" in a labyrinth of time whose passages were an already determined recurrence of the past. A man can only "lose his way" by erring in the disposal of his freedom.

> Beneath English trees I meditated on that lost labyrinth: I imagined it inviolate and perfect upon the secret summit of a mountain, I imagined it obliterated by rice fields or under water, I imagined it infinite, no longer consisting of octagonal kiosks and winding pathways, but of rivers and provinces and kingdoms . . . I thought of a labyrinth of labyrinths, of a sinuous and growing labyrinth that would encompass the past and the future and in some way involve the stars. Absorbed in these illusory

images, I forgot my destiny of a fugitive. For an indeterminate period of time, I felt myself an abstract perceiver of the world.

The second movement of the traverse reiterates the fourth point of irony enumerated above [in section 4] as an ontological delineation of Yu Tsun's perceptions and movements. The refutation of time and encounter with eternity[19] of the last sentence may be described as a self-cosmicizing experience wherein the macrocosmic labyrinth of the universe finds its antithetical opposite in the microcosmic labyrinth of Yu Tsun's being. Thus the entire universe—The Garden—appears suspended, and saturated with a premonition of his personal destiny. However, if the killing of Albert is irrevocable as an event in the future, that future is really only a hidden present and not a real future, and premonitions can be meaningful only if they designate a future that is still free and inviolate. The cosmos is impregnated with a sense of imminency, but this sense is that a future real and inviolate is at hand, the revelations in Albert's library. This is then the inner sense of the experience, which is a refutation of time because it is a refutation of the very "will to power" Yu Tsun has committed to the execution of the irrevocable act. This particular involucrum of irony may deceive the unwary and lead him to suppose that an "inevitable," determined, and necessary or fatal recurrence is arising from the subjective perceptions of the protagonist, and the "indeterminate" content of a real or authentic future from a purely objective interpretation of the story. The reverse, of course, is the case. Yu Tsun is free not to kill Albert up to the last instant of the encounter, and this is the true subjective content of the cosmical premonition and of the final hour.

> For an indeterminate period of time, I felt myself an abstract perceiver of the world. The indistinct and throbbing countryside, the moon, the traces of sunset, pro-

duced an effect in me, as did the gentle downsloping of
the road which eliminated every possibility of weariness.
The evening was intimate and infinite. The road sloped
and forked in the indistinct twilight of the fields. In the
moving to and fro of the wind a sharp and syllabic-like
music, heavily laden with leaves and distances, would
approach and recede.

Intimacy and infinity, the reciprocal revelations of this
evening, are merged and conveyed in the symbolic content of
the strange music in the third "moment" of Yu Tsun's approach. As a fusion of form and sense, of time and space, that
music suspends motion and willing in a *nunc stans* derivable
from Schopenhauer's metaphysics. From this "moment" of
complete immersion in an eternal presentness, a "still center"
of time and the world, the open way in *The Garden* is revealed,
and the content of Yu Tsun's symbols will begin thereupon to
disclose a conflict between the metaphysical contraries *being*
and *becoming*. The Chinese music, as a Borgian simultaneity of
form and multiple meanings, is again expressing the coincidence of the conflicting antitheses of the story, reiterating their
irresolvability, and exposing the directional sense of the story.
Hence the music is conveying the two opposite interpretations
of its own interval of time and place: whether this interval and
present moment is a recurrence of a past event or a unique and
indeterminate metaphysical interconnection of time and place,
race and individual, that has brought Yu Tsun to Albert's gate.
Stephen Albert is playing a record of Chinese music. The
recurring, syllabic-like sounds emitted from the phonograph
are expressing the perfect dialectical identity of both interpretations in a fusion of the story's themes and counterthemes
and a suspension of its conflicting antitheses.
    But the directional sense of the ethical and metaphysical
plot that this "total" fusion is emitting from the gramophone
disc is a recurring reiteration of the indeterminate and unique

element in time: Yu Tsun's freedom to revoke the irrevocable act. The "total" content of that music coming from the center of the labyrinth, associating the present with the past and serving as a premonition of the future, portends the spiritual bond between Yu Tsun and Albert. It identifies, simultaneously, the approaching Yu Tsun and his victim, and confirms our inference that the form in which a past event may be said to be recurring is a tension or conflict between two notions of the cyclical recurrence of events and personalities, an "Oriental" and a "Western" notion of the cyclical or eternal recurrence, the Confucian and the Nietzschean. But now we shall have to conjecture an "objective" and "subjective" frame of reference for each of these notions in order to follow the "total" sense of the dialectical drama. The Confucian, with its basis in the contemplation of natural change, of growth and decay as seasonal occurrences, stresses the ethical "openness" of the pathway to Albert's home, and the Nietzschean, with its emphasis on the tragic inexorability of fate, the metaphysical inevitability of an encounter at the end of an "irreversible" path. The Confucian is pointed to or suggested in the simple presence and attention to natural forms and surroundings, the *Garden*; the Nietzschean, in the inner, compelling effect that nature has on the consciousness of Yu Tsun, here and at the climactic moment of the story. These allusions are compressed in the symbolic content of the music; the notes of the strange and syllabic-like music are Chinese, but its metaphysics are German . . ., compounded of themes taken from Kant, Schopenhauer, and Nietzsche. It is a "dialectical" and "total" music conveyed in the movement of the wind, "heavily laden with leaves and distances," time and space suspended and displaced by sound. The cosmic symmetry of the garden and the rhythm of the music are equated. As Schopenhauer insisted, *rhythm* is in time what symmetry is in *space*. Music, we know also from Schopenhauer, is an objectivization of the will; it is also a displacement and fulfillment of time.

> I considered that a man may be the enemy of other men,
> of other moments in the lives of other men, but not the
> enemy of a country, not the enemy of fireflies, of words
> and gardens, of waterways and sunsets. Then I arrived at
> a tall, rusty iron gate.

Our reactions are being compelled to perceive the step-
by-step displacement of the "irrevocable determination" by an
ironical counter-movement and meaning disclosing the "open
way" to Albert. In the moment Yu Tsun arrives at the tall,
rusty gate his thoughts are a premonition of Albert as the
embodiment of the freedom of his will and being. This is the
"total" meaning of the music, conveying in universal language
the spiritual bond, the brotherhood of men of antithetical
races, and the enigma of their inextricable relations.

The effect Borges intends to sustain is the "total" containment and expression of the story's many meanings at any
given point. Here the totality of meanings is intended to be
released from the fugitive's arrival and passage through the
symbolic gate, the fourth and final "moment" of his approach
to Albert's home.[20] The gate *opens* and *closes*; is the path beyond an open or a closed path? Freedom or compulsion? As a
symbol of Yu Tsun's destiny the tall gate prefigures the towering figure of the archetypal Albert. The Borgian effect is
identifiable as a poetic fusion of antithetical elements: for
instance, Yu Tsun's feeling for nature here is akin to a Taoist
personal identity with the becomingness of nature, but he is
reacting to the landscape of an English countryside, under the
influence of Chinese music and, of course, German metaphysics. His movements suggest a metaphysical emphasis upon
becoming, as do the heuristic symbols, the moon, the sunset;
but the abrupt arrival at the gate suggests the antithetical
absoluteness of being. In the moment he recognizes the music
as Chinese, the chain of premonitions begun on alighting from
the train begin to *recur*, as an antithesis to the reality of events

which are simply *occurring*. If the reader has properly displaced Yu Tsun's symbols he will detect the hint (and the metaphysical implications behind it) in the fact that the Chinese consul Albert is expecting does not show up, but I shall take up this point further along.

> Through the iron bars I made out a grove of trees and a kind of pavilion. I understood suddenly two things, the first trivial, the second all but incredible: the music came from the pavilion, and the music was Chinese. This was why I had accepted it completely without noticing it. I do not remember whether there was a bell, a push-button, or whether I attracted attention by clapping my hands. The sparkling of the music continued.
>
> But from the depths of the intimate structure a lantern was approaching: a lantern whose rays the tree-trunks would successively disclose and then annihilate, a paper lantern in the form of a drum and the color of the moon. A tall man carried it. I did not see his face, because the light blinded me. He opened the gate and said slowly in my language:
>
> —I see the gracious Hsi P'êng persists in amending my solitude. You wish to see the garden, of course?
>
> I recognized the name of one of our consuls and, perplexed, I repeated: —The garden?
>
> —The garden of forking paths.
>
> Something came alive in my memory, and I said, with an incomprehensible certainty: —The garden of my ancestor Ts'ui Pên.
>
> —Your ancestor? Your illustrious ancestor? Please come in.

6

The damp pathway to the house or pavilion zigzagged "like those of my childhood."[21] Albert led the way to his library of "Oriental and Western books," where the gramophone

record was turning beside a bronze phoenix. He observed his guest with a smile; he was very tall and sharp featured; he had grey eyes and his beard was grey. An indefinable some-
thing about him (his archetypal character) suggested a priest and a sailor. He had been a missionary in Tientsin before "aspiring to be a sinologue." They sat down, Albert with his back to the window. Behind him also the hands of a tall circular clock rounded out the hour of their encounter.

> Noticing the time, I computed that my pursuer would not arrive for another hour. My irrevocable resolve could wait.

"Most astounding, the destiny of Ts'ui Pên" . . . , Albert begins, and here the reader must detect the open secret, the "diaphanous mystery" of the encounter: Albert does not know Ts'ui Pên was murdered by a stranger (a foreigner). This is the deduction that supplies the key for reconstructing the meta-physical evidence of the crime. That Stephen Albert does not know the circumstances of Ts'ui Pên's death is the most as-tounding fact about his knowledge of the illustrious ancestor. Put in the simplest terms, that Albert does not know the secret of Ts'ui Pên's murder signifies, in Borges' dialectical design, that Yu Tsun is not "fated" to kill Albert, that he is "free" not to kill him. That Albert does not know Ts'ui Pên was mur-dered by a stranger and a foreigner is then the quantity equal to the "indeterminate" element of time whose imminecy has been the "content" of the symbols of the approach; and this diaphanous but abstruse "negative" to the revelations that are now to be made with mounting hallucinatory clarity, as the hands move toward the moment Madden makes his appearance, becomes the counterpart that supplies us with the "total" apprehension of the events of the narrative.

The Governor of Yunnan province, Albert explains, was learned in astronomy, astrology, and in the interpretation of the canonical books; he was also a chess player, a famous poet, and a calligrapher. But he abandoned these pursuits and renounced his family and official position in order to compose a book and a labyrinth. He isolated himself for thirteen years in the Pavilion of Pure Solitude. When he died, his heirs found only a chaos of manuscripts. The family wished to burn them, but the executor of the will—a Taoist or Buddhist monk—insisted on publishing them.

The enigma of those events taking place a hundred years ago, Yu Tsun recalls, was that the book was a confusing collection of contradictory drafts; the hero died in one chapter but was alive in the next. As for the labyrinth:

> —Here is the Labyrinth, Albert said, and pointed to a tall, lacquered writing cabinet.
> —A labyrinth of ivory! I exclaimed. A minimal labyrinth . . .
> —A labyrinth of symbols, he corrected me. An invisible labyrinth of time. The honor of revealing this diaphanous mystery has been granted to me, a barbarous Englishman. After a hundred years the details are irrecoverable, but it is not difficult to conjecture what happened. Ts'ui Pen could have said on one occasion: *I am withdrawing to write a book*. And on another: *I am withdrawing to build a labyrinth*. Everyone imagined two different things; it occurred to no one that the book and the labyrinth were one and the same. The Pavilion of Pure Solitude rose in the center of a garden, perhaps a garden of intricate design, and this fact may have suggested a physical labyrinth. Ts'ui Pên died; within the borders of his far-flung lands no one ever found the labyrinth. To me, the novel's confusion suggested that it was the labyrinth. Two circumstances provided me with the right solution to the problem. One: the curious legend that Ts'ui Pên had attempted a labyrinth that should be strictly infinite. The second, a fragment of a letter that I chanced upon.

The fragment of the letter, forwarded to him from Oxford, contained the statement: *I bequeath to the several futures (not to all) my garden of forking paths.* Before knowing of the letter's existence, he had asked himself in what way a book could be infinite. A cyclical, circular volume was the only procedure he conjectured, "a volume whose last page would be identical to the first, with the possibility of continuing indefinitely." That circular book, we speculate, would resemble Joyce's *Wake* in several ways. Of the possibilities he conjectured—among them the involucra of the Thousand and One Nights and a platonic, hereditary work transmitted from father to son, "in which each new individual would add a chapter or correct with pious care the page of his elders"—not one seemed to correspond to Ts'ui Pên's contradictory chapters. Then he received the letter and pondered the enigmatic statement. Suddenly he understood: the phrase *several futures (not to all)* suggested the image of forking in time, not in space. A re-reading of the novel confirmed his theory:

> In all works of fiction, each time a man is confronted with several alternatives, he chooses one and eliminates the others. In Ts'ui Pên's almost inextricable novel, he chooses—simultaneously—all of them. Thus, *he creates* varying futures, varying times, which in their turn likewise proliferate and fork. Hence the contradictions of the novel. Fang, let us say, has a secret; a stranger calls at his door; Fang resolves to kill him. Naturally, there are several possible outcomes: Fang can kill the intruder, or the intruder can kill Fang, or both can emerge alive, or both may die, and so on. In Ts'ui Pên's novel all the possible outcomes happen, and each one is a point of departure for other bifurcations. Sometimes the pathways of this labyrinth converge: for example, you arrive at this house, but in one of the possible forms of the past you are my enemy, and in another, my friend. If you will kindly resign yourself to my incurable pronunciation, we shall read a few pages.

Borges intends that we should read here the open, diaphanous secret of his story in this abstruse way of stating it: Albert is hypothesizing a crime that did occur (the murder of Ts'ui Pên by a stranger) and reconstructing a crime about to happen as it is happening (his own murder). In the structure of his story, then, the mystery in Ts'ui Pên's novel that the word *time* unlocks corresponds to our deduction of the elements in his story that Borges has likewise left unstated and indeterminate, but equally self-evident and "inviolate." Our task, like Albert's, is to attempt to "resolve" the inevitable with the indeterminate.

Albert's analysis is thus reiterating the themes of the story in such a way that its "meaning" becomes its refraction in the perceptions of Yu Tsun as he listens to it, which is to say that the analysis is refracting that "labyrinth of symbols," that ethical and metaphysical conflict, which is the consciousness of the Borgian hero. The "content" of the analysis is then the counterpart of Yu Tsun's awareness, a kind of mirror-prism refracting his own perceptions and the act of perceiving them, just as Borges' fiction is a "mirror of enigmas" for ours. Yu Tsun evaded capture for the interval of this hour. Had he been pressed to kill Albert at any given moment before the hour was expended, his atrocious deed would not have been the irrevocable act of destiny it proved to be.

Stephen Albert constructs through conjecture and analysis a metaphysical novel which, as a counterpart to the Western nineteenth-century psychological novel, advances, among other matters, the literary critique by which our story is to be "interpreted." Farther, the novel and its analysis are at the point of converging in time and space, in "reality." The characters of Ts'ui Pên's novel, according to Albert, create different and various futures; that is, they expose the simultaneous and multiple possibilities of personal being in a "literary form" of freedom. They choose all alternatives, but the literary form does not commit them to any one. This literary form is the quintessence of objectivity and freedom and it contains and expresses the "totality," the total potential, of freedom. It is a multidimensional form of literature, of literary creation, and of literary criticism. The characteristic Borgian method of irony is to analyze this hypothetical work as a Chinese novel, incomprehensible, up to now, to the Oriental mind, but accessible, even inevitable, to the Western critical and speculative intellect. Ts'ui Pên's *Garden* is a work of "totality"; its structure expresses the causal equivalence of time, personal will, freedom, and destiny, and it is, inevitably, a structure of consciousness.

> In the bright circle of the lamp I could see his face was that of an old man, but there was something about it unconquerable and even immortal. He read with slow precision two drafts of the same epic chapter. In the first, an army marches to battle across a desolate mountain; the very horror of the shadows and of the stones incites in the army an abhorrence of life, and victory is easily achieved; in the second, the same army crosses a palace where a celebration is going on; to the warriors the shining battle seems a continuation of the celebrating and they achieve victory.

The warring armies are linked of course to the belligerents on the ridges overlooking the Somme, and the significance in Albert's reading these pages is, again, the inevitable "content" refracting the ordeal the hero of consciousness is undergoing. From our objective point of reference the two drafts of the same epic chapter suggest the simultaneous possibility of two different moments in the historical transformation of collectivities approaching or achieving the Caesarian state.

> I listened to those old stories with seemly veneration. Perhaps the stories themselves were less admirable than the fact that they were the work of my race and that a

man from a remote empire should be reconstructing
them for me here, on a Western island, in the course of a
desperate adventure. I remember the closing words, repeated in each draft like a secret command: *Thus did the
ancient heroes battle, their hearts untroubled and their
swords violent, resigned to kill and to die.*

From that moment I began to feel a swarming of human bodies, an invisible and intangible pullulation
around me and in my own darkish body. It was not the
pullulation of the divergent, parallel, and finally coalesc-
ing armies; it was more inaccessible, more intimate, but
in some way prefigured by those teeming armies.

The overt or surface sense of the pullulation is that a
mysterious force is compelling the murderer to the imminent
deed. The armies of Ts'ui Pên's novel and the armies on the
Somme seem to correspond to an impersonal, racial, or collective will, an inexorable imperative overtaking and overwhelm-
ing individual will and conscience. Moreover, the compulsion
appears to shift out of a focus of personal will to a conflict of
impersonal powers. Nonetheless, it would be wrong to suppose that in the pullulation we have a metaphysical "killer
instinct" motivating, in the abstract, all crime and violence.
The dialectical conflict between "fate" and "free will" is being
directed at our apprehension as the perception on the part of
the murderer that the act of murder can only come about as
both the relinquishing of his freedom and his complete
awareness of the consequences of such an act. The imminence
of the convergence of that act and of the apprehension of its
"meaning" is further isolating the protagonist within his
"free" commitment, bearing him to the single, fleeting moment in which the total meaning of the act is its total precep-
tion. In other words, the event in Borges' narrative cannot take
place until the "meaning" of the event becomes coincidental
or simultaneous to it. The ancient heroes of violent swords and
barbaric hearts provide the antithetical charge of irony to the

modern nihilist compelled by his own exertion to be both the self-abasing perceiver and the executor of atrocity. Thus the more compelling the pullulation the more clearly we can displace it with its antithesis: the ethical alternatives left open to a free will. This is the diaphanous circumstance left exposed by the ironical structure and becoming more evident with each of Albert's revelations.

Thus isolated in the involucra of the structural ironies, we see Yu Tsun as both the subject and the object of his actions; "Albert" is only the symbol of his freedom. His dilemma is not one of "fate," but of "fate's" dialectical opposite, the self-awareness of the self-annihilation of personal freedom. I propose to use, as the dialectical opposite of "fate," the term *destiny*. The ironies of destiny, Borges' transvaluation of the ironies of fate, pertain to a drama of this self-willed annihilation of personal freedom. Stephen Albert continues:

> —I do not believe your illustrious ancestor was playing an idle game with his variations. It is entirely unlikely that he should sacrifice thirteen years of his life to the infinite execution of an experiment in rhetoric. In your country the novel is a subsidiary form of literature; in Ts'ui Pên's time it was even a contemptible one. Ts'ui Pên was a novelist of genius, but he was also a man of letters who assuredly did not consider himself a mere novelist. The statements of his contemporaries bear witness to his metaphysical and mystical interests, and his own life amply confirms them. Philosophical controversy usurps a large part of his novel. I know that of all problems none vexed and disturbed him more than the abysmal problem of time. Now, then, this is the *only* problem which does not figure in the pages of *The Garden*. He does not even use the word that signifies *time*. How do you account for this voluntary omission?

I proposed several solutions, all of them insufficient. We discussed them; finally, Stephen Albert said:
—In a riddle the answer to which is "chess," what is

the one forbidden word? I reflected for a moment, then answered:

— The word *chess*.

— Exactly, said Stephen Albert. *The Garden of Forking Paths* is a vast riddle, or parable, whose theme is time; that hidden reason would forbid the mention of the word time. *Always* to omit a word, to resort to inept metaphors or avoidable periphrases, is perhaps the most emphatic way of stressing it. This is the tortuous method the abstruse Ts'ui Pên preferred in each of the meanders of his indefatigable novel.

The mathematical or semantical probability that Ts'ui Pên did not use or mention the word *time* because the precise or relative equivalent of the concept Albert has in mind could not have occurred to him, is the counter and ironical deduction with which one must counter Albert's arguments in order to keep the situation and its "meaning" in suspension. In Albert, the "Western" mind is analyzing what an "Oriental" intuition would never attempt perhaps to reduce to language. One could, of course, coin an explicit term for *time* in Chinese, but the word alone would not express the entire concept of time and the metaphysical consequences Albert has in mind. On the other hand, Albert has evidently taken into account the abstruse practice by which one may indicate the ineffable by intentionally omitting any reference to it. In any case, it is evident that Borges, by exposing Albert's discovery to ironical interpretation and displacement, is indicating the procedure by which we are to detect the inviolate, unstated, and indeterminate relation between the components of his story and arrive at their "solution." *Time* is the inviolate and key word that simultaneously reveals and conceals the mystery of Ts'ui Pên's novel. Similarly, *Albert* is the military secret that simultaneously reveals and conceals the metaphysical solution of our story. Taking Albert's analysis as an example, we can thus infer that our story is also a riddle that is everywhere evident and everywhere concealed, so that the key to it is not so much a "word" as it is a concept, a series of relations expressed ideogrammatically in a metaphysical code name.

The sequence of Albert's[22] analytical statements about Ts'ui Pên's novel is then the sequential revelation to Yu Tsun of the self-evident reasons (ethical and metaphysical) why he should revoke his "irrevocable resolve," but since it is "irrevocable," this sequential revelation will become the absolute and final revelation of why he did not in the instant he fires the bullet that kills Albert.

Our story, then, at its point of resolution, has become a symmetrical design of plot and counterplot, theses and antitheses, meanings and countermeanings, opposing and balancing one another in their mutual opposition. The equation "necessity ← freedom" that we detected in the battleline description "Serre–Montauban," and now the secret simultaneously disclosed and concealed in the riddle and code name *Albert*, are structural reiterations of the irresolvable dichotomy and dilemma to which our apprehension of the story and its events has compelled us: whether the meaning that these events possess is either a totally necessary and absolute order and meaning, or whether they are meaningless, with a "senselessness" as absolute and total as Yu Tsun's brave but atrocious deed.

7

Our alignments of ironical deductions form the counterplot of the story, and the plot and the counterplot are about to converge at that point in the Borgian structure where the free, unique, and indeterminate element of time is nullified and displaced by the "totality of compulsion" of the irreversible event. This point of "totality" will be that fraction of a second in which Yu Tsun fires the bullet that kills Stephen Albert, for only then and there does the "structure" of this event coincide with its "meaning."

The exact moment of the shot, therefore, is the point

where the elements of plot and counterplot and the themes of the story converge, and where the analysis of Ts'ui Pên's *Garden* coincides with the act of murder because it coincides with Madden's arrival outside the library. Hence the firing of the shot will be that moment in Borges' structure when we can suspend the total effect of the name "Albert" because it is the point of total suspension of the story's contents.

The name of the city on the Ancre is, firstly, the secret of British strategy to be communicated to Berlin. The metaphysical secret of the name is contained in the "content" of that period of time on the "bed of iron" and during the search for a person bearing the name in the telephone directory, bringing Yu Tsun and Albert together in these circumstances this night. The relation of Albert to Yu Tsun, the relation in the detective mystery between victim and murderer, is one of personal being; Albert's identity corresponds to the quantity to be expended in the fulfillment of Yu Tsun's destiny. This quantity is Yu Tsun's personal freedom. "Albert" is also the key to the reconstruction of the Goethean accomplishments of the ancestor, and hence the key to the metaphysical secret of Yu Tsun's ancestry. "Albert," then, contains and suspends the various secrets and unknowns of the story and their counterparts. When the reader can apprehend that *Albert* is the ideogram expressing the components of the story and their relations to one another—the multiple levels of symbolical interpretations to which the compressed contents are susceptible and their ironical displacement—he has grasped the total inevitability of Borges' story.

But we are in a position now to see that this total inevitability is the outcome of a free commitment of personal freedom on ethical and metaphysical grounds that disclosed to Yu Tsun's personal will and choice an open pathway. The sum total of ethical and metaphysical details about the event that Borges' structure exposes to our apprehension constitutes its "meaning," but this meaning is not expressed anywhere in the structure just as the "meaning" of Ts'ui Pên's novel is nowhere expressed in the chaotic contents of its contradictory chapters, and just as the universe which we inhabit discloses nowhere its "meaning," but which we nonetheless feel compelled to decipher and conjecture. And of course the "structure" of our universe is the simultaneity of its "form" with its "meaning."

We are also in a position to determine why, in Borges' design of destiny, Yu Tsun's commitment to the irrevocable deed had perforce to occur in an ethical vacuum. Since personal actions and motives and the personal content of experience derive from the free moral choice of individuals, it is from the freedom of personal will that ethical distinctions are derived, and hence the realm or ground of personal freedom is also the realm or ground of value. Moral values are possible because personal will and consciousness can create in the realm of freedom a hierarchy of personal choices. Thus it is that the indeterminate element of time is perceived and experienced by the individual as the metaphysical ground of his capacity to make a free moral choice. But then — and this is the source of the irresolvable predicament perceived in individual consciousness — personal freedom is possible only because chance and contingency are possible in the structure of the universe, and so this that we experience as our personal freedom to act as the good or evil cause of an event is subject to the arbitrary turns of chance. If ethical values cannot exist impenetrable to chance and as part of the absolute structure of our universe in the final degree (as now in our story where we perceive that Yu Tsun is faced with the naked workings of chance), they exist in a metaphysical vacuum, in a vacuum of "nothingness," and our dilemma as individuals who cannot escape moral choices is that our actions and their meaning are at every moment in imminent peril of being *either* annuled by *chance or* displaced by *necessity*.

Now, coming to the point, we see why the intervention of

our ironical reading into the contents of the story must correspond to the equation between the indeterminate element of time and the personal freedom of Yu Tsun, for just as the commitment and disposal of Yu Tsun's freedom is the essential but yet "indeterminate" element in the execution of the plot, just so is our commitment to the deductive process of the Borgian ironies the indeterminate element necessary for activating and completing the counterplot. The reader's apprehension of the predicament of the Borgian protagonist becomes a simulation of that predicament. The story, presenting us with a plot that is more or less its "form," compels us to detect a "meaning," a counterplot, identical with that form, in order to arrive at the apprehension of their dichotomy as a "structure," diaphanous and self-evident, yet as elusive and enigmatic as the universe itself. The irony of Borges, then, pertains to the literary mode by which *simulation* (rather than dissimulation) provides a way of representing our autonomous apprehension of a universal cause and order. We may go even further and say that Borges' unique gifts as a writer of metaphysical fictions have provided stories that are a *simulacrum*, a "total," "hieroglyphic" image of reality.

Borges has thus provided all the epistemological details for apprehending the encounter of Yu Tsun and Albert as an "event." We are about to witness the criminal event in such a way that we can "know" from it the laws of causality governing human motives and actions. As the hands of the clock at Albert's back move toward the moment of Madden's arrival, the analysis of Ts'ui Pên's *Garden* is providing the self-evident cause of the crime. The various movements antithetical to one another (the hands of the clock, Madden's approaching) are moving toward their point of imminent convergence, and the inexorable revelation developing for the Borgian hero is the *either/or* of moral choice and the imminent forking of the open path. Since Yu Tsun is "free" to revoke the irrevocable act, which of *The Garden's* forking paths is the way?

We recall that when Yu Tsun knocked at the tall, rusty gate the towering figure of Albert appeared abruptly, breaking the sequence of motions sustained by the "circular" continuity of the music: "But from the depths of the intimate structure a lantern was approaching. . . . A tall man carried it." Presently, when Madden appears outside the library, we shall read: "In the yellow and shadowy garden I saw a man; but the man was strong like a statue, but the man was approaching along the pathway and he was Captain Richard Madden." The antithetical sense of these breaks, or turns, as stressed by the conjunction *but*, are the plural forkings of time refracted in the labyrinth of the hero's consciousness. They set off the interval of time (one hour) between the moment Albert first appears and the moment when Madden appears, and the forking paths of time converge and cut off all escape.

Albert, as he continues his analysis, is virtually analyzing the motives of a hypothetical murderer as a resolution of the personal being of the man before him, himself as the victim, the present scene as the time and place, of a crime about to happen; but, moreover, all as the perceptions of the man before him, as those perceptions converge on the act. This "ontological analysis," clearly, as it proceeds from the novel to the image of the universe, is carrying on an outrageous parody and indictment of itself and of those flaws inherent in all "literary criticism," and the recourse to deductions and hypotheses in the solution of detective plots.

> I have collated hundreds of manuscripts, I have corrected the errors that the negligence of copyists has introduced, I have pondered and conjectured the plan of this chaos, I have re-established (I believe I have re-established) the original order, I have translated the entire work, and I am convinced that he never once uses the word *time*. The explanation is obvious: *The Garden of Forking Paths* is an incomplete, but not false, image of the universe as conceived by Ts'ui Pên. In contrast to Newton and Scho-

penhauer, your ancestor did not believe in a uniform, absolute time. He believed in infinite series of time, in an organic and vertiginous web of times paralleling each other, diverging and converging. This plurality of times approaching one another, forking or breaking away, or by-passing one another through the centuries, embraces *all* possibilities. We do not exist in the majority of these times; in some you exist and I do not; in others I but not you; in yet others, both of us. In this one, with which chance has chosen to favor me, you have arrived at my house, in another, on crossing the garden, you have come upon my dead body; in another, I am saying these same words, but am an error, a phantasm.

The ironical opposition between the "form" of this analysis and its "meaning," between our plot and counterplot, is bringing to the focus of a self-evident "structure" our perception that the "meaning" of the event cannot be other than our apprehension of its "form." Yu Tsun is both the object and the subject of this analysis; the refracted "content" of the analysis is this encounter with the towering archetypal Albert as a confrontation with the enigma of the self. The counterplot calls for any number of deductions based on this "content." For example: from the point of view of the subject, the subject Yu Tsun does not necessarily exist in the time in which his acts are compelled and not free; he may be an "error" or "phantasm." Or, conversely, the probability exists that the events of his entire life may be so ordered or aligned in the vertiginous web of simultaneous times that all or nearly all his actions may be determined, or that one single action decide his destiny; or, moreover, the probability exists that *one* action perpetually imminent is the form by which he perceives himself in time. In any case, the total sense of the analysis refracted in his consciousness is that each one of the times possible for Yu Tsun postulating a probable encounter with Albert corresponds to a potentiality of personal being; each one of these simultaneous times postulates a different Yu Tsun, a different person, who meets and faces Albert. The guest who finds Albert's body in the garden (struck down by the enigmatic Hsi P'êng, the Chinese consul who did not show up?) is another Yu Tsun, another being.

By the time Albert pronounces the words "error" (in one dimension of time, we infer—this one?—his theory is wrong) and "phantasm," few literary critics will miss the point, he is speaking like the prototypal "ontological" critic requisite for the stories of Borges, but whose relation to their contents, because they provide for their own displacement, they render highly precarious. Literary analysis has been displaced by metaphysical speculation, and metaphysical speculation by the imminency of the moment about to be made metaphysically real.

> — In all of them, I said, not without an uneasy trembling, I am deeply grateful for your reconstruction of the garden of Ts' ui Pên.
> — Not in all, he murmured with a smile. Time is forking perpetually toward innumerable futures. In one of them I am your enemy.
> Again I felt that pullulation. I had the feeling the humid garden surrounding the house was oppressively saturated with invisible persons. Those persons were Albert and I, secret, toiling, and multiform in other dimensions of time. I looked up and the dim nightmare dissipated.

To get the complete idea of the conflict that is occurring between the Borgian antitheses we have to sense the way Yu Tsun is perceiving that conflict as an opposition between a "reality" of his will and its representation. The pathways of Albert's analysis, the multiple dimensions of time, are converging in reality as that reality is being determined by Yu Tsun's moral choice and personal will. Refracted in his consciousness, they indicate not that he is "totally" compelled or fated to kill Albert, as the pullulation overtly suggests, but that, perceiving his profound moral indebtedness to Albert, and recognizing the archetypal transcendence of their encounter, he is free to revoke his atrocious plan. The pullulation Yu Tsun feels is the oppression of his own perceptions, now totally isolated by the ordeal of moral choice. But, conversely, this same pullulation conveys the sense of a recurrence of impersonal or immemorial urges of race and blood, a compulsion of collective fears and hates, because it prefigures the imminent displacement of freedom by the "totality of compulsion," now symbolized by the figure of the implacable pursuer.

The nightmare does not dissipate, we infer: it assumes the shape of another nightmare, presenting us with the final version of the hero's dilemma: if Madden had not appeared at this precise instant, would he have revoked his plan and spared the life of the unique, Goethean being who embodies his freedom because he possesses, inviolately, the metaphysical secret of his ancestry?

> In the yellow and shadowy garden I saw a man; but the man was strong like a statue, but the man was approaching along the pathway and he was Captain Richard Madden.
> —The future already exists, I replied, but I am your friend. May I see the letter again?
> Albert got up. He was tall, and he opened the drawer of the towering cabinet; he turned his back to me for a moment. I had my revolver ready. I pressed the trigger with utmost care: Albert fell without a sound, instantly. I swear his death was instantaneous: a flash.

The "timing" of Albert's murder is perforce the coincidence of its "form" and "meaning." In the restricted sense of style and literary craft that "form" expresses Borges' own private need to create an order of cause as impenetrable to chance as the human mind can devise and a symmetry of logic and imagination as autonomous and inevitable as is possible to attain within the confines of a given literary form. But this literary form is of course also its own meaning, so that inevitably we find form simulating meaning, and meaning simulating form, which is to say that we apprehend the climax of the story as the simultaneity of its literary form with its ethical and metaphysical meaning. The structural ironies of "The Garden" are the operative ingredient of this simultaneity, and hence they are always disclosing in their interval something about the process of our apprehending them, as well as conveying their "insoluble" meanings. The painstaking details of style and structure in Borges' stories are ultimately an obsession with the conveyance of a way of apprehending that aspires to be, in its own way, total and absolute. This is why the ironical in his stories has little to do with mockery, and that little with the gratuitous exposure of the fallibility of our own powers and modes of understanding and our sensibilities.

The ironies of destiny, as we have called them, unlike the ironies of fate of yesteryear, do not subject his characters to the "mockery" of a cosmic order or an omniscient being. The details of style and structure in "The Garden," moreover, serve to deflect any impulse to see Yu Tsun as a victim derided by an impersonal order of cause in the universe. Yu Tsun perishes in the "labyrinth of symbols," the invisible labyrinth of times, simulating his and our apprehension of the coincidence of the "form" of the crime to its "meaning," not because he kills Albert for a nullity of motives, but because he attains, if only for the fleeting moment of its execution, an apprehension of the act realizing his own destiny that only an omniscient or infallible, god-like intelligence may possess. The act of murder—in this Garden of Knowledge—is one and the same with the apprehension of its "meaning," and the revelation of its total consequences, past and future, and the fallibility of the Borgian hero (like Albert's and ours) is intellective.

Yu Tsun, of all human beings in the universe, alone possesses the "total knowledge" of this event that his knowledge of Ts'ui Pên's death and the revelations of Albert's analysis comprise together. On the level of metaphysical cause, then, the Chinese spy is the "inevitable" killer of Albert because he is the bearer of the Secret that this event, simultaneously, reveals and conceals. While arriving at the "solution" of the story and its mystery, we find that we can explain and clarify all that can be clarified and known intellectively about the crime,[23] but that in doing so. we are infallibly exposing our precarious decipherment to the imminent perils of the diaphanous unknown on whose paths human events take place, and of which our apprehension and Borges' artifice are only a simulation, or, if this term is still strange, a *simulacrum*. "Our acts are our symbol,"[24] Borges has said, and Yu Tsun, in the labyrinth of consciousness, "lost his way" because, bearer of the Secret and "abstract perceiver of the world," he looked into the mystery concealed in the labyrinth of symbols which is the universe, and perished, in order that his destiny may be read there as a sign, a hieroglyph of the ineluctable and inscrutable.

# BORGES 3

*We (the undivided divinity which acts within us) have dreamt the world. We have dreamt it resistant, mysterious, visible, ubiquitous in space and firm in time; but we have consented in its architecture to tenuous and eternal interstices of non-reason in order to know that it is false.*[25]

In the next attempt at a detective story Borges arrived at the easeful, consummate stylization of nearly all his techniques. The third-person narrative of "Death and the Compass" (1942)[26], an underhanded concession to literary convention, is the surface manner of a structure attempting to displace the archetypal "mystery" of all detective fictions. It is one of Borges' most stylized efforts, the surface manner providing the reader with a relatively easy access to the perplexities of structure. I shall not go into an extended analysis of the story because a good discussion of it is available,[27] and because I think I have already put before the reader the widest as well as the narrowest contexts of Borges' irony. The stories I take up in this chapter offer particular problems and degrees of refinement. My intent is to disclose, for each story, the central, pivotal point on which the whole irony rests, the point suspending the total "inevitability" of the structure.

In "Death and the Compass" we have an archetypal detective plot displaceable at the point where the reader can infer the total sense of Borges' allusions to an antinomy of symbolic knowledge, the point of irony suspending the mystery of "the names of God." The stylization is so complete that, in spite of the surface manner, a bare outline of the plot is impossible without a recital of the counterplot. For our purpose we need not attempt to extricate one from the other. We can safely approach the story as a particular stylization of the structure of consciousness. To get to the sense of the stylization, we shall have to reduce the components of the detective fiction to an abstract meaning—in the last paragraph to an "invisible, unending line"—and to see the structure of an "inevitable" solution fitting the series of crimes as the structure of fallible human powers committed to reading the transcendental "content" of symbols. In the archetypal detective plot, Erik Lönnrot, the detective, and Red Scharlach, the gunman, are the "inevitable" antagonists, matching powers of cunning and intelligence, each dedicated to the eradication of the other. The basic clue exposing the reader's reactions to the tensions of an irresolvable antinomy is that the gunman traps and kills the detective. The antithetical points of similarity between them allude to one "criminal archetype." The rivalry is suspended in a conflict of antithetical and mutual displacements about the symbolic quantities *three* and *four*.

On the 4th of December, Doctor Yarmolinsky, the delegate from Podolsk to the Third Talmudic Congress, is found murdered in his room in the Hôtel du Nord. The detective's mind, eager to venture on the solution, is committed to proceed by the hypotheses of pure reason, to premise an "inevitable" solution corresponding to an "inevitable" cause and premeditated motive for the crime, and excluding a decisive intervention of chance. The inspector, Franz Treviranus, whose conjectures are commonplace, guesses the true state of affairs from the evidence—a matter of chance—and, later, the spurious nature of the third crime, which takes place on the night of February third, at a point southeast of the first. The second crime, the murder of Yarmolinsky's assassin, takes place on the night of January third, in a remote corner of the western suburbs. The three crimes, as the letter from "Baruch Spinoza" *alias* Red Scharlach, asserts, have a perfect symmetry of time and place. When superimposed on a map of the city, the three places form an equilateral triangle. Three crimes, or "sacrifices," give us one kind of mystical or symbolic unity.

A fourth crime at a point South, which "Baruch Spinoza" said would not take place, introduces a perplexing set of ironical relations. The fourth crime, "inevitable" by the compass at the villa of Triste-le-Roy, makes possible two equilateral triangles by the drawing of an "invisible" and displaceable line between points East and West. The two triangles are identical, in more than one sense, and are therefore one and the same. The same fourth point, of course, provides the rhombus figure of the paint shop, the harlequin costumes, and the window lozenges of the mirador of the villa of Triste-le-Roy. Now, if we focus our attention on the radical antithesis between the quantities three and four in their geometrical representation, the antithetical tensions of the story will reveal the irresoluble symbolic conflict activated and contained in the single, reiterated figure. This conflict is, again, a refraction of consciousness, as indicated in the dizzy moment Lönnrot fixes his perceptions on the rhomboid diamonds of the window, and Scharlach and his men appear from "nowhere" to kill him.

> By way of a spiral staircase he came to the mirador. The evening moon shone through the lozenges of the windows; they were yellow, red, and green. A frightening, bewildering memory halted him.
> Two men of short stature, ferocious and stout, pounced on him and disarmed him. (154)

The stylized effect is brought off by the abruptness of the transition between the two paragraphs; the men break upon Lönnrot abruptly at that moment in which his perceptions connect the lozenges of the window to the rhombs of the paint shop and the harlequin costumes, and to the moment he drew the rhombus figure on the map and determined the site of the fourth crime with the compass. Simultaneously, he has intuited that *he* is the victim of this "inevitable" fourth crime, and that this very intuition has displaced the idea that occurred to him on the train but that he rejected: that Scharlach himself might be the fourth victim. The men pounce on him as if they materialized from that intuition provoked and symbolized by the lozenges.

This is the point in the reading of the story, the center of the labyrinth, where the reader can displace the detective mystery and perceive the archetypal mystery of symbolic knowledge alluded to in the conflict of *three* and *four* and the "invisible, unending line" to which all quantities and the conflict itself can be reduced. The rhombuses simultaneously contain the triangles and are displaceable by them. The "predicament" of symbolic knowledge alluded to is that the same figure or symbol can contain two antithetical orders of meaning, a trinity and a tetragram, a mystic, equilateral triangle and the Tetragrammaton.

Lönnrot rejects Treviranus' conjecture that Yarmolinsky has been the victim of chance and mishap, but the evidence that magnetizes his mind, the unconcluded sentence, *The first letter of the Name has been uttered*, has come about precisely because of the element of chance he rejects. He extracts an "inevitable" motive from Yarmolinsky's book, the *History of the Hasidic Sect*. His purely "rabbinical explanation" produces the purely rabbinical motive which his mind premised and Scharlach deduced as that premise: the Hasidic sect has sacrificed Yarmolinsky in the hope of discovering the Secret Name. The detective's mind, then, is fallible from within its own reasoning. In Borges' dialectical conflict Lönnrot is simultaneously the detective proceeding according to the deductions of pure reason and the "inevitable" victim of those deductions as deduced by his antagonist. The fallibility of the detective's mind is expressed diagrammatically in the rhombus figure by the simultaneity of the relations between points three and four, the third crime and the fourth crime. The killing of the detective by the gunman is simultaneously the third crime and the fourth crime. The total irony indicates that Lönnrot was certain to be Scharlach's victim according to both orders of symbolic meaning in the "sacrifices"; he is the third victim of the triangle of crimes contained simultaneously in the rhombus or tetragram of crimes in which he is the fourth victim and Scharlach the sham third. Moreover, this antithetical symmetry is possible because it is perceptible to the pure intellect as the precise equilibrium, a mutual dislocation of one by the other, of chance and the "inevitable" solution.

The antithetical sense of this equilibrium is the symbolic "content" dislocated by the paradoxical situation in which the gunman solves the mystery of the crimes for the detective and for the reader. Scharlach read in the columns of the *Yidische Zaitung* that Lönnrot was studying the names of God in order to come across the name of Yarmolinsky's killer. The editor's simplification, without scrutiny, can pass as another occurrence of chance, but under pressure it will expose its antithetical content and a "fallible," atheistic editor to go with the fallible detective. In the popular edition of Yarmolinsky's *History of the Hasidic Sect* the gunman read that the fear of uttering the Name of God had given rise to the doctrine that the equilateral Name is all-powerful and secret, and learned that some Hasidim, in search of the Secret Name, had gone so far as to make human sacrifices. He deduced that Lönnrot would conjecture the Hasidim had sacrificed the rabbi, and set out to justify that conjecture. He executed a sequence of crimes which could be seen as a mysterious sequence of either three *or* four, but which are in fact three *and* four, or three *in* four, because the third one is a sham or simulacrum. In the murder taking place in the carnival atmosphere of February third, Scharlach played the part of the victim with the tripart identity, "Gryphius-Ginzberg-Ginsberg." The scrawled evidence left behind contained a plurality of meanings, any one of which can be read in an absolute, symbolic sense: *The last of the letters of the Name has been uttered.* The hoax deceived Lönnrot, who deduced, as Scharlach intended, that it was the third in the series of "sacrifices" and that a fourth was also inevitable, since the "purely rabbinical" explanation demanded a fourth crime to correspond to the fourth day of the month as computed by the Hebrews and the four points of the compass and the Tetragrammaton. The sham crime, then, is the ironical, displaceable quantity which gives us Lönnrot as the "inevitable," fallible victim in either the tri or tetra order of symbolical symmetries of time, place, and identities. Its function as the total irony is to dislocate from one "absolute" symbolic context the contrary symbolic context, and to sustain, in the reader's mind, the conflict of mutual dislocations from the one geometrical figure of the rhombus as the structural meaning of the story. The total irony can be activated at any point in the story; any given point of the structure, like the interconnected letters of the Secret Name, will reveal its infinite, simultaneous, and "inevitable" connections with all the others.

The archetypal detective mystery, to which the mysterious element in all detective fictions can be reduced by this catalytic irony, is the predicament of the human intellect committed to deciphering the enigmatic and ultimately elusive order of the universe. The predicament and its human reality is the mystery, and this is Borges' theme in the stylized play between the "dusty Greek word" and the outwitting of the detective. The effect of the dislocating irony is to create a constant play between the mystical inevitability of the four-letter secret Name and the total inevitability of the events of the story. The story, with all its complicating symmetries, is actually possible as a direct third-person narrative because Borges has managed to ironize from every direction his own techniques for producing the "total inevitability."

The order of the crimes, three *or* four, or three *in* four, within a period of ninety-nine *or* one hundred days, has been a secret collaboration between detective and gunman; the crimes are so precise as to place, time, and identity of the victims, even to the precise problematical adjustments between them dependent on the dislocating function of the "hiatus" of irony, that the perfect solution can hardly be other than the eradication of the reasoning mind which first prefigured them. The detective's powers, in the archetypal sense, are committed to reasoning order out of mystery. The gunman knew all along there was no mystery in the real events, but his hatred for the rival and the desire for vengeance compelled him to create a semblance, a simulacrum of mystery, no less authentic or ingenious than the efforts of authors of detective fiction. The mystery exists in the detective's mind as an ineludible reality to be grappled with and overcome. The detective is committed, on an ontological plane, as Yarmolinsky and the Hasidim on a mystical or superstitious plane, to fathom the absolute secret, "the Secret Name." He is the victim of Scharlach's simulacrum of a mystery because he intuits the everlasting, ineluctable symmetry or order of which their antithesis and rivalry is a symbol.

Our story, again, works out as if it were a riddle. The irony of Lönnrot's destiny is the symbolic "content" dislocated from the unutterable Name by the jarring implications of the sham crime. But the total irony is that the components with which we grasp that there is a riddle to be solved are reiterating the elusiveness and insolubility of the ultimate mystery. This is the antithetical sense with which every detail of the story is charged. The impression of a total inevitability can be traced to the completeness of the stylization playing for ironical effects between the chance "form" of Yarmolinsky's sentence and the absoluteness of its "content," the ineffable Name; between the journalistic sensationalism of human sacrifices committed to the end of learning the name of God and the even more sensational exposure of the theological, epistemological, and ontological postulates implicated in the intelligential act of the detective, the pure reasoner, who foresaw but failed to prevent the murder which would be his own.

Every detail about the crimes conveys the antithetical sense of the whole; every detail, like the unfinished sentence on Yarmolinsky's typewriter, can refract under pressure into a plurality of meanings: the stylized reiterating of the color red, the elusive character of the Hôtel du Nord, the contents of Yarmolinsky's books, Scharlach's brother, who corresponds to the second of the identical triangles, the vast impersonality of the city, a stylized version of Buenos Aires. Every fact about the crimes is charged with a potentially "infinite" meaning and relation to the others, offering the reader an inexhaustible source of surprises. To recite the inevitable connections of any one of them to all the others would amount to a total reconstruction of the story. The reader can undertake the task and abandon himself to it with the foreknowledge that he will find himself in a maze whose every point reiterates the center.

Finally, behind the third-person narrative of "Death and the Compass" we can discern the complete impersonality of the narrator. That impersonality, to the reader intimate with Borges' ways and sensibility, is conveyed in the quality of the perceptions which establish and release the metaphorical unity of, for instance, the odor of eucalypti, "the interminable odor of the eucalypti," or the images of Lönnrot's exploration of the villa of Triste-le-Roy. The narrator refers to himself and his locale only once. The self-reference is a signature stroke of irony: "To the south of the city of my story there flows a blind little river" (152). The effect of the total irony dislocates the Buenos Aires of fact and relocates it as a creation of dream within our fiction. The supposed realistic reference is in the reverse direction, from dream to fact.

Between the plot and the counterplot, the triangle and the rhombus, the third day of the month and the fourth, and corresponding to the hiatus which, as the Hasidim reason, indicates the hundredth name of God and corresponds to the Absolute Name, lies the shifting, elusive expanse of irony on which Lönnrot was led to betrayal by his deductions. This area of unspecified bounds, activated by our reactions, is actually the indeterminate region, with its depth and surface, on which we construe and reconstruct the intuition and the conjecture of Borges' story. The indispensable requirement for grasping the quality of his irony is to perceive that the total inevitability of the plot is produced by construing or inferring the counterplot; thereon the reader discovers that the total irony releases from the simultaneity of his perceptions a sense of vast, primeval areas of meaning, stretching apart "doomsday and death." Then come counter-shocks of meaning to jar the events of the story into a final adjustment of an ironical reading.

2

In the volume *The Aleph*, a collection of stories from the
period 1944–52, "Emma Zunz" is the farthest removed from
elements of fantasy, unreality, or dream, a fact Borges emphasizes.[28] The actions of Emma Zunz are related as a third-person
narrative in the sense and order of a crime fiction striving for
surprise, climax, and anticlimax by a narrator whose surreptitious presence, knowledge of certain facts, suppression or
unexplained ignorance of others, constitute the decisive element in the concretion of the story's structure; that is, the
decisive element in the structural antithesis of plot and counterplot, as apart from Emma Zunz's actions. The outcome of
the structural antithesis, as apart from the outcome for Emma,
gives us a total inevitability resulting from the interconnections of time, place, compulsion, motive, and identities. The
story, then, may be seen as the subtle incorporation into a
structure of consciousness of the requirements of both a crime
fiction and the realistic, third-person narrative.

The total irony of the story awakens the reader's impulses
to the vast disproportion between what Emma intended to
accomplish in the exchange of her virginity, as just cause for
killing the man responsible for the disgrace of her father, and
the outcome of events for her. The structure of consciousness
intrudes upon and displaces the crime story sense and technique at the points where we can infer the inevitable fallibility
in the events corresponding to the fallibility of the motives of
the eighteen-year old girl.

Emma works in the textile factory, in Buenos Aires, of
which Aarón Loewenthal is part owner. On a Thursday afternoon she receives a letter, posted in Brazil, from a stranger
informing her of the death of Manuel Maier, presumably by
suicide. The stranger, a boardinghouse friend of the deceased,
does not know that Maier's real name is Emanuel Zunz and
that Emma is his daughter. Emma later destroys the letter, and

evidently the Buenos Aires police remained completely ob-
livious to any connection between the death that motivated
Emma's plan and the shooting of Loewenthal. For, again, the
central character is the bearer of a secret, and the possession of
this secret and the sense of power it provides expose her fallibility. The secret Emanuel Zunz confided to his daughter that
"final night," six years previously (at the age of her puberty),
was the sworn assertion that Loewenthal, at the time the
manager of the factory, was the thief of the embezzled funds — of
which Emanuel Zunz had been accused, convicted, and dis-
graced. Emma's obsession to inflict a just punishment on
Loewenthal, her plan and its execution, are based entirely on
her father's sworn word. We are probably right in assuming
that she lost her mother at an early age. For Emma the bonds
between her and her father are inviolate, but, as readers, we
may allow ourselves the sophistication that incest is involved.
In order to avenge her father in accordance with her plan and
the justification for it, no connection must be suspected between the disgrace and death of her father and her shooting of
Loewenthal on the part of anyone, not even her closest friends,
except her victim (and the reader, the narrator, and God). For
all concerned, as for God, she must have an inviolate reason
for killing him.

"She did not sleep that night and when the first light of
dawn defined the rectangle of the window, her plan was already perfected (60)." Somewhere along the intricate workings
of her mind that night, so intricate a part of the vigil of her
consciousness that we can only express it crudely where
Borges discreetly committed it to abstruse silence, her father's
sworn word of innocency, his honor among men and before
God, equated itself to her own purity before men and God, his
blemished honor to her unblemished girlhood, according to
the secret workings of her being, moved by the love and ven-
eration, perhaps even the obsession, that only a daughter may
keep for her father when she has repulsed any thought of him

or feeling originating even remotely in sex; somewhere along the movement of her being it became evident to her that the intimate possession of her body was the thing to be sacrificed to the end of consummating the secret vengeance and the righteous triumph. She would submit to the horror of giving herself to a man in the way that would preserve the purity of her motive and cause. For it was essential that in killing Loewenthal and accusing him before the courts of human justice which had passed sentence on her father she have an unquestionable motive and its incontestable proof. The man to whom she will give herself in the hours immediately preceding an appointment with Loewenthal must not know who she is, nor care to know; he must be a man who cannot possibly connect her with the worker who shoots Loewenthal, as the newspapers are sure to report, after he deceived her outrageously and attacked her. She must not be punished for shooting him, for she is an instrument in the execution of divine justice. Her sacrifice is righteous in the sight of God. Her motive is secret and pure, a thing between her and her father.

She has conceived a plan and a justification for it as perfect as the rectangle of light at the window. The reader of Borges, by recognizing its symbolic "content," will read that too-exact realistic detail as an allusion to the labyrinth of consciousness on whose precarious paths she compels herself to an inexorable destiny. The events of Friday, as she had probably foreseen, provided two circumstances of utmost importance to her plan. There were rumors of a strike at the factory, and Emma, as before, made known that she was against all violence. After work she went with Elsa Urstein, her best friend, to enroll in an athletic club for women and underwent a medical examination. On Saturday morning the other circumstance on which her plan depended presented itself. She read in *La Prensa* that the ship *Nordstjärnan*, out of Malmo, would sail that night. Then she phoned Loewenthal and insinuated that she had some information about the strike she wanted to tell him without the other girls knowing, and promised to stop by his office at nightfall.

The narrator's careful compression of plot and counterplot, insuring the total inevitability of the outcome, has enclosed the psychological explanation of Emma's motive within a sociological circumstance. On the superficial plane apparent to the public, Emma was an employee on whose loyalty to her fellow workers Loewenthal infringed while violating the trust due to his position as owner. The truth, of course, is very much the reverse. Emma and Loewenthal are moral enemies, but with this in common: both assume God's righteousness to be their cause. "Loewenthal was very religious. He believed he had a secret pact with the Lord, which exempted him from doing good in exchange for prayers and piety (64)." The antithesis between them has a theological context to which the unconcealed symmetries in the adventitious realism are to be referred: their claim to share God's righteousness is the exposed source of their fallibility as human beings because it is the source of their feeling of power. The public's disbelief in Emma's accusation, which the incontestable evidence will overcome, is based on the assumption that the bald, corpulent, respectable, and recently widowed factory owner can not have had an erotic interest in the girl. Moreover, as his intimate friends know, his true passion is money.

In order to defend himself from thieves Loewenthal kept the iron gate to the factory yard locked and a dog in the yard and, as everyone knew, a revolver in the drawer of his desk. To shoot Loewenthal with his own revolver is Emma's stratagem. The symbolic "content" of that revolver, the indispensable prop of the crime story, is multiple and refractive along the lines of the dialectical symmetry. Once the absolute sense of Borges' realistic details lies exposed we can assume, quite rightly, their inevitability as their inevitable meaning. The revolver, of course, has a sexual significance, but it has lain innocently in Loewenthal's drawer for many years without the slightest suspicion of sexual symbolism. Could Emma have foreseen what the revolver, that instrument of justice prefigured by her consciousness making her plan possible, would become in the fateful moment she would point it at Loewenthal and force him to confess? Could she have foreseen that the revolver, like the money she tears up in her feelings of hate and loathsomeness, would resolve themselves into ineradicable reminders of her falling and of the guilt uniting her dishonor to her father's?

An interesting element about "Emma Zunz" is the inverse direction of its symbolism. The usual procedure for Borges is to compel the reader to dislocate a symbolic "content" from a particular disclosure as the counteracting effect of its dialectical opposite. Here we do not have an evident dialectical opposite provoking the antithetical tensions and their irony; we have only the subtlest allusion to one. Consequently we find the irony working directly on the realistic detail and upon our impulse to respond to the realism of the action. The peculiar refinement of the story is the subtlety of the dislocating effect of the irony on the realistic detail. For instance, the details which fix our attention on the objects, a letter, a revolver, hidden in drawers. Emma hides the letter in a drawer "as if in some way she already knew the ulterior facts (59)"—that is, as if she were already guilty of the thing for which her guilt is going to be so great. The revolver in Loewenthal's desk drawer is the indispensable weapon in her plan. Before she thinks out her plan that night the revolver is "already" the inevitable connective back to the letter. "She had already become the person she would be (59)." Where the symmetries of inevitability insinuate themselves, as the dialectical opposite of the adventitious realism, we are compelled to displace the realism of, for instance, the revolver and the money the sailor leaves for Emma, as symbols of her destiny, and, finally, by referring them to the outcome, to dislocate their "content." The process is all the more engaging because Borges has restricted himself to a bare minimum of props for staging a drama of dialectical tensions whose purpose it is to give us the inner, eternal structure of the action.

On Saturday afternoon Emma made her way to the waterfront and to the Paseo de Julio, the brothel district.

> To relate with some reality the events of that afternoon would be difficult and perhaps unrighteous. One attribute of the infernal is its unreality, an attribute which seems to mitigate its terrors and which aggravates them perhaps. How can one make credible an action hardly believed in by the person who experienced it? How recover that brief chaos which today the memory of Emma Zunz repudiates and confuses?    (61–62)

In order to preserve the purity of the horror of what she was doing Emma chose from the men of the *Nordstjärnan* a coarse one for whom she could have no feelings of tenderness.

> The man led her to a door and then to a murky entrance hall and then to a tortuous stairway and then to a vestibule (in which there was a window with lozenges identical to those of a house she lived in as a child with her parents) and then to a passageway and then to a door that closed behind her.    (62)

Behind the closed door, as the space-time reiteration of the labyrinth theme suggests, Emma's girlhood presided over by the figure of her venerated father came to an end in the consummation of the act which cannot ever end in the desolation of her consciousness. In that room outside of time did Emma think *once* of her dead father? "My own belief is that she did think once, and in that moment her desperate undertaking was imperiled (62)." In that moment she thought of her father *and* her mother, and the exposure of her parents to the bleakness of her action revealed their union as the origin of this horror she had inflicted upon herself. In that moment her father's sex blemished her purity and contaminated forever her womanhood. Emma could not have foreseen that her fallibility lay in exposing her virgin's motive to the successful execution of her plan to avenge her father.

> The man, a Swede or Finn, did not speak Spanish; he was an instrument for Emma as she was for him, but she served for pleasure and he for justice.    (63)

Her first act, after the man left, was to tear up the money "as before she had torn up the letter." The oblique meaning of the act consigns her father to the depths of her nausea and her hatred for men.

Having made her way to Loewenthal's office without being noticed, as her plan required, not her father's vengeance but her own was foremost in her obsessive compulsion, although she kept repeating to herself the accusation now pathetically devoid of meaning. Loewenthal, innocent in this matter, was to feel the brunt of her guilt and hatred. The Emma who shoots him more or less heedless of the motive that originally justified the act, fires the revolver to eradicate the man who now becomes, like her father, the indirect cause of her dishonor. Loewenthal dies before she finishes her accusation: "I have avenged my father and they cannot punish me . . ." She never knew whether he understood at all.

> The dog's barking reminded her that she could not, yet, rest. She disarranged the divan, unbuttoned the coat on the cadaver, took off the bespattered glasses and left them on the filing cabinet. Then she picked up the telephone and repeated what she would repeat so many times again, with these and with other words: *An incredible thing has happened . . . Mr. Loewenthal had me come over on the pretext of the strike . . . He abused me, I killed him . . .*
>
> The story, in fact, was incredible, but it imposed itself

on everyone because substantially it was true. True was
Emma Zunz' tone, true her shame, true her hate. True
also was the outrage she had suffered; only the circumstances were false, the time, and one or two proper
names.    (65 – 66)

The final paragraphs simultaneously release the multiple,
interconnected ironies and position them in relation to the
ironic destiny of guilt and humiliation Emma inflicted on
herself in exchange for her chastity. Loewenthal probably died
without knowing why Emma killed him, but then there is no
one single, exact explanation as to why she did. Her motive
was not the one for which she sacrificed her chastity; hence
she murdered him for an offense he never committed, unless
we can conjecture a metaphysical explanation in which he is
more than the indirect cause of her dishonor. Emma's accusation is incredible, yet it imposed itself on everyone because it
is "substantially" correct. The public, meanwhile, accepted
Loewenthal's guilt for an outrage for which Emma's father is
equally to blame. Loewenthal was killed by a revolver which
he kept for his own defense, but Emma was betrayed and
dishonored by the very thing by which she justified her act of
violence. She exchanged her virginity not for righteousness
but for guilt, and her secret (unknown to any persons but
Borges and his reader) shall never cease to be the terrible thing
it is because it is a reality between her and God.
     The total inevitability of these interconnected ironies (and
I have mentioned only enough of them to make my point)
rests implicitly upon our understanding that Emma's chastity,
as a metaphysical, not biologic, reality is her inviolate relation
to God. The total irony assigns this absolute meaning to the
outcome of her actions or no meaning at all. The inevitability
of the ironical symmetries of time, place, names, and identities
gives us either a meaning and a moral order in the events
which can be seen as "infinite" and absolute and pointing to a

meaning and order beyond themselves, or else a completely
meaningless order, implicating the mind and imagination
which conceives and gives it shape. The "reality" of the events
of the story moves into the final focus in our apprehending
that the ironies construct and sustain the irreconcilability of
these two orders of interpretation.

3

"The God's Script" (1949),[29] by all counts one of the most
original, is — it may be said almost axiomatically — the most
successful of Borges' stories. One or two others represent a
greater effort in craftsmanship, but even "The Immortal" falls
short of a total exactitude or equivalence in its effects. I am
even tempted to call "The Script" the paradigm or archetype of
Borges' accomplishments in the short prose fiction, if only to
emphasize that it is the most nearly perfect fusion and
compression of his themes, resources, and techniques conceivable, the dialectical tensions assuming a finely sharpened
parabolic sense and direction. I shall leave to the end of my
discussion what I have to say about it as a parable of this or
that, because any such attempts depend on insights into the
total irony of the structure.

The story takes place, if it can be said to take place at all,
in Mexico at the time of the Spanish conquest of the Aztec
empire. As in the case of "The Garden," we have a revelatory
account in the first person, by a prisoner, Tzinacán, the Aztec
magician-priest of the pyramid of the god Qaholom. Pedro de
Alvarado, known to history as the ruthless and brutal lieuten-
ant of Hernán Cortés, while searching for a fabulous and secret
treasure, came upon the pyramid of Qaholom at dusk. His
men captured and tortured the magician-priest; before his
very eyes they wrecked the idol of the god, but Tzinacán did
not reveal the location of the hidden treasure. They lashed
him, deformed and broke his body, and threw him into a

prison. The torture of his imprisonment, worse than death, has lasted many years. The narrative, an account of the effects on his body, mind, and spirit of these many years, reveals how Tzinacán deciphered the magical script of his god. Borges has fancied for Tzinacán an intuition and mentality, a *Weltanschauung*, that one could not, with any plausibility, attribute to an Aztec priest. Embedded in Tzinacán's cabalistic, theological, and mystical cogitation (see the Epilogue to *El Aleph*), for example, is this oblique reference to the existentialism of the twentieth-century Spanish philosopher, José Ortega y Gasset: "a man is, by and large, his circumstances . . ."

Having developed a long analysis of "The Garden," which broke the splendid continuity of the very sequences under discussion, I shall not attempt a similar effort here, but shall provide the complete text of the brief account in a version as faithful to the quality of the effects of the original Spanish as I can manage. To get the full effect, one must be prepared to read "The Script" as an uninterrupted concatenation of symbols building up to a climax that, simultaneously, annuls and consummates itself. The opening phrase, *La cárcel es profunda y de piedra*, has the charge of emotive and symbolical connotations usually associated with poetry. The circular prison, a domed pit, is divided into two adjacent cells by a high wall, with an opening in it covered by an iron grating (evidently a gate that can be raised from above); his cell is one side of this underground pit; in the other side his jailers have put a jaguar that, but for the grating, can tear Tzinacán to pieces instantly.

## THE GOD'S SCRIPT

The prison is deep and of stone; its form, that of a nearly perfect hemisphere, though the floor (also of stone) is somewhat less than a great circle, a fact which in some way aggravates the feelings of oppression and of vastness. A dividing wall cuts it at the center; this wall, although very high, does not reach the upper part of the vault; in one cell am I, Tzinacán, magician of the pyramid of Qaholom, which Pedro de Alvarado devastated by fire; in the other there is a jaguar measuring with secret and even paces the time and space of captivity. A long window with bars, flush with the floor, cuts the central wall. At the shadowless hour [mid-day], a trap in the high ceiling opens and a jailer whom the years have gradually been effacing maneuvers an iron sheave and lowers for us, at the end of a rope, jugs of water and chunks of flesh. The light breaks into the vault; at that instant I can see the jaguar.

I have lost count of the years I have lain in the darkness; I, who was young once and could move about this prison, am incapable of more than awaiting, in the posture of my death, the end destined to me by the gods. With the deep obsidian knife I have cut open the breasts of victims and now I could not, without magic, lift myself from the dust.

On the eve of the burning of the pyramid, the men who came down from the towering horses tortured me with fiery metals to force me to reveal the location of a hidden treasure. They struck down the idol of the god before my very eyes, but he did not abandon me, and I endured the torments in silence. They scourged me, they broke and deformed me, and then I awoke in this prison from which I shall not emerge in mortal life.

Impelled by the fatality of having something to do, of populating time in some way, I tried, in my darkness, to recall all I knew. Endless nights I devoted to recalling the order and the number of stone-carved serpents or the precise form of a medicinal tree. Gradually, in this way, I subdued the passing years; gradually, in this way, I came into possession of that which was already mine. One night I felt I was approaching the threshold of an intimate recollection; before he sights the sea, the traveler feels a quickening in the blood. Hours later I began to perceive the outline of the recollection. It was a tradition of the god. The god, foreseeing that at the end of time there would be devastation and ruin, wrote on the first day of Creation a magical sentence with the power to ward off those evils. He wrote it in such a way that it would reach the most distant generations and not be subject to chance. No one knows where it was written nor with what characters, but it is certain that it exists, secretly, and that a chosen one shall read it. I considered that we were now, as always, at the end of time and that my destiny as the last priest of the god would give me access to the privilege of intuiting the script. The fact that a prison confined me did not forbid my hope; perhaps I had seen the script of Qaholom a thousand times and needed only to fathom it.

This reflection encouraged me, and then instilled in me a kind of vertigo. Throughout the earth there are ancient forms, forms incorruptible and eternal; any one of them could be the symbol I sought. A mountain could be the speech of the god, or a river or the empire or the configuration of the stars. But in the process of the centuries mountains are leveled, the river changes its course, empires undergo mutations and havoc, and the configuration of the stars varies. There is change in the firmament. The mountain and the star are individuals, and individuals perish. I sought something more tenacious, more invulnerable. I thought of the generations of cereals, of grasses, of birds, of men. Perhaps the magic would be written on my face, perhaps I myself was the end of my search. That anxiety was consuming me when I remembered the jaguar was one of the attributes of the god.

Then my soul filled with pity. I imagined the first morning of time; I imagined my god confiding his message to the living skin of the jaguars, who would love and reproduce without end, in caverns, in cane fields, on islands, in order that the last men might receive it. I imagined that net of tigers, that teeming labyrinth of tigers, inflicting horror upon pastures and flocks in order to perpetuate a design. In the next cell there was a jaguar; in his vicinity I perceived a confirmation of my conjecture and a secret favor.

I devoted long years to learning the order and the configuration of the spots. Each period of darkness conceded an instant of light, and I was able thus to fix in my mind the black forms running through the yellow fur. Some of them included points, others formed cross lines on the inner side of the legs; others, ring-shaped, were repeated. Perhaps they were a single sound or a single word. Many of them had red edges.

I shall not recite the hardships of my toil. More than once I cried out to the vault that it was impossible to decipher that text. Gradually, the concrete enigma I labored at disturbed me less than the generic enigma of a sentence written by a god. What type of sentence (I asked myself) will an absolute mind construct? I considered that even in the human languages there is no proposition that does not imply the entire universe; to say *the tiger* is to say the tigers that begot it, the deer and turtles devoured by it, the grass on which the deer fed, the earth that was mother to the grass, the heaven that gave birth to the earth. I considered that in the language of a god every word would enunciate that infinite concatenation of facts, and not in an implicit but in an explicit manner, and not progressively but instantaneously. In time, the notion of a divine sentence seemed puerile or blasphemous. A god, I reflected, ought to utter only a single word and in that word absolute fullness. No word uttered by him can be inferior to the universe or less than the sum total of time. Shadows or simulacra of that single word equivalent to a language and to all a language can embrace are the poor and ambitious human words, *all, world, universe.*

One day or one night—what difference between my days and nights can there be?—I dreamt there was a grain of sand on the floor of the prison. Indifferent, I slept again; I dreamt I awoke and that on the floor there were two grains of sand. I slept again; I dreamt that the grains of sand were three. They went on multiplying in this way until they filled the prison and I lay dying beneath that hemisphere of sand. I realized I was dreaming; with a vast effort I roused myself and awoke. It was useless to awake; the innumerable sand was suffocating me. Someone said to me. *You have not awakened to wakefulness, but to a previous dream. This dream is enclosed within another, and so on to infinity, which is the number of grains of sand. The path you must retrace is interminable and you will die before you ever really awake.*

I felt lost. The sand burst my mouth, but I shouted: *A sand of dreams cannot kill me nor are there dreams within dreams.*

A blaze of light awoke me. In the darkness above there grew a circle of light. I saw the face and hands of the jailer, the sheave, the rope, the flesh, and the water jugs.

A man becomes confused, gradually, with the form of his destiny; a man is, by and large, his circumstances. More than a decipherer or an avenger, more than a priest of the god, I was one imprisoned. From the tireless labyrinth of dreams I returned as if to my home to the harsh prison. I blessed its dampness, I blessed its tiger, I blessed the crevice of light, I blessed my old, suffering body, I blessed the darkness and the stone.

Then there occurred what I cannot forget nor communicate. There occurred the union with the divinity, with the universe (I do not know whether these words differ in meaning). Ecstasy does not repeat its symbols; God has been seen in a blazing light, in a sword or in the circles of a rose. I saw an exceedingly high Wheel, which was not before my eyes, nor behind me, nor to the sides, but every place at one time. That Wheel was made of water, but also of fire, and it was (although the edge could be seen) infinite. Interlinked, all things that are, were, and shall be formed it, and I was one of the fibers of that total fabric and Pedro de Alvarado who tortured me was another. There lay revealed the causes and the effects, and it sufficed me to see that Wheel in order to understand it all, without end. O bliss of understanding, greater than the bliss of imagining or feeling. I saw the universe and I saw the intimate designs of the universe. I saw the origins narrated in the Book of the Common. I saw the mountains that rose out of the water, I saw the first men of wood, the cisterns that turned against the men, the dogs that ravaged their faces. I saw the faceless god concealed behind the other gods. I saw infinite processes that formed one single felicity and, understanding all, I was able also to understand the script of the tiger.

It is a formula of fourteen random words (they appear random) and to utter it in a loud voice would suffice to make me all-powerful. To say it would suffice to abolish this stone prison, to have daylight break into my night, to be young, to be immortal, to have the tiger's jaws crush Alvarado, to sink the sacred knife into the breasts of Spaniards, to reconstruct the pyramid, to reconstruct the empire Forty syllables, fourteen words, and I, Tzinacán, would rule the lands Moctezuma ruled. But I know I shall never say those words, because I no longer remember Tzinacán.

May the mystery lettered on the tigers die with me. Whoever has seen the universe, has beheld the fiery designs of the universe, cannot think in terms of one man, of that man's trivial fortunes or misfortunes, though he be that very man. That man *has been he* and now matters no more to him. What is the life of that other to him, the nation of that other to him, if he, now, is no one. This is why I do not pronounce the formula, why, lying here in the darkness, I let the days obliterate me.


It was inevitable, in this drama of consciousness, that the prisoner Tzinacán should conclude that the god's script was writ there on the jaguar's fiery skin; that, as he aged and his mind grew darker, his flesh and spirit weakened, the ordeal should sunder his personal being; inevitable, also, that a revelation of secret designs in the universe, with its illumination of love and pity, should justify his torturous existence, and reconcile him to the horror of death-in-life: for the ultimate meaning of the universe that a man may possess cannot be other that his own destiny.

The correlations between cause and effect, between beginning and outcome, in Tzinacán's ordeal are so exact, in his telling of it, that their sum total is one and the same with their inevitability. That is, their inevitability derives from the Borgian exactitude between the order of the experiences and events disclosed and the order in which they are narrated. The irony of the story coincides with and thus reiterates this inevitability, from the scale of the whole down to small details. It is suggested first in the details of the oppressive form of the stone chamber—the imperfection in the shape of the floor, the barred window, the total darkness with its instant of light at noon. Its implications begin to emerge as we learn the details of the prisoner's precarious existence next to the jaguar and the circumstantial process wherein he first recalls the tradition of the god, and determines that the secret, destined for a chosen one at the end of time, is writ there on the moving beast. Their totality heightens as we follow the prisoner's hallucinatory attempts to decipher that arcane "text," that "fearful symmetry" consisting of a design of lines and spots (*rosetas jeroglíficas*) which he sees always in motion, through the iron bars, for an instant of light. Then, totally evident, the implications focus on the crux of the matter: the problematical relation of the deciphering mind of the human subject to the absolute "content" of the magical script. The total irony of the story, one and the same with the totality of Tzinacán's destiny, can thus be seen as pivoting the absolute "content" of the god's script on the circumstantial process of decipherment.

The exactness between form and meaning in "The Script" has produced what one may call the Borgian paradigmatic structure of consciousness. By this I mean that at any level of interpretation the "content" of the displaceable symbols will be indivisible from the content of the story as a whole. Hence, in this paradigmatic structure, the fallibility of the hero inheres in the "totality" of the attempt of the powers of consciousness, will and understanding, memory and language, to compel their own transcendence. The consciousness of the hero attempts and accomplishes nothing less than the very annihilation of its powers through their consummation.

Reiterative, pervasive, the irony creates the effect of irreconcilable extremes between the starting point of the story and its close. But this effect is the result of tensions *progressively* elaborating an account whose total meaning is grasped *instantly* in the moment the story reaches its climax, in the disclosure: "This is why I do not pronounce the formula." The antithetical sense of the tensions, at their apex, is a concatenation of symbols revealing, or releasing, a meaning which simultaneously annuls and sustains, by means of the effect of a total reiteration, the entire dialectical design. The god's script, as conceived and deciphered by the prisoner, a formula of "forty syllables, fourteen words," containing the total meaning and power of the universe, and, of course, of language, is, therefore, Borges' paradigmatic symbol within the total symbolism of his story.

The most apparent of the antithetical tensions is the one we can perceive between the *ultimate sense* of the account and its *progressive*, or *sequential, sense*. The sequential sense conveys in ordered progression the when and why, where and how, the prisoner deciphered the all-powerful arcanum. The ultimate sense reveals that its discovery and possession is the reason for the account itself. Consequently, the antithetical sense of each disclosure is that each is simultaneously an evocation of the ordeal undergone by the prisoner, and a reiteration of the ultimate effect of possessing the script, and of the inner, eternal circumstance of his imprisonment. The inevitability of the sequential sense (its presciential order or concatenation) is determined by the ultimate sense, but the latter, once the final displacement comes about in a reader's mind and feelings, will be a retroaction, the sequential concatenation in reverse.

Upon completing the story, the reader perceives that its beginning is its inevitable ending, and, conversely, that the ending is the inevitable beginning. One is led to conclude that Borges has epitomized in the structure the thematic antithesis of being and its coming-to-be in time. In the piece "Borges and I" we read: "Spinoza understood that all things wish to persist in their being; the stone eternally wants to be a stone, and the tiger a tiger."[30] But the time dimension in our story is suspended, like stormy spray in a still seascape, in the infinite space-time present of mystical illumination. Some may see it, and the cyclical night of imprisonment, as an "unreal" or "magical" time. I read it as a dimension of consciousness.

Tortuous dream, chimerical self-delusion, metaphysical phantasy, mystical ecstasy—all apply to Tzinacán's abysmal ordeal. But one should stress that the prisoner has obeyed an inner compulsion, a commitment of self, that brings him, at its culmination, to a soul-shattering confrontation with an archetypal dimension of being. The act of transcendence implicit in the mystical vision of the wheel, or circle, annuls the force and value of his personal motives—hate, vengeance, worldly power—and his will to realize them.

The total exactitude of Borges' effects in "The Script," I suggest, arises from a number of equivalences of symmetries and antitheses, of which the most evident is the equivalence of the personal or individual dimension of being to the sequential sense of the disclosures, and the impersonal or archetypal dimension of being to their ultimate or instantaneous sense. An overall, exact displacement of the individual by the archetypal, or impersonal, is my explanation for its complete success. Once we look at the story in this fashion, we can detect the two sets of antitheses operative in a structure of hieratic symbols which seems impenetrable because the time dimension is actually a dimension of being, that is, of consciousness. I call it Borges' paradigmatic structure of consciousness because it conveys in symbolic form that tendency of his intellect and imagination to construe the ultimate value of an individual life as an emanation of a single, all-inclusive universal archetype.[31] But the confrontation is a conflict, and for individual consciousness its outcome equivalent to death. These remarks, purposely exploratory, anticipate the theme of "The Immortal," perhaps the most hermetic of Borges' fictions.

The compressed contents of "The Script" can be expanded, evidently, to a critique on man in his world, a critique fusing metaphysics, theology, and occultism, anthropology, semantics, and literary symbolism along a narrow, tenuous band. In the other direction, in the sense of a parable, the story is susceptible to various readings; a parable of modern, existential man; of the scientific intellect obsessed by dreams of power; of the writer in Spanish America inured to the degrading tyranny of dictatorships. Perhaps this last possibility is a link between the impersonality of the story and Borges' personal existence in the Argentina of the 1940's.

# BORGES 4

*Music, states of happiness, mythology, faces belabored by time, certain twilights and certain places, try to tell us something, or have said something we should not have missed, or are about to say something; this imminence of a revelation, which never does come off, is, perhaps, the esthetic phenomenon.[32]*

The theme of "The Immortal," Borges tells us, is "the effect that immortality would have upon men"; the story offers us "a sketch of an ethic for immortals."[33] If our responses, aroused by this unparalleled effort in the short narrative, can approach the exacting quality of the intuitions and perceptions which have conceived and organized the story, we shall arrive at an apprehension of its antitheses, movements, and tensions as an agon, or conflict, between the personal and the archetypal dimensions of being, and this agon, or conflict, as the necessarily irreconcilable antithesis which, under the Borgian aspect of things, constitutes human consciousness. The impenetrability of the story, we shall then verify, corresponds to the completeness with which the significance of the events as a personal narrative are displaced by a impersonal meaning. The immortality Borges has conceived for the immortals of his story is neither the immortality of a hereafter of religious belief nor the biological immortality of the species, but the much more precarious immortality of human consciousness. They are immortal in time, not out of time or in eternity; hence the despair and horror with which individual consciousness confronts such an existence, and hence that "ethic for immortals" that equates a deathless impersonality to the uniqueness of a personal death.

In the succession of events in the narrative of the Roman tribune Marcus Flaminius Rufus, whom we know to be, also, Joseph Cartaphilus, we have a sequential movement corresponding to the unique and indeterminate reality of personal experience. In the disintegration of the contents of his narrative with which the story closes, we have the climactic eruption to the surface of a countermovement, which has run continuously beneath the personal narrative, and corresponds to the archetypal entity—Homer—of which that personal experience and existence are a prolonged intimation. The apprehension of this structure of antithetical movements turns upon the intricate irony that compels us to infer, simultaneously on various levels, the inverse relations and the reciprocal displacements between the impersonal, or archetypal, sense of the personal disclosures and the personal, irretrievable sense which brings to life the abstract and archetypal; to infer, that is, the conflict, or antagony, of tensions constituting an individual consciousness. Because the irony is operative as a total and simultaneous confrontation of the personal and the archetypal, it can be described as the total irony to which, in the final analysis, the multiple meanings of the story and their antithetical relations to one another are to be referred. This total irony, we may say then, is the catalyst we are impelled to activate once we have committed our responses to tracing the dialectical motions of Borges' imagination.

The apperception of this irony, as we should expect, is not a circumstantial matter uncomplicatedly dependent on the subjectivity of private perceptions, but a deliberate component of the fiction to which we must respond if the very integrity of the story as a work of literary art and of its author are to be at all accessible to us. The fiction, as it presses toward the surprise conclusion, reduces the autobiographical account to a heap of mutilated words, intrusions, or thefts, interpolations, isolated images, and decomposed symbols, the debris to which the Borgian imagination has disintegrated the very thing it set out to create. The structure of movement and countermovement, creation and disintegration, is the generic expression of Borges' mind and imagination, the structure of thought and feeling with which he communicates that range of intuitions implying a compulsive, impersonal character in what is assumed to be most spontaneous and subjective, free and intimate, in literary creation. In the end, or, as his Immortal says, "when the end draws near," tradition and language reduce and absorb into one impersonal and anonymous body the most inimitable and personal of feelings and experiences. In "The Immortal" Borges has carried out to an unqualified degree that tendency—or better, that necessity—of his inventiveness to provide for its own ironical and critical displacement.

The Immortal of the story is the immortal poet who stands at the beginning or very near the beginning of the Western literary tradition in which Borges' immersion is so complete and self-conscious. But "The Immortal" is also the story of "two men," or rather, of two archetypes of immortality, the immortal poet and the "everlasting Jew." Homer has been many men to the collective consciousness of mankind. He is, or persists, as an immortal in the only critical sense that is accessible to the consciousness of living men. The transformations of the Wandering Jew throughout legend and literary history risk becoming just another rehearsal of folklore motifs unless brought into a similar perspective. Just who or what Homer is or means in world literary tradition and collective or historical consciousness is a "Homeric Question," which has undergone transformation and reiteration in a context larger than any one of the adherents of the various theories propounded to explain the *Iliad* and the *Odyssey* would have cared to consider. Borges conjectures a fiction that manages to allude to the multiple aspects of the Homeric Question and their entire development, although the Question itself is only peripheral to his theme, by confronting an individual who is Homer with an archetype who is the same Homer in a symbolic succession of events spanning the centuries of the Homeric tradition. By presenting his fiction as authored by Joseph Cartaphilus, he alludes not only to "Semitic origins" and "collective authorship," but likewise to the immortality of Jewish letters. A curious page in De Quincey's Essays, where we find Solomon and Homer, the elder Temple and the "great Homeric temple" of the *Iliad*, paired in the thousandth year before Christ, suggests a fundamental link in Borges' design.[34]

The story of "The Immortal" consists of five short chapters preceded by an explanatory note and followed by a Postscript dated 1950. The note explains that in June 1929, in London,

Joseph Cartaphilus, a Smyrnian antiquarian, offered the Princess of Lucinge the six volumes in small quarto of Pope's *Iliad*. She exchanged a few words with him at the time she received them. He was, she said, a man "of singularly vague features"; he handled various languages "with fluency and ignorance." The few details advanced about his appearance are, of course, a calculated attempt to define archetypal features of a legendary figure. In October of the same year she learned from a passenger of the *Zeus* that Cartaphilus had died at sea while returning to Smyrna, and had been buried on the island of Ios. She found the manuscript, written in English and consisting of five short chapters, in the last volume of the set. The sense behind these disclosures is that, in the twentieth century, the individual who is the immortal creator is a dealer in antiques of the Homeric tradition, dealing "not in art, but in the history of art," and that he dies, a mortal, in 1929.[35] "Joseph Cartaphilus" is of course the name the Wandering Jew bears when he first appears in England in the Latin chronicle of Roger of Wendover for the year 1228.[36] Since the "original" of Cartaphilus' account is in English, a translation, like ours, back into English contrives to restore it. The "original," we are told, "abounds in Latinisms," another allusion to the Latin chronicle as well as to English eighteenth-century prose styles.[37]

• • • •

The opening phrase, "As far as I can recall, my labors began . . .," prefigures an archetypal memory behind the personal *I* and a span of time and memory extending back in parallel currents from two moments: the present moment (ca. 1922) of recall and the moment of the events occurring in the reign of Diocletian.

In the first chapter we read that the Roman tribune, on a sleepless night in a garden in Thebes Hekatompylos on the banks of the Nile, in the last years of the third century, learned from a mysterious horseman the existence of a secret river that "purifies men of death," and of the secret City of the Immortals located in the extreme Occident, at the end of the world. The tribune recruited a large expedition to find the City, but the ordeal of survival in the African desert overwhelmed his men; they deserted, mutinied, and plotted to kill him; finally he was forced to flee with a few loyal soldiers. Then he lost contact with these men and wandered over the burning desert for days. One morning he saw, in the distance, the mirage-like forms of pyramids and towers. As he lost consciousness from thirst and exhaustion, he fell into a nightmare in which he could perceive the surface lines of a water jar that ever evaded his reach.

> Unbearably I dreamt of an exiguous and nitid labyrinth: in the center was a water jar; my hands could almost touch it, my eyes could see it, but so perplexing and intricate were the curvatures that I knew I would die before touching it.

The one element to which we can reduce the tribune's account of his labors is the strange compulsiveness of the anxiety that impelled him to seek the secret City and of the anxiety of this ordeal of extricating and recalling the events of the search. The search was a hallucinatory exertion of personal will, courage, and powers of endurance. Moved by the anxiety and precariousness of personal existence, its perishability exposed to the impassive but cruel forces of the cosmos, the tribune and his men were driven by the obsession to be immortal, to survive forever the ordeal of human existence subject to the inexorable disintegration of time, by drinking from a secret river of pagan magic. The ordeals, or labors, of the tribune appear to us as a personal anxiety, but the compulsion behind the anxiety, as we discover from the ironical interconnections of the chapters at the story's close, designates the impersonal entity whose immanence we become aware of when we perceive the potential symbolic transparency of the series of disclosures.

The events of this chapter begin on a sleepless night and

conclude in a nightmare of an interminable, soul-consuming day. The tribune thrust himself upon the search out of the frustration and inaction of an unwarlike existence: "Fever and magic consumed many men who, magnanimously, coveted the steel." The entire expedition, save its leader, perished in the desert wastes. The expedition is actually the personal quest of the tribune, and the labors he speaks of comprise a personal epic of consciousness. The account, which appears to be a painful attempt to recall those events on the part of an individual, is potentially a series of intimations of the archetypal and symbolic memory which is the compulsion behind the personal anxiety to recall. Behind the restlessness, anxiety, and desperation to find the City of the Immortals is the compulsion of an immortal will. The individual who was the Roman tribune Marcus Flaminius Rufus could not have known, on that sleepless night in a garden of Thebes, that his determination to find the secret City was an intimation of an archetypal will.

2

The quality of Borges' extraordinary art resides in the tension he can maintain between the autonomous, spontaneous charge of a revelatory impulse and its effect as compulsive and inevitable. The sustained tension, which appears to be a suspension or equilibrium of contrary forces, is in fact the sustained reiteration of their antithetical confrontation, rising in intensity and pressing toward an ever imminent climax. This quality communicates the anxiety of the tribune as the irreconcilable conflict between the irreducible experience of the subject who feels, suffers, thinks, and acts in an existential duration of time, and the meaning of that feeling, suffering, thought, and action in the absolute sense of time and being. The antagony, or conflict, arises because the tribune's disclosures possess both a personal "content" and a symbolic "con-

tent" which are antithetical to one another. The personal
"content" integrates the personal sense of his actions and
experiences into a narrative movement configuring the
uniqueness of a personal destiny. The symbolic "content"
disintegrates that uniqueness by betraying those actions and
experiences as archetypal instances, as the immanence of a
symbolic being. The effect of this conflict—the simultaneous
integration and disintegration of "contents" within a single
disclosure and then within the complete design of the five
chapters—is an acute sense that the antagony is about to
shatter itself and produce a revelation of transcendental attributes, and that it would do so, for our impulses are awake and
stirred to that possibility, if only the literary symbols before us
could cease to be what they are, that is to say, symbols, and no
more, of an unfathomable reality. For our expectations have
been produced by the ironical opposition between the autonomous, revelatory charge and its effect as compulsive and
inevitable; and it is this irony operative in our perceptions
which activates the symbolic potential of the narrative, and it
is for this reason that we shall be unable to extricate the higher
symbolism of the story from the surreptitious irony activating
and stipulating it. At the present point in the narrative, then,
the tensions between the charge and the effect provoke us to a
series of sustained expectations of an ultimate sense to the
antagony of which the tribune's horror, solitude, and anxiety
are the immediate substance.

When he awakened from the nightmare, he found himself
in an oblong niche (or grave), with his hands tied behind his
back. The disclosure is intended as a spontaneous revelation of
a personal experience. But both the experience and the disclosure are evidently symbolic. Further, the very form of the
disclosure reiterates the antithesis between the personal sense
of the experience and its symbolic attributes by attempting a
simultaneous integration and disintegration of "form" and
"content."

> When finally I *unwound* myself from this nightmare, I
> found myself lying with my hands *bound* in an oblong
> niche no larger than a common grave, shallowly exca-
> vated into the sharp escarpment of a mountain.

I have italicized the words that designate the antithetical
condition of the awakening, an *unwinding* and a *binding*, a
figurative action and a literal result, a personal impulse and a
result symbolic of compulsion.

The sense of the disclosure is that the experience is both
an awakening out of the nightmare and an involuted collapse
into another hallucinatory, unreal state of consciousness. The
awakening, it can almost go without saying, is a kind of resurrection (implying a death of sorts), a symbolic action, as are
all the actions, movements and gestures of the story. But the
individual who is Flaminius Rufus executes these actions, and
experiences the anguish and dread of discovery, because,
according to the Borgian design of destiny, "he does not know
who he is." His actions are archetypal and mythical, but they
cannot appear as such to the subject who executes them or
recalls them. Farther, the Borgian subject experiences their
archetypal and impersonal substance, in the moment of confrontation, as a horror not unlike death, causing dread and
anguish. At this point in the narrative, the fiction itself is
possible because the tribune expresses a personal anxiety and
the peril and insecurity of a personal destiny. "I felt a painful
throbbing in my breast, I felt that I was burning with thirst."
From the niche, he saw, running along the base of the mountain, an impure stream, clogged with debris and sand, and
beyond, "beneath the first sun or beneath the last," the
unmistakable City of Immortals. Around him he saw a
hundred or so niches similar to his and from these and from
shallow pits in the sand "emerged gray-skinned men, with
scraggly beards, and naked . . . I thought I recognized them:
they belonged to the bestial breed of the troglodytes, who

infest the shores of the Arabian Gulf and the Ethiopian caves; I was not amazed that they could not speak and that they devoured serpents."[38]

Thirst impelled him to hurl himself recklessly, his eyes closed and his hands tied behind his back, down the slope to the debris-clogged stream, the river whose waters grant immortality. The contrast between the wretched condition of the man who in delirium slakes his thirst, like an animal, in the brackish stream, and the marvelous magical property he acquires, is an antithesis proceeding from the pathetic fragility of personal existence and running counter but parallel to the wretched condition of the troglodytes, who inspire repulsion but are the Immortals, and as such the ethical as well as the physical symbols of immortality. The condition of the stream itself is symbolic of the contrast between the immortality possessed by the troglodytes and ethical values founded on personal uniqueness and mortality. The symbolic transparency of the scene, then, prefigures the transvaluation of ethics implied in the immortality the tribune acquires, unknowingly, at this moment.

> Before collapsing again into sleep and delirium, inexplicably I repeated some Greek words: *the rich Trojans of Zelea who drink the dark waters of Aisepos . . .*
> I do not know how many days and nights wheeled over me.

In chapter V of the story we are told the Greek words are a Homeric fragment, and in the context of chapter V, where the entire personal content of the account disintegrates, they are there an "intrusion" or a "theft." In the context of chapter II, where the irony and the pathos focus on the adverb "inexplicably," they are an exertion of memory and designate an action and a symbolic "content" of that action. In this context the tribune recalls the words in irreconcilable opposition to the archetypal entity—Homer—of which they are an intimation.

Behind the restlessness that impelled him to reach the City and to find the Immortals we infer the impersonal compulsion which has designated his journey and exploration a symbolic approach and confrontation with Homer; that is, with the troglodyte who follows him out of the primitive village, like a faithful dog. The representation of consciousness as a labyrinthine nightmare is so usual in Borges' stories that the reader may overlook the significance of this perplexing technique. The sense of the involuted nightmares, which dislocate and remove from reality the events and actions, is actually designating something very much like the antithesis of both dream and reality. I refer to a state of super-awareness, of intense or heightened vigilance, where will and memory may assume the same hallucinatory aspect of certain actions performed in such a state, or images produced by the mind and symbols intuited. If the matter were susceptible of being determined in such a fashion, the reader could attempt to count the precise number of involutions of dream within dream, or delirium within delirium, in which the events of the tribune's narrative occur. At a given point in those involutions the physical presence of the Immortal Homer becomes evident, but by every indication of those spirals designating the labyrinth of consciousness he appears as a purely symbolic entity, who, at the moment he speaks (in chapter III), reverses the direction of the narrative; and from that point, like an illumination, the intimations of his presence diffuse throughout the account and render it the ironic fabric of symbols at the point of an imminent revelation. That intense vigilance, sustained to an almost unendurable degree, is the normal state of consciousness of the Immortals, of the troglodyte Homer, who follows the tribune to the base of the plateau on which the City stands, and waits there, like Argos for Ulysses, for the period of the exploration; that is to say, maintains a symbolic vigilance corresponding to the personal experience of the tribune in the City and the revelation of the meaning of its atrocious architecture.

Toward midnight, I set foot on the black shadow of its walls, bristling on the yellow sand with idolatrous forms. I was halted by a kind of sacred horror. So abhorred by man are novelty and the desert that I was glad one of the troglodytes had accompanied me to the last. I closed my eyes and awaited (without sleep) the light of day.

The exploration of the City offers us the most luminous instance of an antagony between the individual and archetypal aspects of being, between the personal ordeal and the impersonal revelation which discloses itself as the compulsive content of that ordeal. Paradoxically, the luminosity is due to the vortex of multiple reiterations of the labyrinthine situation. As a personal experience, the exploration is an ordeal of the spirit, of horror, solitude, anguish, and the sense of the absolute desolation of the individual in a meaningless world. As a symbolic action it is the rite of passage of man through his own microcosmic structure designed as an archetypal replica of the universe. Three stages, consisting of an antithesis between the physical form and its effect of desolation upon the spirit, comprise it: a descent, an ascent, and a final illumination. This illumination, refractive in an ironic sense in the forthcoming ethic of the Immortals of which it is an anticipation, concludes thus:

> *This City* (I thought) *is so horrible that its mere existence and perdurance, although in the midst of a secret desert, contaminates the past and the future and in some way jeopardizes the very stars. As long as it lasts, no one in the world can be valorous or felicitous. I do not wish to describe it; a chaos of heterogeneous words, the body of a tiger or bull in which teeth, organs, and heads would pullulate monstrously in mutual conjunction and hatred can (perhaps) be approximate images.*

In the final illumination we have the extremes of mortal insecurity and distress elicited from the confrontation with the "form" of its absolute meaning. The tribune feels horror, fear, and repulsion because he discerns that the Immortals who conceived and erected the atrocious place have invested with form and order a structure expressing the void of meaning, the senselessness, of the universe. As an immortal creation, the palace represents, not a creation of order out of chaos (this had been the original City the Immortals destroyed), but the reverse, a mocking, formalized reiteration of the senselessness of any order, symmetry, or opposition in the face of the total absence of meaning in the universe. It expresses the negation of the possibility of order, physical or moral, and, hence, of value. It excites horror and repulsion in the individual because the endless incompleteness of its monstrous reiterations formalizes the very element of uncertainty or indeterminateness which the individual experiences as his own realm of choice and freedom, and as providing the possibility of happiness and the attainment of personal qualities—courage, honor, virtue, intelligence. The architectural atrocity, we know from the context of chapter IV, was conceived by Homer. The final illumination, in the context of the entire narrative, is then the encounter of an individual consciousness with its own archetypal structure, its meaning.

The anxiety of the tribune throughout his search for the Immortals has been the sustained presentiment of the revelation that, as a subject who wills and suffers in the expectation of fulfilling personal desire and personal destiny, he is but an immanence of an immortal and mythical entity, and that his thoughts and actions, insofar as he is their cause or subject, are but anticipations of an impersonal will and an archetypal memory. Or, to put it in the context of the present moment of the story, the tribune's anxiety is the sustained presentiment of the impending revelation of an archetypal dimension of being determining personal destiny. Consciousness itself is, then, according to Borges' configuration, the antagony between personal will and feeling, anticipating in future time the fulfillment of personal freedom, and the imminent, inexorable effacement of that freedom and its possibility by a compulsion proceeding from the immemorial, generic being *Man* which every individual bears within him both as an identity and a stranger. What the tribune anticipates is not the "content" of freedom in future time, but the inevitability of the displacement of his freedom by an impersonal compulsion.

The third stage, at its consummation the empathy of despair, signifies that it is the end, or purpose, behind the compulsion of the anxiety that has brought Flaminius Rufus, from the sleepless night in Thebes, face to face with the architectural prescience of an immortal consciousness.

The personal account conveys the tribune's anxiety as an ordeal of will in the time dimension of the events, and as an ordeal of memory in the time dimension of the narrative. The tensions within the narrative do not arise, however, from any opposition between projections of will and memory, for they convey parallel meanings, and carry forward the sequential and personal movement of the narrative. The tensions within the narrative proceed from the irreconcilability between the autonomous, personal value of the experiences and disclosures, their perishability and irretrievability, and the compulsiveness of the movement running counter to the sequential, which determines these experiences and disclosures as mythical and archetypal. This is the structure of a sustained antagony between the integration of personal experience and personal destiny in existential time, and its simultaneous disintegration or displacement by the anonymity of archetypal symbols; the ironic structure of consciousness which Borges has attempted to contain and delineate in the sequence of five chapters or contexts, in which each executes its own integration and the disintegration of the preceding chapter or context, the total sequence constituting the symbolic transparency of an individual consciousness and destiny. To say that the tensions of this structure constitute an irreconcilable antithesis is to recognize that, under the Borgian aspect of things, consciousness is an inexorable compulsion in time, a continuum of tensions resolvable only in the annihilation of the living subject.

3

Each of the five chapters, then, delineates the antagony in a precise, sequential context within the total context. In chapter I we have obscure and distant *intimations* of the symbolic entity of Homer in the personal ordeal of the tribune. In chapter II those intimations are pressed to the point of an imminent *revelation* in the extremes of anguish, horror, and despair in the exploration of the City, which is the spatial aspect of the encounter with the Immortal Homer as the vigil the troglodyte maintains is the time aspect. In chapter III we have the *confrontation* of the individual and the archetypal, and the climax of the personal ordeal of the tribune in the moment the troglodyte reveals himself as the immortal creator of the *Odyssey*.

The apprehension of the movements and tensions sustaining the confrontation is a matter of perceiving the ironical inevitability of each of the tribune's disclosures and their counterpoints, and of following the indirectness of the process of accumulative and antithetical displacements. When the tribune emerged from the last hypogeum he found the troglodyte tracing signs on the sand; he would study them and correct them, but then he erased them, as if annoyed by the game. The brutish creature appeared to exist in a world of the most insensitive, primitive humanity. He could not express, not even in mute gestures or expressions, the least indication of feeling or thought. But his presence and companionship relieved the acute sense of loneliness and desolation of the tribune. "He looked up at me, seemed not to recognize me. But so great was the solace that overwhelmed me (or so great and fearful my loneliness) that I had the thought that this rudimentary troglodyte who looked up at me from the floor of the cave had been waiting for me." The troglodyte led the way back to the village, and that night the tribune conceived the plan of teaching him to speak.

The humility and wretchedness of the troglodyte brought to his mind the image of the moribund old dog of the *Odyssey*, and he gave the troglodyte the name Argos and tried to teach it to him. The disclosure is ironical (it is, in fact, a composite of involuted ironies) because what appeared to be a fortuitous recollection was inevitable, since the troglodyte and the tribune are the two aspects of the same consciousness, separated by an expanse of centuries and sundered by an abyss of what and how they can feel; and because, as in what followed, the prolonged, ineffectual attempt to teach the sphinx-like creature the name Argos, the images, intuitions, and imaginations that occurred to the tribune, in the sequence and duration of the attempt, which lasted many years, were intimations of the absolute knowledge possessed by the archetypal mind of the troglodyte. The signs that the troglodyte traced on the sand, we infer from the context of chapter IV, were conceivably the symbols of a superhuman speculation which may well have touched, if only fleetingly, on the very confrontation taking place, in which case the existence of the tribune would have been a mere configuration of that immortal mind.

> Motionless, his eyes inert, Argos seemed not to perceive the sounds I tried to inculcate in him. But a few steps from me, he seemed to be far away. Lying on the sand like a small and ruinous lava sphinx, he let the heavens revolve over him indifferently, from the twilight of dawn to that of evening . . . I thought that Argos and I participated in different universes; I thought that our perceptions were alike, but that he combined them in another way and devised other objects with them; I thought that perhaps for him there were no objects, only a vertiginous and continual play of exceedingly brief impressions.

> I thought of a world without memory, without time; I considered the possibility of a language without substantives, a language of impersonal verbs or indeclinable epithets. Thus the days perished and with them the years, but one morning there happened something akin to felicity. It rained, with a powerful slowness.

But to consider the ironical sense of the tribune's disclosures and efforts is to become aware of the counter-tensions which define, in the futile and exasperated bewilderment of the tribune, the counter-ironical implication in the Borgian delineation of an archetypal entity. Argos' insensitivity and his wretched condition are a circumstantial feature of his immortal existence. His physical condition is as pathetic as the efforts of the tribune to penetrate his abstract thinking.

When Argos, or rather, Homer, speaks, excited to the most primitive ecstasy by the cloudburst in the desert, he stammers the phrases that are (as the expression of his condition, an immortal roused to naked sensations) equally as inevitable, and hence doubly pathetic in their symbolism, as the image of the faithful dog lying on the dung heap.

> *Argos, Ulysses' dog.* And then, also without looking at me: *This dog lying on the dung heap.*
> We accept reality easily, perhaps because we intuit that nothing is real. I asked him what he knew of the *Odyssey*. The usage of Greek was painful for him; I had to repeat my question.
> *Very little,* he said. *Less than the poorest rhapsodist. It must be a thousand and one hundred years since I invented it.*

I will not attempt to analyze the multiple ironies deflected from this, the climactic disclosure of the narrative; the ironies are evidently attempting something quite beyond analysis: the activation of meanings simultaneously revealed and disclosed as the refractive evanescence of symbols expended in the impossible effort to make literature express what it cannot express, the very transfiguration of its symbols into the higher reality where they are no longer symbols but that unfathomable reality itself. The effect of the ironies, consequently, is an instability of meanings sustained by their mutual oppositions. The troglodyte facing Flaminius Rufus reflects the mythical identities of Homer, Ulysses, and Argos as opposed and yet as one. The total effect of the ironies, again, is that of an irreconcilable antithesis provoking reactions of horror and consternation to the picture of the immortal creator compelled by the effects of time to recall his immortal creation in the image of the old dog lying on his own dung heap. But the disintegrating picture, moreover, integrates the context in which we shall be obliged to consider the value of personal literary creation in relation to "the ethic for immortals."

### 4

"Everything was made clear to me that day." The context of chapter IV is the elucidation of the events and experiences of chapters II and III, divesting those events and experiences of their suspensive and mysterious attributes, and thus provoking a disintegrating effect upon their unique and personal significance. Flaminius Rufus did not know he was immortal until the morning of the downpour, many years after he drank from the impure stream. Since the narrative moves forward through the sequential, accumulative displacements of the personal by the mythical and impersonal, the precise context of the personal pronoun "I" undergoes a series of intricate transformations throughout the five chapters or contexts. In the "I" of the personal identity of chapter I we perceived the contrapuntal intimations of an impersonal entity. In the "I" that elucidates the enigmas surrounding the troglodytes, the river of immortality, and the City, we perceive that the relations have changed; that the personal identity of Flaminius

Rufus is now the counterpoint to the impersonal tone of the entity who says: "To be immortal is commonplace. . . The divine, the terrible, the incomprehensible, is to know that one is immortal." This impersonal identity now relates the life story of Homer and the history of the Immortals and expounds their way of life, and, as the foundation of their ethics, the concept of the world as a system of precise compensations.

To know oneself to be immortal is to possess an immortal consciousness capable of knowing every experience, every thought and feeling, however base, perverted, virtuous, or noble, possible to the entire human race. Within a span of infinite time an immortal man is capable of every evil and of every good, and all things, evil or fortunate, that can happen to a man shall happen to him. To an immortal consciousness all actions are just, but also indifferent. There are no moral or intellectual merits or values because there are no personal distinctions, no personal situations, felicities, insecurities, destinies; no personal creations or inventions. To that immortal consciousness all actions, experiences, and situations are but echoes of others in the past or anticipations of others which are to occur in the future. Nothing is new or unique, and a single immortal man is all mankind.

> Homer composed the *Odyssey*; if we postulate an infinite period of time, with infinite circumstances and changes, the impossible is not to compose, at least once, the *Odyssey*. No one is anyone, one single immortal man is all men. Like Cornelius Agrippa, I am god, I am hero, I am philosopher, I am demon and I am world, all of which is a tedious way of saying that I am not.

To know oneself immortal is to postulate oneself as the anonymity and impersonality of mankind, to experience archetypal being as a reality of non-being.

The Immortals were invulnerable to pity because they were all-but-invulnerable to suffering. For them consciousness

consisted of the absorbing exertions of pure speculation, a
state of intense intellectual alertness and vigilance, which was,
for them, nonetheless, a complex state of pleasure.

The ethic of the Immortals discloses itself as the ironical
counterpart to the personal ordeal of the tribune because these
impersonal disclosures, conveyed in a tone of detachment and
indifference, are the expression of the same individual who
underwent the ordeal of will and who recounted it as an ordeal
of memory, conveying the extremes of anxiety, horror, and
despair of mortal existence. Consequently, now fully apprehending the movements of the story, we anticipate that the
ironical displacement of these disclosures is in turn forthcoming, but that, in this case, a personal identity and mortal
existence will constitute the antithesis: the search for a river
that shall restore mortality, the ordeal of an immortal being to
find death.

> Among the corollaries of the doctrine that there is no
> thing which is not compensated by another there is one
> of very little theoretical importance but which induced
> us, towards the end or beginning of the tenth century, to
> disperse ourselves over the face of the earth. It can be
> stated in these words: *There exists a river whose waters
> grant immortality; in another region there must be another
> river whose waters efface it.* The number of rivers is not
> infinite; an immortal traveller who traverses the world
> will finally, one day, have drunk from all of them. We
> proposed to discover that river.

What appears to be an equilibrium of mutual compensations between death and immortality, personality and mythical
being, is, of course, not an equilibrium at all, but the reiteration of their irreconcilability which can end only in the death
of the individual. To know oneself to be immortal is incomprehensible because it is the knowledge that consciousness is
an inexorable compulsion in time, and that an immortal con-

sciousness is neither a refutation of time nor a transfiguration of being.

The structure of tensions inevitably irreconcilable, a Borgian literary counterpart to the poised instability and disequilibrium of baroque art and music, determines that the Immortals will divest themselves of their immortality, and this action, by their ethic, is devoid of any intrinsic importance or value. This is pathetic, of course, as the end to which immortality leads; and it is ironical, because now the direction of the pathos is reversed, and the ordeal of Flaminius Rufus becomes an intimation of the personality of the archetypal creator, Homer.

> Death (or its allusion) makes men precious and pathetic. They are moving because of their phantom condition; every act they execute may be their last; there is not a face that is not on the verge of dissolving like a face in a dream. Everything among mortals has the value of the irretrievable and the perilous. Among the Immortals, on the other hand, every act (and every thought) is the echo of others that in the past preceded it, with no visible beginning, or the faithful presage of others that in the future will repeat it to the point of vertigo. There is nothing that is not as if lost amidst indefatigable mirrors. Nothing can happen only once, nothing is preciously precarious. The elegiacal, the solemn, the ceremonial, do not hold for the Immortals. Homer and I separated at the gates of Tangier; I think we did not even say goodbye.

5

The elucidations of chapter IV conclude with the discordant displacement of its own contents, accomplishing, however, in the final sentence, as a reiteration of the close of chapter III, the moment of precise opposition between Flaminius Rufus and Homer by which we know that they are identical in the sense that the archetype is immanent in the individual. Once we become accustomed to the ironical interconnections of events, of time and place, we see that their inevitability rises from the antithetical directions of the sequential movement, denoting the personal significance of the events, and of the countermovement, which protrudes now in the climactic displacements of chapter V. The impersonality prefigured in chapter I, revealed as immanent in the atrocious palace in chapter II, and confronted in the figure of the troglodyte in chapter III, asserts itself directly here in the tone of impassive indifference and detachment, as the antitheses of the anxiety of the tribune's ordeal. The countermovement, as it completes the overall antithesis of the story's theme, is in one respect the complete disintegration of the preceding contexts, but by this very effect it insures our understanding that the story is integrating itself at another level, the level at which the five contexts must be considered together as the total confrontation of the individual and the archetypal in a structure attempting to represent the simultaneous integration and disintegration in temporal duration of an individual consciousness. For this reason, then, the confrontation of chapter III, the central chapter of this seemingly impenetrable artifice, must be seen as the paradigmatic situation of the over-all structure and the situation symbolized implicitly at any given point in the story.

But now, in order to attain fully to that level of prehension, it is incumbent that we recognize that each context or chapter, as a unit, bears an ironic opposition to each of the others, which insures the interconnectedness of the whole. Like the mirrors spoken of by the tribune, each chapter deflects the contents of the others, and the whole presents us with a simultaneity of meaning in opposition to the sequentiality of experiences and events in the life span of the Immortal. The events of the story span at least sixteen centuries; nearly eleven centuries more if we count the complete age of the Homeric epics. Now, neither the esthetic pleasure derivable from the story nor the appreciation of the ideas represented in it depends upon our entertaining the slightest doubt in our minds whether that expanse of time and events could really constitute a single life time (much less a series of incarnations or avatars), and not because the story is purportedly a fantastic one, but because it is a symbolic one. The time span of the story is not an esthetic issue, but the coherency of the contexts as a symbolic, not simply a narrative unity is. That coherency Borges has attained indirectly through the ironical interconnectedness of the contexts, that is to say, the simultaneous refraction among them of a total symbolic meaning.

When we recognize that the contexts, from the intimation of the impersonal to the displacement of the personal by the impersonal, refract one another with the indirectness of irony, we become aware that the meaning of their interconnectedness, of the whole they constitute, is a symbolic meaning of which we would be unaware without the irony. To perceive that the sequential, accumulative displacements of the story accomplish their own simultaneous refraction is, then, to apprehend the irony to which Borges has pressed the antitheses of his structure in order to make possible the total confrontation of the individual and the archetypal dimensions of being.

The structure of the story, therefore, is not merely an opposition of meanings but their tensile interactions, inciting and constantly perplexing our perceptive impulses. And it is this interaction, set off by the clash of ironic indirectness, which produces the effect of an impending revelation about to disclose a further, all-embracing symbolism that we perceive imminent just beyond our grasp. The irony brings about this effect because, as it is dislocating one irreconcilable from another, it is disclosing to us the depth at which our own perceptions are provoked to infer their simultaneous validity. The irony reveals itself, by its function, as the activator of symbols which find their different and, at times, widely separated levels in our intuitions and reactions. That imminent symbolism which we intuit lies just beyond what we perceive at any given moment is the effect of the irony approaching its total possible effects. The symbolic potential of Borges' structure, then, has the peculiar quality of being inseparable from the irony, its activator. In our story, as in others of consummate workmanship, Borges brings us by the devious path of ironic indirectness to the threshold of a symbolism of superior and even transcendental attributes, but he does so by insuring that the symbols shall be delivered to us with the stipulations of irony. The quality of his art, to a great extent, can be attributed to the depth at which the tensions of this ironic stipulation compel us to activate the symbolic potentiality of his stories.

The first section of chapter V purports to narrate the events in the life of Flaminius Rufus-Cartaphilus from the eleventh century to 1921 as the continuity of the Homeric tradition through diverse languages and literatures in its multiple aspects, alluding, with deliberate inclusiveness, to the epic themes of war and adventure, the philosophical and esoteric interpretations of the Homeric poems, and the controversies and speculations about their origins and authorships. The subject, the "I", of these disclosures, we perceive, once we overcome our initial perplexity, is an impersonal entity to whom the lives of Flaminius Rufus and Cartaphilus serve as contrapuntal identities.

In 1921, on a journey (from England) to Bombay (the opposite direction of the horseman from beyond the Ganges of the first chapter), the Immortal discovered, on the outskirts of a port on the Eritrean coast, the stream whose waters restored him to mortality. The helpful note at the bottom of the page, put there by the editor Borges, suggests that "the name of the port has been erased." To call our attention to the name of the port in this way was almost unnecessary; for, by the inevitable symmetries of time and place, if the port is not the present site of ancient Berenice (the location of the tribune's camp facing the Red Sea in the first chapter) we know that it should be, since every symmetry of the story is meant to reiterate the theme of irreconcilability of opposites in the movements of recurrence and repetition, that irreconcilability being the persistence of their motions. The act of drinking of the waters of mortality is related in a tone of an impersonal, everyday felicity as the antithesis to the hallucinatory event in chapter II. "Once again I am mortal, I repeated to myself, once again I am like all men. That night, I slept until dawn."

There follows the disclosure — "After a year's time, I have re-read these pages" — by which we learn that the preceding document was written, most likely, in the year 1922;[39] that is, just after the Immortal recovered his mortality, a circumstance which might explain, for those demanding this sort of veri-similitude, the extremes of personal feeling in the early chapters and the (pathetic) indifference and impassive detachment of the last paragraph.

In the second section, a self-analysis of the entire docu-ment but especially of the section just preceding, Cartaphilus attempts an explanation of the disturbing, unreal element of his autobiography, the apparent intrusion of another man delineating himself into his account. At this point, where the ironic opposition between the three identities, Flaminius Rufus, Cartaphilus, Homer, becomes clear, the over-all anti-thesis of the story is completed. *"The history I have narrated seems unreal because in it are mixed the events of two different men."* What follows is the dislocation of the identity of Flam-inius Rufus from Joseph Cartaphilus, who now speaks of the tribune with complete objectivity, as if the opposition be-tween them were that of an author and a character he had created. We perceive that he is speaking in this manner be-cause he no longer possesses a self, a personal identity. But the concealed sense of these displacements is that Homer is the entity which defines the separate identities of Flaminius Rufus

and Cartaphilus because he is the archetype the former disclosed as identical with himself and that the other still experiences as himself. Hence the Cartaphilus who concludes the
account has been Homer and Ahasuerus, the immortal poet
and the everlasting Jew. The experiences of everyman incar-
nate, bearer of the generic consciousness of man, he no longer
possesses an identity of his own. Because the impersonality of
an immortal consciousness is irreconcilable with individual
identity, for death is what bestows on personal life its final,
irretrievable uniqueness, Cartaphilus consigns himself to the
greater and everlasting immortality of anonymity and oblivion. The resources of language itself, how much less those of
conventionalized literary expression, contain no images that
can express or approximate to an absolute impersonality and
anonymity—we recall the incredible, wretched condition of
the troglodyte—as a living, articulate presence. To have
reached such a state of "impersonal" self-expression is to have
exhausted the very possibility of expression, the personal
content of language and experience. Cartaphilus, here a symbol of the literary artist of the early twentieth century, a dealer
in literary antiques, the most precious of which are words,
concludes:

> When the end draws near, there no longer remain images
> of recall; only words remain. It is not strange that time
> should have confused the words that once represented
> me with those that were symbols of the fate of him who
> accompanied me for so many centuries. I have been
> Homer; shortly, I shall be No One, like Ulysses; shortly, I
> shall be all men: I shall be dead.

Cartaphilus, in his analysis, begins by displacing the
personal content of the Homeric borrowings in the ordeal of
Flaminius Rufus, thereby divesting the events themselves of a
unique, personal significance, and concludes by divesting the
images of recall which constitute his narrative of any but an

archetypal content. By considering the multiple refractions of this development and the contexts of the first three chapters, we infer that in writing these chapters he was not "recalling" events but prefiguring their mythical and symbolic "content." Like the ordeal of recall, the present analysis must be read as a series of intimations of the symbolic character Homer, who remains throughout always in character—that is, a symbol of human consciousness and an archetype of the immortal creator. This series, refracted in chapters I and II and there allowing us to infer that the compulsion the tribune obeys is an intimation of an archetypal entity, is here completely divested of any emotive tension; yet for this reason they express a counter sense to the earlier compulsion: the pathetic fragility of an impersonal consciousness.

When we compare Cartaphilus' final disclosure and the Postscript of 1950 reporting the scrutiny of the document by Dr. Nahum Cordovero (a rather erudite critic, but incapable of coping with higher Borgian symbolism), and his conclusion that the entire document is apocryphal, with Borges' concluding comment, we are in a position, with these three pointers, to respond to the total irony of the confrontation. I shall cite only Borges' final comment:

> In my judgment, the conclusion is inadmissible. *When the end draws near,* Cartaphilus wrote, *there no longer remain images of recall; only words remain.* Words, displaced and mutilated words, words of others, were the meagre alms left to him by the hours and the centuries.

Cartaphilus, disturbed by the intruding references to Homer, points them out as if they were circumstantial contaminations, due to the inherent falseness of the poetic method and the corruptive nature of memory. We apprehend, nonetheless, that they were inevitable and have some notion as to why, but an impersonal mind sees this fact in reverse direction to ours, and this incompatibility, with its dislocating

effect, is the ironic opposition between the sequential and
countermovements of the story at its close. Cartaphilus has
written, as a personal narrative, an account which is equally
the impersonal narrative of Homer; and his document, in all
its pathetic self-effacement, expectancy and transparency, may
stand as a Borgian paradigm of the creative process of literature, as well as a twentieth-century re-creation of Homeric
themes.

Dr. Cordovero's inference, that the entire document is
apocryphal, is, then, precisely half the truth. In its conception,
the entire narrative is meant to be a fabric of interpolations, a
seemingly incidental assortment of quotations and references,
but in fact a dense symbolic interweaving of literary tradition,
seen in its continuity as a circumstantial equation between
oblivion and memory at any given point. The Postscript, a
parodistic indictment of his own baffled critics, is only Borges'
ironic manner of pointing this out to us. What Borges does not
point out, however, is that he has executed a structure of
"intrusions or interpolations" that not only evokes a myth and
a whole literary tradition within a specific emotive context,
like Eliot's in *The Waste Land,* and represents a symbolic consciousness within a pattern of temporal duration and recurrence, like Joyce's in *Finnegans Wake,* but that provides us also,
with marvelous economy, with a complete set of refractive
contexts by which we can approach the myth, re-experience
the tradition, apprehend the operative concepts of time and
memory, and attempt to decipher the symbol. In the fabric, the
interpolations, activated as symbols through their ironic re-
fractibility, possess simultaneously a personal and an impersonal sense, and out of the ironic opposition there emerges an
artifice of symbols providing us with an unceasing source of
surprise precisely because the irony has insured that the effect
will be that this disclosure of the total meaning of the symbols,
which yet constantly eludes our grasp, is still constantly imminent; but a narrative of such deviousness, one must admit,

would be beyond the critical sensitivity of a Dr. Cordovero.

It is this irony of baroque elegance, then, which brings into focus, as an interconnected whole, the integration of an impersonal identity and memory through the disintegration of a personal history; the resolution of life as "form," withstanding the dissolution of time and death in mortality rather than in immortality, and the imperishability of a single, unique individual life through the perishability of language and memory. As a Borges hero of consciousness the Immortal drinks first from the river of immortality and enters upon and becomes identical with an archetypal existence which can yet only express itself, pathetically, through the tensions of his effaced individual "I"; then he seeks, finds, and drinks from the river whose waters restore him to mortality; he dies, consigned to the "nothingness" of death that completes the meaning of life as "form." The ironic structure of simultaneity of meanings insures, as a symbolic cohesion, the total confrontation of the individual and the archetypal by which we intuit intimately, and always perforce just beyond our grasp, the unfathomable meaning and mystery behind all symbolism; but that meaning and that mystery can be none other than our own experience of ourselves as individuals and yet as Man and his destiny in the world.

*NOTES*
*INDEX*

*NOTES*
*James Joyce: The Way of Irony to the Threshold of Myth*

1. See *The Workshop of Daedalus, James Joyce and the Raw Materials for "A Portrait of the Artist as a Young Man,"* Collected and edited by Robert Scholes and Richard M. Kain (Northwestern University Press, 1965), pp. 56–74; pp. 65–66. The material was published earlier in *Yale Review,* 49:355–367 (1960).

2. See Richard Ellmann, *James Joyce* (New York: Oxford University Press, 1959), pp. 149–153.

3. *Correspondance* (*Oeuvres complètes,* Paris, 1926–33), [Letter of May, 1852] II, p. 407. See Harry Levin, "*Madame Bovary*: The Cathedral and the Hospital," *Essays in Criticism,* 2: 23 (1952); *The Gates of Horn* (New York: Oxford University Press, 1963), p. 269.

4. *Correspondance* [Letter of January, 1854], IV, p. 15.

5. *Feuilles détachées, Oeuvres complètes,* ed. H. Psichari (Paris [19--]), II, p. 1160. See Haakon M. Chevalier, *The Ironic Temper, Anatole France and His Time* (New York: Oxford University Press, 1932), pp. 46–47.

6. Chevalier, *The Ironic Temper,* pp. 3,5 ff.

7. Ellmann, *James Joyce,* p. 199; *L*[II] 81.

8. The asterisk refers one to Theo. Spencer's note: "The changed wording is written in pencil in the margin, perhaps at a later date than that of the MS."

9. See the review Joyce wrote on *Catilina* in 1903, CW 98–101, and the comments of the editors, Ellsworth Mason and Richard Ellmann.

10. See Ellmann, *James Joyce,* p. 201.

11. *Ibid.,* pp. 154–155, 180.

12. *Ibid.,* pp. 154–155.

13. *Ibid.,* p. 241; *L*[II] 219. The letter to Stanislaus Joyce, undated, was probably written in March 1907.

14. *Dublin's Joyce* (London: Chatto and Windus, 1955 [Indiana University Press, 1956]), p. 43.

15. Introduction and Notes to *Chamber Music* (Columbia University Press, 1954).

16. See Ellmann, *James Joyce,* pp. 181, 300–301.

17. Letter to Grant Richards, May 5, 1906, *L*[II] 134.

18. See S. L. Goldberg, *James Joyce* ([Edinburgh, Oliver and

Boyd] New York, Grove Press, 1962), ch. 2, p. 39; Marvin Magalaner and Richard M. Kain, *Joyce, The Man, the Work, the Reputation* (New York, 1962), ch. 4; Hugh Kenner, *Dublin's Joyce*, ch. 5; Marvin Magalaner, *Time of Apprenticeship, The Fiction of Young James Joyce* (New York and London, 1959), ch. 3; William York Tindall, *A Reader's Guide to James Joyce* (New York, 1959), pp. 3–49; Harry Levin, *James Joyce, A Critical Introduction* (New Directions, 1960), pp. 29ff; and David Daiches' study in *The Novel and the Modern World* (University of Chicago Press, 1960), ch. 4.

19. See Fritz Senn's article on Joyce's scrupulous use of words: "'He Was Too Scrupulous Always,' Joyce's 'The Sisters,'" *James Joyce Quarterly*, (hereafter referred to as *JJQ*), 2:66–72 (Winter 1965).

20. See Clive Hart's important discussion of the parallel between the close of "Eveline" and the close of *Finnegans Wake*, in *Structure and Motif in "Finnegans Wake"* (London: Faber and Faber, 1962 [Northwestern University Press, 1962], pp. 53–55; hereafter referred to by the short title *Structure*.

21. Letter to Grant Richards, May 5, 1906, *L*II 134.

22. Florence L. Walzl points out the advanced state of ironic inversion in the religious symbols of this story: "Symbolism in Joyce's 'Two Gallants,'" *JJQ*, 2:73–81 (Winter 1965).

23. See A. Walton Litz, *The Art of James Joyce, Method and Design in "Ulysses" and "Finnegans Wake"* (London: Oxford University Press, 1961), p. 2; Ellmann, *James Joyce*, pp. 274–275.

24. *James Joyce*, ch. 15; see p. 262.

25. *Ibid.* See also John V. Kelleher, "Irish History and Mythology in James Joyce's 'The Dead,'" *Review of Politics*, 27:414–433 (July 1965); and a detailed reading by Florence L. Walzl of the closing passage: "Gabriel and Michael: The Conclusion of 'The Dead,'" *JJQ*, 4:17–31 (Fall 1966).

26. "The *Portrait* in Perspective," in *James Joyce: Two Decades of Criticism*, ed. Seon Givens (New York [1948] 1963), pp. 154–155; *Dublin's Joyce*, ch. 8; also A. Walton Litz, *The Art of James Joyce*, p. 3.

27. The most recent discussion is F. Parvin Sharpless,

"Irony in Joyce's *Portrait*: The Stasis of Pity," *JJQ*, 4:320–330 (Summer 1967). See also, in this issue of *JJQ*, the statements by James Naremore on pp. 336–337. The earlier commentaries are: S. H. Poss, "A Portrait of the Artist as Beginner," *University of Kansas City Review*, 26:189–196 (Spring 1960); Robert E. Scholes, "Stephen Dedalus: *Eiron* and *Alazon*," *Texas Studies in Literature and Language*, 3:7–15 (1961); S. L. Goldberg's statements in *The Classical Temper, A Study of James Joyce's "Ulysses"* (London: Chatto and Windus, 1961 [New York: Barnes and Noble, 1961]), pp. 109–111, and in *James Joyce,* ch. 3; Maurice Beebe, "Joyce and Stephen Dedalus: The Problem of Autobiography" in *A James Joyce Miscellany, Second Series,* ed. Marvin Magalaner (Southern Illinois University Press, 1959), pp. 67–77; a passing diagnosis by Harry Levin in "Symbolism and Fiction," *Contexts of Criticism* (Harvard University Press, 1957), p. 193; and, of course, Hugh Kenner's opinions noted above.

28. My statements are based on Ellmann's in *James Joyce,* pp. 274–275, 283, 361, 365.

29. See Robert S. Ryf, *A New Approach to Joyce, The "Portrait of the Artist" as a Guidebook* (University of California Press, 1962), pp. 165ff.

30. "A Portrait of the Artist," p. 60. See note 1 above.

31. See Robert Martin Adams, *Surface and Symbol, The Consistency of James Joyce's "Ulysses"* (New York: Oxford University Press, 1962), p. 250; the statements by S. L. Goldberg in *The Classical Temper,* pp. 33–36, and by Mark Schorer in "Technique as Discovery" in *Forms of Modern Fiction,* ed. Wm. V. O'Connor (University of Minnesota Press, 1948), p. 22.

32. On the labyrinth images and theme see David Hayman, "Daedalian Imagery in *A Portrait . . .*" *Hereditas,* Seven Essays . . .," ed. Frederic Will (University of Texas Press, 1964), pp. 33–54; H. M. McLuhan "Joyce, Aquinas, and the Poetic Process," *Renascence,* IV, no. 1 (1951), p. 9, or *Joyce's "Portrait", Criticisms and Critiques,* ed. Thomas E. Connolly (New York, 1962), pp. 257–259.

33. Hugh Kenner, *Dublin's Joyce,* p. 132.

34. *James Joyce,* p. 63; see also *The Classical Temper,* pp. 33ff.

35. "Introductory: The Zeit Geist," *Transition, Essays on Contemporary Literature* (London, Hogarth Press; New York, Viking Press, 1926), pp. 3–16. When Edwin Muir, on page 37, says "It was because he [Joyce] went back so far to the fundamentals of art that his book had its enigmatic, primal atmosphere, and seemed, in spite of its modernity, hoary with years," he is underscoring the "mythical quality" of *Ulysses*; see p. 38.

36. Quotations are from *James Joyce, A Critical Introduction*, rev. ed. (1960), p. 68

37. *Ibid.*, p. 73.

38. *Ibid.*, p. 124.

39. *Ibid.*, p. 134. See also Frank Budgen, *James Joyce and the Making of "Ulysses"* (Indiana University Press, 1961), p. 284.

40. *Dublin's Joyce*, p. 11.

41. *Ibid.*, p. 207.

42. *Ibid.*, p. 10.

43. *Ibid.*, p. 209.

44. *Ibid.*, p. 242.

45. *Ibid.*, p. 256.

46. See note 27 above. Page references to *The Classical Temper* are indicated within parentheses following the end of each quotation.

47. *Fabulous Voyager, James Joyce's "Ulysses"* (New York, 1959), ch. XIII. A scholarly discussion of Joyce's irony by Father William T. Noon appears in *Joyce and Aquinas* (Yale University Press, 1957), pp. 88ff.

48. *James Joyce and the Making of "Ulysses,"* p. 257. To another correspondent Joyce wrote: "I like the episode myself. I find it of a tranquilising spectrality," *L* 176. Stuart Gilbert, *James Joyce's "Ulysses," A Study* (New York, 1960), p. 370, and Frank Budgen, p. 258, both report that "Ithaca" was Joyce's "favorite episode."

49. See Rudolph Von Abele, "*Ulysses*: The Myth of Myth," *PMLA*, 69:358–364 (1954).

50. After S. L. Goldberg's arguments (*Classical Temper*, pp. 300ff), it hardly needs saying that there are numerous aspects only partially successful, some even defective, in

*Ulysses*, but these (in my opinion) pertain chiefly to Joyce's attitude toward matters or events other than the intensity with which his main characters are drawn and the elaborate means used to bring the drama of their relationship to a focus. In the final analysis it is the human depth of the life-like complexity of Bloom and Stephen that contains and communicates the intimacy and artistic value of Joyce's exploration of conjugal love, fatherhood, Ulyssean constancy and resourcefulness.

51. See the remarks by Clive Hart, *Structure*, pp. 25ff, and by R. M. Adams, *Surface and Symbol*, pp. 41 and 147.

52. Clive Hart, *Structure*, p. 49.

53. There is, needless to say, an ironical dimension in *Exiles*, but it does not offer the interest or the novelty of the prose works. One can only agree with the majority of Joyce's critics that his play is of much less importance than his prose narratives.

54. *The Classical Temper*, p. 263.

55. This essay on Joyce's irony was completed many months before I saw William Blissett's on Joyce and Wagner: "James Joyce in the Smithy of his Soul" in *James Joyce Today, Essays on the Major Works*, ed. Thomas F. Staley (Indiana University Press, 1966), pp. 96–134. Mr. Blissett anticipates, in various passages, a portion of what I have to say on irony and myth. The vantage point is his, because he has, as an approach to Joyce, Wagner's fusion of myth and music to start with; but he richly deserves the rewards. Of *Ulysses* he says: "If the literary symbol is the Wagnerian myth writ small . . . Joyce re-expands the literary symbol into myths to rival Wagner's. His mode is, of course, comic and ironic while Wagner's is heroic and tragic (p. 121)." "What has been asserted about the musicality of Joyce's art [in *Ulysses*] . . . applies the more strongly to . . . *Finnegans Wake*, which indeed can only be read and described on such assumptions . . . for what in the *Wake* is not leitmotif, what is not myth? (p. 127)."

56. Richard Ellmann, "The Limits of Joyce's Naturalism," *Sewanee Review*, 63:567–575 (1955); the parallel passages in *James Joyce* appear on pp. 562–563.

57. I have found Northrop Frye's speculations helpful,

but needless to say my assumptions about myth and the mythical are broader than those he considers, and the manner in which I apply them to a specific author more restrictive. In *Anatomy of Criticism* see pp. 42–43 and 136–137.

58. My approach to the structure and "total meaning" of *Finnegans Wake* is schematic and speculative to a degree, but based on a comprehensive estimate of the findings and insights of a number of Joycean scholars and critics. I am indebted most directly to Clive Hart, James S. Atherton, David Hayman, A. Walton Litz, Richard Ellmann, M. J. C. Hodgart, and John V. Kelleher. I have acknowledged my specific indebtedness to them, and to other critics and scholars, in the notes below. In some cases my acknowledgment appears in the text above.

59. The *Wake* is a work of reconciliation in at least two very definite contexts. In the context of Joyce's personal attitude toward Ireland it represents the attainment of a paternal-like tolerance rather evidently proportionate to the impulse to treat themes of Irish legend and history as comedy and burlesque, as is apparent from the very first sketch set down for the book in March 1923, the "King Roderick O'Conor" piece. See M. J. C. Hodgart, "The Earliest Sections of *Finnegans Wake*," *The James Joyce Review*, 1: 3–18 (1957); David Hayman, ed., *A First Draft Version of "Finnegans Wake"* (University of Texas Press, 1963), pp. 6, 21.

In the context of a twentieth-century "resurrection myth," Joyce's structure of cyclical recurrence and ironic vision reconcile the naturalistic representation of individual destinies to a mythical configuration of human destiny as proposed by, or deducible from, the advances of psychology and anthropology into the areas of knowledge and the interpretation of experience once occupied exclusively by religion. It is the second of these contexts to which the usual discussions of the cyclical structure as a fusion of the One and the Many, or of the *Wake* as a contemporary myth with a mystico-scientific nucleus, are to be referred, but all such interpretative discussions, it seems to me, must rest necessarily on an implied recognition of the first. Another context, a corollary of the first, would explain the *Wake* as a result of Joyce's coming to terms with both the ambition and the limitations of his art at the apex of its maturity.

Still another context, the personal and confessional, is delineated by Ruth Von Phul in "Circling the Square: A Study of Structure," *A James Joyce Miscellany*, 3rd ser., ed. M. Magalaner (Southern Illinois University Press, 1962), pp. 239ff. James S. Atherton has an illuminating passage in *The Books at the Wake* (New York: Viking Press, 1960), pp. 23–24.

60. William Irwin Thompson points out that the *Wake* "is stereotypal, not archetypal; the structure, with its concern for the circle and the square, has archetypal pattern, but the language and the stories do not." "The Language of *Finnegans Wake*," *Sewanee Review*, 72:82 (1964).

61. The case for the year 1932 is detailed briefly by Vivian Mercier in "In the Wake of the Fianna," *A James Joyce Miscellany*, 3rd ser., pp. 230–231. See also Nathan Halper's arguments in favor of the year 1922: "The Date of Earwicker's Dream," in *Twelve and a Tilly*, Essays . . . ed. Jack P. Dalton and Clive Hart (London, 1966), pp. 72–90.

62. *James Joyce's Scribbledehobble, The Ur-Workbook for "Finnegans Wake,"* ed. Thomas E. Connolly (Northwestern University Press, 1961), p. 104.

63. "Quest and Cycle in *Finnegans Wake*," *The James Joyce Review*, 1:39–47 (1957). Quotations are from pp. 44–47. Also in *Fables of Identity* (New York: Harcourt, Brace, World, 1963), pp. 262–264. A parallel passage appears in *Anatomy of Criticism*, pp. 323–324.

64. Two volumes of essays on Joyce appeared in 1966, containing new, valuable expert opinion on the *Wake: Twelve and a Tilly, Essays on the Occasion of the 25th Anniversary of Finnegans Wake,* eds. Jack P. Dalton and Clive Hart (London: Faber and Faber, 1966); *James Joyce Today, Essays on the Major Works,* ed. Thomas F. Staley (Indiana University Press, 1966). In *James Joyce Today* see Clive Hart, "*Finnegans Wake* in Perspective," pp. 135–165. Also his articles "The Elephant in the Belly: Exegesis of *Finnegans Wake*," *A Wake Newslitter*, no. 13, May 1963; and "The Hound and the Type-bed: Further Notes

on the Text of *Finnegans Wake*," *A Wake Newslitter*, n.s. vol. III, no. 4 (August 1966), in part a reply to Jack Dalton's essay "Advertisement for the Restoration," in *Twelve and a Tilly*, pp. 119–137.

65. *Structure*, p. 115.

66. *Ibid.*, p. 36.

67. "Joyce Digested," *Accent*, 5:182 (Spring 1945).

68. I quote from Breon Mitchell's paraphrase in "The Newer Alchemy: Lord Rutherford and *Finnegans Wake*," *A Wake Newslitter*, n.s. vol. III, no. 5 (October 1966), pp. 96–102. Mitchell fails to mention the defecation motifs in the passage.

69. I do not wish to give the impression I am minimizing Joyce's labyrinthine obscurity; I could hardly do that, or the "immense labour of exegesis," as Walton Litz (*The Art of James Joyce*, p. 73) names the process, which even the best of Joyce's readers must devote to his text before the effect of simultaneity becomes easeful and familiar. On the other hand, I think it is necessary to insist that our labors of exegesis pertain to the quantitative elaboration of Joyce's themes and in many cases, as indispensable as they are, go no further than the mere enumeration of them.

70. See Clive Hart, *Structure*, p. 51.

71. David Hayman, "From *Finnegans Wake*: A Sentence in Progress," *PMLA*, 73:154 (March 1958).

72. The phrase is Samuel Beckett's, *Our Exagmination . . .* (New Directions, 1962), p. 14.

73. My drawing is an Archimedean spiral "stylized" after Brancusi's "Symbol," that is, the direction of revolution is clockwise, and the fourth revolution terminates at the point where it intersects the initial line. It should surprise no one that Brancusi's abstract is as old as the Spiral of Archimedes; or that Archimedes' Book of Spirals should furnish, as an equivalence between mathesis and myth, an exegetical device for *Finnegans Wake*. Archimedes, or his ghost, makes one appearance at the *Wake*: "archimade levirs of his ekonome world" 230.34.

Brancusi's "Symbol of Joyce" served as the frontispiece in *Tales Told of Shem and Shaun* (Paris: Black Sun Press, 1929

[1930]). According to Caresse Crosby, the book did not appear until the Spring of 1930; see *The Passionate Years* (London, 1955), pp. 195–197; Ellmann, *James Joyce*, pp. 627–628, 803.

Richard Ellmann remarks that the symbol is a "curleycue intended, as Brancusi said later, to express the *'sens du pousser'* which he found in Joyce; the sense of enigmatic involution is also conveyed" (*James Joyce*, p. 627). It is my impression that Brancusi made the drawing "Symbol of Joyce" before he made the metal spiral called "Portrait of James Joyce," photographed in Carola Giedion-Welcker, *Constantin Brancusi*, trans. Maria Jolas and Anne Leroy (New York, 1959), p. 198; or, if the metal spiral was done first, it was named after the drawing. See also Richard M. Kain and Alan M. Cohn, "Portraits of James Joyce: A Revised List," *JJQ* 3:206–207 (Spring 1966).

The Musée National d'Art Moderne, in Paris, owns two drawings by Brancusi that are probably preliminary sketches for the two studies done in 1929 and mentioned in *L 279*. I am indebted for this information to Marielle de Lavilléon, who is in charge of cataloguing Brancusi's works for the Museum; she also informs me that the metal spiral is missing.

74. *James Joyce: Two Decades of Criticism*, ed. Seon Givens (New York: Vanguard Press, 1963), p. 9. There are several versions of the story. This one, I gather, was original with Joyce. See *L 279, 312*; and Ellmann, *James Joyce*, p. 627.

75. Hart, *Structure*, ch. 2; pp. 73–75.

76. "Quest and Cycle . . ." (See note 63).

77. See the remarks by Clive Hart, *Structure*, pp. 14, 38–43, 188; by Walton Litz, *The Art of James Joyce*, p. 44.

78. My task, and the task of future exegetes, has been made immeasurably easier by Clive Hart's *A Concordance to "Finnegans Wake"* (University of Minnesota Press, 1963), and Adaline Glasheen's *A Second Census of "Finnegans Wake"* (Northwestern University Press, 1963).

79. "From Work in Progress," *Contact Collection of Contemporary Writers* (Paris [1925]), pp. 133–136.

80. See note 59 above.

81. "From Work in Progress," pp. 135–136.

82. See note 72 above.

83. See Atherton, *The Books at the Wake*, pp. 227, 243.
84. See Hart, *Structure*, p. 186.
85. Claude Lévi-Strauss, "The Structural Study of Myth," in *Myth, A Symposium,* ed. Thomas A. Sebeok (Indiana University Press, 1958), p. 51 (1965 ed., p. 83).
86. Ernst Cassirer, *An Essay on Man* (Yale University Press, 1944), p. 81.
87. Hart, *Structure*, p. 130.
88. "From *Finnegans Wake*: A Sentence in Progress," pp. 136 – 154. See note 71 above.
89. Atherton, *The Books at the Wake*, pp. 114ff.
90. See Eugene Jolas, "My Friend James Joyce" in *James Joyce: Two Decades of Criticism*, pp. 11 – 12.
91. Hart, *Structure*, pp. 83 – 95.
92. *Ibid*, p. 68.
93. *Ibid*, p. 206.
94. See also Clive Hart's Index of Motifs, *Structure*, p. 231.

*Jorge Luis Borges: The Ways of Irony in the Labyrinth of Consciousness*

1. "Cabe sospechar que la realidad no pertenece a ningún género literario; juzgar que nuestra vida es una novela es tan aventurado como juzgar que es un colofón o un acróstico." Address to the Society of Argentine Writers in 1945 on occasion of its Award of Honor to Borges for *Ficciones.* Published in *Sur,* n. 129 (1945), pp. 120 – 121.

The best introductions to Borges for English readers are those by Paul de Man, *New York Review of Books*, Nov. 19, 1964, pp. 8 – 11, and James E. Irby in *Labyrinths* and *Other Inquisitions* (cited below). For the student of Borges' works the following bibliographies are available: a very useful one compiled by Ana María Barrenechea, and included in *La expresión de la irrealidad en la obra de Jorge Luis Borges* (Colegio de México, 1957), only part of which appears in the English translation of this work: *Borges, The Labyrinth Maker*, ed. and trans. Robert Lima (New York University Press, 1965); also

Nodier Lucio y Lydia Revello, "Contribución a la bibliografía de Jorge Luis Borges," *Bibliografía argentina de artes y letras* 10/11 (1961), pp. 45ff; (in French) in the volume of *L'Herne* (1964) devoted to Borges, pp. 487–516; and the review article on Miss Barrenechea's book by James E. Irby in *Nueva Revista de Filología Hispánica*, 16:125–132 (1962).

To date the following works by Borges are available in book-form in English:

*Labyrinths, Selected Stories and Other Writings*, ed. Donald A. Yates and James E. Irby, with a Preface by André Maurois (Norfolk, Conn.: New Directions, 1962); augmented edition published in 1964 as New Directions Paperbook 186. Page references below to the 1964 edition are indicated with the short title *Labyrinths*. Yates and Irby provide a skeletal bibliography of Borges' works and a partial list of translations of poems, stories, or essays available in English and in several other languages.

*Ficciones*, edited and with an Introduction by Anthony Kerrigan (New York: Grove Press [London: Weidenfeld and Nicolson], 1962); the complete text of *Ficciones* (Buenos Aires, 1956) translated by several hands. I refer to this volume as *Ficciones*, Eng. trans., etc.

*Dreamtigers*, translated from *El hacedor* (*The Maker*) by Mildred Boyer and Harold Morland (University of Texas Press, 1964).

*Other Inquisitions, 1937–1952*, trans. Ruth L. C. Simms, Introduction by James E. Irby (University of Texas Press, 1965; New York: Washington Square Press, 1966). Page references below are to the latter edition.

*A Personal Anthology*, edited and with a Foreword by Anthony Kerrigan (New York: Grove Press, 1967; London: Jonathan Cape, 1968).

Except where noted otherwise, I quote and translate from *Obras completas de Jorge Luis Borges* (Buenos Aires, Emecé Editores), and refer to these volumes with the symbol *OC*. All translations from Borges are my own. In my text I furnish a complete translation of "The God's Script" (*La escritura del dios*), which is the translation published in *Labyrinths*. This translation, and the excerpts translated from "El jardín de senderos que se bifurcan," "La muerte y la brújula," "Emma Zunz," and "El inmortal," are authorized and reprinted by kind permission of New Directions Publishing Corporation, New York, Publishers of Jorge Luis Borges, *Labyrinths*, Donald A. Yates and James E. Irby, eds., and Laurence Pollinger, Ltd., London. Page references to *OC* are followed in my notes by references to the corresponding passages in the book-form translations available in English.

A complete English text of the other four stories included in my study will be found as follows:

"The Garden of Forking Paths," in *Labyrinths* and *Ficciones*.

"Death and the Compass," in *Labyrinths*, *Ficciones*, and *Personal Anthology*.

"Emma Zunz," in *Labyrinths*.

"The Immortal," in *Labyrinths*.

2. Prologue to "Artificios" (Postscript, 1956) in *Ficciones, OC* (1956), p. 116. *Ficciones*, Eng. trans., p. 105. For another list of books and authors see *Discusión, OC* (1957), p. 165.

3. Numerous instances could be quoted where Borges speaks of his literary indebtedness. The following forms part of the address quoted above in note 1: "For many years I thought I had been reared in a suburb of Buenos Aires, a suburb of venturesome streets and visible sunsets. The truth is I grew up in a garden, behind a long wall, and in a library of illimitable English books. Palermo of the knife and guitar loitered on the streetcorners (so I am told) but they who populated my mornings and furnished pleasant horror to my evenings were Stevenson's blind buccaneer, dying under the horses' hooves, and the traitor who abandoned his friend on the moon and the voyager of time, who returned from the future with a withered flower, and the genius imprisoned for centuries in the Solomonic waterjug, and the Veiled Prophet of Khorasan who concealed his leprosy behind jewels and silk. More than thirty years have passed, the house where those fictions were revealed to me has been demolished, I have travelled to and from the cities of Europe, I have forgotten

thousands of pages, thousands of irreplaceable human faces, but often I think that, essentially, I have never left that library and that garden. What have I done since, what shall I yet do, but weave and unweave stories derived from those stories?" Cf. Prólogo, *Evaristo Carriego, OC* (1955), pp. 9–10.

4. "Yo diría que barroco es aquel estilo que deliberadamente agota (o quiere agotar) sus posibilidades y que linda con su propia caricatura." Prologue, 2nd ed., *Historia universal de la infamia, OC* (1954), p. 9.

5. The first essay of the volume bearing the same title, *Historia de la eternidad,* 1st ed., 1936, 2nd ed., *OC,* 1953.

6. The concluding essay of *Otras inquisiciones, OC,* 1960; *Labyrinths,* pp. 217–234; *Other Inquisitions,* pp. 180–198.

7. See "Dos esquinas: sentirse en muerte" in *El idioma de los argentinos* (Buenos Aires, 1928); *Otras inquisiciones, OC,* pp. 245–248; *Labyrinths,* pp. 225–227; *Other Inquisitions,* pp. 188–190.

8. See page 162. On Borges' notions of a "circular time" see Roger Caillois, "Les thèmes fondamentaux de J. L. Borges," *L'Herne* (1964), pp. 211–217.

9. Prologue to *Ficciones, OC,* p. 12; Eng. trans. pp. 15–16.

10. "El primer Wells," *Otras inquisiciones, OC,* pp. 126–127; *Other Inquisitions,* p. 91.

11. *Otras inquisiciones, OC,* p. 256; *Labyrinths.* pp. 233–234; *Other Inquisitions,* p. 197. For an earlier discussion than mine of Borges' irony see Rafael Gutiérrez Girardot, *Jorge Luis Borges, ensayo de interpretación* (Madrid, 1959), pp. 82–120.

12. Note on M. Davidson, *The Free Will Controversy* (London, 1943), in *Discusión, OC,* pp. 176–177.

13. In the volume published by *Sur* and bearing the same title: *El jardín de senderos que se bifurcan* (Buenos Aires [1941], 1942). The stories comprising this volume now form the first part of *Ficciones.*

14. *Ibid.,* Prologue (dated Nov. 10, 1941), p. 7. My translation of the story is based on this edition. I am indebted to Anthony Boucher for permission to use his translation of "The Garden" (*Ellery Queen's Mystery Magazine,* August, 1948, pp. 311–322) as a basis for revising mine. Mr. Boucher ex-

plained to me that, with Borges' acquiescence, he had changed the name of the English sinologist in the story from "Albert" to "Corbie" (the name of a village just east of the point where the Ancre joins the Somme) because he felt that it was very improbable that only a single listing would appear under Albert in a London telephone directory. His apprehension I found less surprising than Borges' acquiescence. Early in the story we are told that the two German spies are in Staffordshire, and we are not led to assume that the directory Yu Tsun consults is a London directory; it is a local one, perhaps from a city in the Midlands. Other details are equally plausible. The Gazetteer in *The Times Survey Atlas of the World* (1922) lists a Fenton in Staffordshire; described in *Encyl. Brit.*, 11th ed. (1910), X, 260. However, Borges' intentions are not to bring off a reasonably plausible detective fiction. His purpose in arranging precise facts and details may well be to mislead or deflect, if not confuse, his reader's impulse to grasp a given detail as ostensibly "probable" or "realistic."

15. Granted the reference to Liddell Hart's *History* is wholly for purposes of fiction, it seems necessary, for the sake of the minimum degree of plausibility, to insist on a date in June 1916, because July 24–29 was part of an extremely dry period on the Somme front and because, after the attack of July 1 and the subsequent British advance, a German defense line Serre-Montauban could not have been drawn on July 24th. "Serre-Montauban" does designate a front line on July 1st and an alignment of thirteen British divisions.

I suspect (if the error is not deliberate) that a transcribing or private oversight of sorts is involved. If we correct "junio" for "julio de 1916," an *n* for an *l*, we have a plausible date on which to support the fiction. The closest situation I find in Liddell Hart's *History* to Borges' "facts" appears on page 314 of the Boston edition, 1935. There we read that a bombardment began on June 24th and that the attack (of thirteen divisions) intended for June 29th was postponed until July 1st. June 24–29, as the account in the *Official History* compiled by Sir James E. Edmonds (London, 1932, "1916," vol. I [vol. V:1], pp. 302–303) will disclose in detail, was a period of fog, thunderstorms, and rain. Liddell Hart's *History* is one of the books Borges diligently annotated ca. 1940, *Discusión, OC,* p. 165.

16. See "El ruiseñor de Keats," *Otras inquisiciones, OC,* pp. 165–169; "The Nightingale of Keats," *Other Inquisitions,* pp. 127–130.

17. I have dealt elsewhere with the labyrinth theme in Borges' stories: "The Labyrinths of Jorge Luis Borges," *Modern Language Quarterly,* 20:259–266 (1959).

18. See Burton Watson, *Ssu-ma Ch'ien, Grand Historian of China* (Columbia University Press, 1958), pp. 101–104. The idea of a *Chinese* labyrinthine garden is apparently an invention of Borges. All of the features of a Chinese garden mentioned by Yu Tsun, pavilions, meandering pathways, watercourses, the "mountain," are common to the gardens of China; likewise the conception of a garden laid out with cosmological and mythological aspects. (See Osvald Sirén, *Gardens of China,* New York, 1949, pp. 70–84; Edward Schafer, *Tu Wan's Stone Catalogue of Cloudy Forest, A Commentary and Synopsis,* University of California Press, 1961, p. 5.) But a garden laid out on a "labyrinth" plan has never been a Chinese practice and a Chinese garden-book-labyrinth is apparently only conceivable as the Borgian parodistic notion of what the Western mind and sensibility can read into the irregular and unexpected intricacy of Oriental linear design. The Chinese elements in Borges' story comprise a "puzzle" of bewildering perplexity, which a Western intellect will be compelled to decipher by hypothesizing a solution of the "inscrutable." The disparity between the Chinese conception of an intricate garden as an imitation of nature and a Westerner's conception of a cosmological labyrinth-time derived from it are the basis for Albert's fallibility in the story. The coincidence of *thirteen* British divisions in the attack on the Somme and *thirteen* years spent by Ts'ui Pên on his novel is a numerology playing on Borges' "Chinese puzzle" theme. The "Montauban" of the battle-line description is the "inevitable" Borgian coincidence and connective to the cosmic mountain of Chinese garden symbolism. The "mountain" is appropriately hidden in the compression of themes in the passage:

Algo entiendo de laberintos: no en vano soy bisnieto de aquel Ts'ui Pên, que fué gobernador de Yunnan y que renunció al poder temporal para escribir una novela que fuera todavía más populosa que el *Hung Lu Meng* y para edificar un laberinto en el que se perdieran todos los hombres. Trece años dedicó a esas heterogéneas fatigas, pero la mano de un forastero lo asesinó y su novela era insensata y nadie encontró el laberinto. Bajo árboles ingleses medité en ese laberinto perdido: lo imaginé inviolado y perfecto en la cumbre secreta de una montaña, lo imaginé borrado por arrozales o debajo del agua, lo imaginé infinito, no ya de quioscos ochavados y de sendas que vuelven, sino de ríos y provincias y reinos.

19. See p. 123 and notes 7, 8 above.

20. An amiable reader of these pages in typescript remarked that Borges' "Garden," with its center, gate, and pathways, ought to have suggested the symbolism of medieval literary gardens to me. I agree. But the associations of garden symbolism —from the Garden of Eden (knowledge of good and evil) to Gethsemane (betrayal)—are universal (and exceedingly various). Borges' story is of course about a quest in a garden, a quest for knowledge, or knowing, about an act of murder that becomes a cognitive act. And is it necessary to remind ourselves that murder and garden are connected etymologically in our word *assassin?* In the legendary garden of Hassan ben Sabbah there grew the hashish that inspired his followers to murder. J. E. Cirlot's *Dictionary of Symbols* (New York: Philosophical Library, 1962, p. 110) tells us "the garden is the place where Nature is subdued, ordered, selected and enclosed. Hence, it is a symbol of consciousness as opposed to the forest, which is the unconscious. . . " It does seem that Borges' fusing of irony and symbolism has certain precedents in the medieval tradition. See, for instance, D. W. Robertson, Jr., "The Doctrine of Charity in Mediaeval Literary Gardens," *Speculum*, 26:24–49 (1951).

21. Our story speaks only of a grove of trees, but in *Ashgrove* these are probably ashtrees, and perhaps even an ash plantation laid out as curiously as the network plantations

recommended by Sir Thomas Browne in *The Garden of Cyrus,* a book of more than passing interest for Borges. Albert's trees would then be laid out in the form of the "quincuncial lozenge." Our inference is borne out by the zigzagging pathway and the light from the lantern crossing among the trunks as Albert approaches the gate. Borges puts the lozenge form to clever use in "Death and the Compass," where it is a geometrical symbol for his labyrinth.

22. The probability exists that Albert may be completely wrong in his analysis. If he is wrong, the source of his error is the deduction that Ts'ui Pên's novel and the labyrinth were one and the same. But the story also contains the countersign to this objection, and this countersign is the evident flaw in Albert's knowledge (the "inviolate" revelation revealed ironically in his revelations): the fact that he does not know Ts'ui Pên was murdered by a stranger and a foreigner. By reading the "meaning" of this inviolate flaw correctly, that is, as evidence of Albert's fallibility, we arrive at the "correct" interpretation of his analysis. His analysis is a deduction of Ts'ui Pên's intentions and the novel's "meaning," and therefore our analysis and apprehension must be that the analysis is to be deduced as the "meaning" of the event taking place in our story, and for this reason the probable solution of the Chinese novel.

23. In a note to the essay "On Chesterton," we read: "Not the explanation of the inexplicable, but only of the confusing is the task that, generally speaking, writers of detective fictions undertake." *Otras inquisiciones, OC,* p. 122; *Other Inquisitions,* p. 88.

24. See *El Aleph, OC* (1957), "Biografía de Tadeo Isidoro Cruz," p. 55.

25. "Nosotros (la indivisa divinidad que opera en nosotros) hemos soñado el mundo. Lo hemos soñado resistente, misterioso, visible, ubicuo en el espacio y firme en el tiempo; pero hemos consentido en su arquitectura tenues y eternos intersticios de sinrazón para saber que es falso." "Avatares de la tortuga" (1939), *Discusión, OC,* p. 136; *Otras inquisiciones, OC,* p. 156; *Labyrinths,* p. 208; *Other Inquisitions,* p. 120.

26. "La muerte y la brújula," first published in *Sur*, no. 92 (1942), and now included in the second part of *Ficciones*. A translation by Michael Brailove appeared in *Occident* (Berkeley, Calif., Spring, 1962), pp. 49–58. Page references in my text are to *Ficciones, OC* (1956), pp. 143–158.

27. In Marcial Tamayo and Adolfo Ruiz-Díaz, *Borges, enigma y clave* (Buenos Aires, 1955), ch. 2.

One of the books authored by Doctor Yarmolinsky, and pondered by Lönnrot, is entitled *Vindication of the Cabala.* Ten years before he wrote "Death and the Compass," Borges published an essay with the title "Una vindicación de la Cábala," *Discusión* (1932), *OC*, pp. 55–60; and in 1940 the essay "The Mirror of Enigmas," "El espejo de los enigmas," in *Otras inquisiciones, OC*, pp. 171–175; *Labyrinths*, pp. 209–212; *Other Inquisitions*, pp. 131–134. These two essays, in particular, prefigure some of the ideas brought off brilliantly in "Death and the Compass" and "The God's Script". My translation of the earlier essay appeared in *Gnomon*, no. 2, Spring 1967 (Gnomon Press, Lexington, Kentucky): "'A Vindication of the Cabala' by Jorge Luis Borges, A Translation with Notes," pp. 23–27.

28. Epilogue to *El Aleph, OC*, p. 171. Page references in my text to "Emma Zunz" are to *OC* (1957), pp. 59–66.

29. "La escritura del dios," published in *Sur*, no. 172 (1949), and collected in *El Aleph, OC*, pp. 115–121. In the address cited in note 1, above, Borges described several stories that, at the time (1945), were in draft form. Two of them were "The God's Script" and "The Immortal," whose first title was "Los inmortales" (see Miss Barrenechea's Bibliography in *La expresión de la irrealidad* . . . p. 161).

30. "Spinoza entendió que todas las cosas quieren perseverar en su ser; la piedra eternamente quiere ser piedra y el tigre un tigre." *El hacedor, OC* (1960), p. 50; *Labyrinths*, p. 246; *Dreamtigers*, p. 51.

31. It is interesting to compare the dialectical movement of the ideas expressed in some of Borges' essays ("El sueño de Coleridge," *Otras inquisiciones, OC*, pp. 25–30, *Other Inquisitions*, pp. 13-17, for example) with the imaginative projection

of these ideas in his stories. In his essays the personal destinies which are seen more or less as intimations of an archetypal entity are the lives of poets and writers—Shakespeare,
Flaubert, Coleridge.

32. "La música, los·estados de felicidad, la mitología, las
caras trabajadas por el tiempo, ciertos crepúsculos y ciertos
lugares, quieren decirnos algo, o algo dijeron que no hubié-
ramos debido perder, o están por decir algo; esta inminencia
de una revelación, que no se produce, es, quizá, el hecho
estético." *Otras inquisiciones, OC,* "La muralla y los libros," p.
12; *Labyrinths,* p. 188; *Other Inquisitions,* pp. 3–4.

33. In the Epilogue to *El Aleph* (Buenos Aires, 1952), the
collection of stories of which "El inmortal" is the first in order.
An earlier version of this analysis, completed in February 1963,
appeared in French in the volume of *L'Herne* devoted to Borges
in 1964. It may be of interest to compare my analysis and the
commentary by Jacques Réda, "Commentaire de *L'Immortel* de
Jorge-Luis Borges," *Cahiers du Sud,* 49th Yr., no. 370 (Febru-
ary-March 1963), pp. 435–455.

34. "Homer and the Homeridae," *Collected Writings of
Thomas De Quincey,* ed. D. Masson (Edinburgh, 1890), VI, 27.
The "everlasting Jew" of legend is not "immortal" until the
day of Christ's death. I suggest that in order to think of Solo-
mon-Ahasuerus, in the story, as a parallel to Homer we need
to see their combined legendary existence as an archetype of
the persistence of Jewish traditions, at least in Christian mentality. De Quincey, *Writings,* III, 438–440 (mentioned in the
"Postscript, 1950"), and I (1889), 42–43, was a source for other
details in the story. The student of Borges will find many
interesting hints about his writings in Ronald Christ, "Jorge
Luis Borges, An Interview," *Paris Review,* no. 40 (Winter-
Spring 1967), pp. 116–164; on De Quincey see p. 161: the
passage referred to (*Writings,* I (1896), 129) is quoted in the first
paragraph of the essay "The Mirror of Enigmas."

35. I am indebted to Marcial Tamayo and Adolfo Ruiz
Díaz (*Borges, enigma y clave,* pp. 94–96) for several insights.
However, I disagree with these authors on several points of
interpretation. Their reservations are explained away if we

subordinate the questions of personal and historical chronology to a symbolical unity.

36. An English translation of the passage from Roger of Wendover's *Flores Historiarum* is available in George K. Anderson, *The Legend of the Wandering Jew* (Brown University Press, 1965), pp. 18–19. See also Anderson's article "The Wandering Jew Returns to England," *Journal of English and Germanic Philology*, 45:237–250 (1946), esp. p. 239–240. Henceforth Borges' story must be accepted as a literary embellishment of the legend. Enrique Anderson Imbert points out that, as Borges has worked a reference to Cornelius Agrippa into his story, perhaps his source for some details has been the strange *Chronicles* by David Hoffman of the last century, where a conversation between Cartaphilus and Agrippa is reported, "Nueva contribución al estudio de las fuentes de Borges," *Filología*, 8:7–8 (1962). Hoffman's work has the title *Chronicles Selected from the Originals of Cartaphilus, The Wandering Jew, Embracing a Period of Nearly XIX Centuries* (London, 1853), and includes the account by Roger of Wendover followed by the account of the conversation between Cartaphilus and Agrippa (vol. I, pp. x-xvi). G. K. Anderson (*Legend of The Wandering Jew*, 1965) describes Hoffman's book at length, pp. 153–160.

37. Some other details: Cartaphilus has written in English because he shares with Englishmen the qualities of an extravagant individualism known as "eccentric." Perhaps one of the literary antecedents of Borges' immortals is Swift's struldbrugs in *Gulliver's Travels* (III, ch. 10).

38. The serpent as a traditional symbol of immortality is appropriate, I guess, even as food for immortals. Many of Borges' symbols in the story have the nightmarish aspect of his City of the Immortals.

39. The date 1922 has undoubtedly a personal significance for Borges: Cartaphilus loses his immortality and commits his experiences to writing at the very time Borges begins his own literary career.

# INDEX

Agrippa, Henry Cornelius, 232, 264
Ahasuerus, 239, 263. *See also* Cartaphilus
Albert (France), 137, 142, 152, 176
Albert, Stephen (in "Garden of
  Forking Paths"): as Goethean
  archetype, 144, 153, 167, 180, 182;
  name as ideogram, 143, 176
*Aleph, The*, 195, 204
Apprehension, act of, xvii, 12, 50, 51
  of multiple meanings: and "Ithaca," 52–54, 56; in *Wake*, 70, 72,
  82; and symbol for total form of,
  76; exegetical diagram of, 74–75,
  83, 90; and perception of irony,
  74; resolution of as myth, 57, 78,
  90–91, 104–109 passim
Apprehension, mode of: explained,
  13; in *Dubliners*, 15, 22; in *Portrait*,
  25, 31–32; in *Ulysses*, 47; as *stasis*,
  54; and Joyce's styles, 55; in *Wake*,
  107; in Borges, 125; and irony, 126
"Approach to Al-Mu'tasim," 124
Aquinas, Thomas, 7–8
Archimedean spiral, 74, 75, 252
Archimedes, 252
Atherton, James S., 67, 250, 251

Beckett, Samuel, 91
Blissett, William, 249
Bloom, Leopold: 29, 35, 38, 50, 51;
  Joyce's irony toward, 52–53; in S.
  L. Goldberg's interpretation of
  *Ulysses*, 42, 44, 46–47; in H. Ken-
  ner's, 39, 40–41
Bloom, Molly, 35, 42, 44, 69
Bloom, Rudy, 38, 46–47
Bloy, Léon, 122
Borges, Jorge Luis: essays and sto-

ries compared, 123–124; stories
compared to mathematical problems, 130; literary sources of, 122,
256, 258, 263, 264; impersonality,
194; Joycean poem, xi; translator
of Joyce, x
  motifs: archetypal characters:
detective and criminal, 187–192;
Goethean, *see* Albert, Stephen;
Homeric, *see* Cartaphilus; destiny,
156–158, 177, 184, 209, 222, 226;
eternity, encounter with, 123,
162–163; labyrinth, 142, 153–159
passim, 170, 183–184, 197, 200,
225; memory, 218, 219–220
time: cyclical, 160–164 passim,
211–212; simultaneous times, 174,
179, 180; refutation of, 132; irreversibility of, 152
  narrative art: iterative form, 121,
125, 127; conjecture in, 120, 148,
157; effects on reader, xix, 119,
128–129, 178, 220–221, 237; humor, 123; symbolism, 126–128,
137, 199, 242, 260, 264
irony: operations of, 126, 131; and
symbols, 128, 221, 230–231, 236–
237; and counterplot, 178; involution, as counterpoint, 151–155,
173, 229; displacement of meaning, 121, 146, 174, 228; and "totality" of meaning, 187, 190–194
passim, 202, 210–211, 216
Borges, Jorge Luis, and Joyce, James,
compared: as writers, ix–xii,
119–120; style and techniques,
xii–xiii; use of irony, xiii, xvi,
xvii, xix; representation of consciousness, xviii
Brancusi, Constantin, 74, 75, 77, 83,
252–253
Browne, Sir Thomas, 261

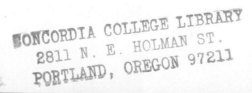